MANAGEMENT-MINDED SUPERVISION

BRADFORD B. BOYD
Management Institute
University of Wisconsin

McGRAW-HILL BOOK COMPANY
NEW YORK
ST. LOUIS
SAN FRANCISCO
LONDON
TORONTO
SYDNEY

MANAGEMENT-MINDED SUPERVISION

Library of Congress Catalog Card Number: 68-13510

ISBN 07-006940-9

678910   MAMM   74321

To my wife, Marianne

PREFACE

If an executive could isolate himself with a newly appointed first-line supervisor for several days, discuss with him what it means to be a manager, explain to him the full scope of his new responsibilities, and suggest approaches to problems that will confront him, that executive would begin to answer the question so many have voiced, "How can we get our supervisors to think and act like managers?" Unfortunately, few managers can take the time needed for a thorough orientation to the management viewpoint. Fewer still do take the time, and the unsatisfied desire for management-minded supervisors is intensified.

Conservatively we estimate that seven million men and women will be promoted to supervisory positions in the coming decade—seven million who will come to understand that the supervisor is management at its closest point of contact with the productive employee. To some the management frame of reference will come naturally, to others acceptance of management responsibility will come slowly and painfully, and there will always be those who never really become "members of management." In any event, the need for management-minded supervisors in business, industry, and government exists today as it never has before and will become more and more pronounced as the management population increases. To this growing need, then, this book is addressed.

Certainly no one could be vain enough to presume he has answered the need, but it is my sincere hope that *Management-minded Supervision* will make a contribution. Almost two decades of working and associating with managers at all levels, both in their plants and in the university environment, has helped me develop an insight into what management wants from its supervision. This book is written for the supervisor, and hopefully it sets forth his responsibilities, his problems, his challenges, and his opportunities in a realistic, honest management perspective. I have tried to say what most executives want to tell their supervisors about being a manager by discussing the challenges a supervisor faces from a practical rather than theoretical standpoint.

The book is built around three major needs of the supervisor—

management-mindedness, leadership, and job knowledge. Research and day-to-day work with foremen and supervisors from hundreds of organizations have helped define these needs. Our institute conference rooms have provided a laboratory in which we could refine methods of supervisory development.

The reader will soon come to know Burt Hall, the supervisor of an assembly department in a fictitious manufacturing plant. Burt provides, I hope, the only fiction in the book. Each chapter begins with a problem, or as an optimist would say, an opportunity that faces Burt. A composite of thousands of good foremen across the land, Burt Hall has his strengths and his weaknesses. As the reader proceeds, he will find himself sharing Burt's viewpoints many times and wondering how Burt can be so wrong in other situations. Burt should stimulate thinking and personal evaluation of the reader's own management practices and attitudes. Although he is a supervisor in a manufacturing plant, Burt faces problems that might confront retail store supervisors, government department heads, or supervisors of white-collar, sales, or technical personnel. He is a first-level manager.

Although this book is written for the foreman or supervisor, I hope others will find value in it. The training director who wants to set up a program on the basics of supervision for his own organization may find it helpful to use the case studies which precede each chapter to initiate his own group discussions. The employee who wants to become a supervisor should be able to gain some helpful knowledge about the position he seeks. Members of management interested in orienting the new supervisor to the management viewpoint may find here some of the things they want to say. Personnel men seeking to develop potential supervisors in presupervisory training programs may find approaches in this book to give some direction to those programs. And the student who seeks to understand the role of the supervisor in the management hierarchy will have access to a point of view shaped by twenty years of working with managers in business, industry, and government.

The viewpoints and opinions expressed in this book are my own, yet I lay no claim to originality. Who really knows when an idea was conceived, when a philosophy was developed or an opinion molded? It would be impossible to acknowledge individually those who have contributed to this book because it begins with the thousands of supervisors who have attended institutes at the University of Wisconsin and shared their experiences, problems, and opinions. The literature in the field of management has certainly helped shape the thinking reflected on these pages, as have consultants, professors, and managers who have served our program so well as discussion leaders. My associates at the Management Institute also have contributed substantially over the years to the philosophy that is contained in this book. To the many firms who have cooperated in research projects or who have accorded me the opportunity of conducting supervisory development programs in their plants goes a special word of thanks.

Recognizing the difficulties of giving individual recognition, I still feel that three such expressions of gratitude must be made. Clayton G. Orcutt, of the State of Wisconsin's Industrial Commission and formerly an associate in the Management Institute, did more than anyone I know to keep my thinking and my vocabulary oriented to the supervisor. His common sense and practical approach have provided me through the years with an example I have been proud to follow. His counsel helped me greatly to develop empathy for the supervisors for whom this book is written.

Professor Norman C. Allhiser, Director of the Management Institute, provided the encouragement and support that was needed to start and complete this book. His direction of the Management Institute over the past decade, more than anything else, has molded my own management-mindedness.

An especially warm word of appreciation goes to Mrs. Gladys Dahl, who has so capably handled the administrative work of our Supervisory Institutes. Her dedication has contributed immeasurably to the smooth functioning of our section. To an already heavy work load she cheerfully and enthusiastically added the burden of preparing the manuscript.

Bradford B. Boyd

CONTENTS

MANAGEMENT-MINDED SUPERVISION

PART
ONE

MANAGEMENT—MINDEDNESS

Business without profit is not business any more than a pickle is candy.

CHARLES F. ABBOTT

Success or failure in business is caused even more by mental attitude than by mental capacities.

WALTER DILL SCOTT

CHAPTER
ONE

DEVELOPING MANAGEMENT-MINDEDNESS

Why is there so much concern for developing management-mindedness? It comes simply from a widely held belief that the way a person thinks determines the way he acts and that all supervisors should be concerned with acting and functioning like managers.

We can discount the tendency of some to think that the supervisor's job is declining in importance. A conservative estimate is that six to seven million new supervisory positions will be filled in the coming decade. Consider the words of Edward C. Schleh, author of *Management by Results*.

If management is to do an effective job in coordinating all of the activities of an enterprise to sound accomplishment of company objectives, its prime approach should be based on the first-level requirements. What is required at the first-level operation is in the long run the final result of the enterprise. All of the planning work along the way is usually of little value unless the first-level people turn out something worthwhile and sell it at a worthwhile price. This emphasis on first-level operation is one of the first and cardinal requirements of any management approach and should be paramount in the decisions of managers at every level.*

THE CASE OF BURT HALL

Just one more month to go and a decision about Burt Hall, supervisor of Assembly Department B, would have to be made.

* From "Management Based on the First Level," in *Management International,* International Review for Management and Managerial Sciences.

Burt had been made supervisor on a jointly agreed-upon probationary basis. He still had an inactive membership in the union and would retain his seniority if either Burt or management decided that he should return to his old job.

Perhaps the phrase "either Burt or management" contributed to the problem, for both Oscar Palmer, plant manager, and Ray Ford, assembly superintendent, felt that Burt just hadn't taken hold as "a member of management." Burt, unaware of their concern, also felt deep down that he was not doing the job for which he had so much enthusiasm just five months ago.

A top producer, intelligent, well liked, and properly motivated, Burt was a unanimous choice when the vacancy in Department B was created. "A natural for the job" is the way Ray Ford concluded his recommendation of Burt. Everyone involved in Burt's selection felt the same way. It wasn't hard to sell Burt on the job. He did, however, express some concern about whether he could take the tremendous responsibility and whether he could boss his old buddies. That was when the probationary arrangement was worked out. No one really thought that it was any more than window-dressing. Now, five months later, this face-saving arrangement provided the basis for the discussion between Mr. Palmer and Ray Ford. Burt was also doing some soul searching.

Things started out smoothly enough for Burt. The people in his department liked him—they always had. He knew the work to be done, and no one minded taking orders from him. While he felt a little uneasy bossing people at first, he soon gained confidence. He demonstrated that he could take production schedules and transform them into completed orders. He knew his job was production coupled with good quality and low costs. This was where he concentrated his efforts. He was rewarded by encouraging comments from Ray Ford on his excellent production record.

It hurt, then, whenever anything or anybody interrupted the smooth flow of production. Burt was quick to show his displeasure—not by shouting but by scowling and silence. Changes, for example, irritated him. "They can't get production if they keep monkeying around with methods," he complained to several of his assemblers.

Specials got under his skin because they took longer. Burt couldn't see why standard lines couldn't be made to work. Ray Ford told him once that the company took great pride in accommodating customers, but Burt still felt they could sell the customer on adjusting to standard lines. It was important to recognize the company's overall goals and customer demands, Ray told him. Burt agreed, but said that a man had to have his own goals and that his was to make his department the most productive in the plant. Burt's interest in production was commended by Ray with a caution not to lose sight of the total picture.

When the union objected to restudying a job on which a new method had been installed, Burt sided with it. He knew there would be a fuss, and he wanted to avoid anything which might disrupt production. The labor contract permitted the setting of new rates on a job whenever a new method or new equipment was installed. Burt and the steward argued that there wasn't enough of a change to warrant a new study. Management had felt that the rate had been out of line for some time. The new method gave them the opportunity they had been waiting for. Burt reluctantly supported the new study. His reluctance gave Mr. Palmer the first reason to question Burt's promotion.

As time went on there were other occasions when Burt's attitude reflected his feeling that he stood between management and his employees—a part of neither. He saw himself as being fair to both sides. His employees perceived him as a company man—all production and costs. Mr. Palmer and Ray Ford developed the feeling that he was a "loner"—out to set a mark for himself. No one, including Burt, had any doubts that he had changed since taking over.

Burt found it difficult to pin down just when or why he began to feel this job wasn't his cup of tea. He had started out with an overwhelming desire to succeed. There hadn't been any major problems or blow-ups. Relationships with his buddies and fellow workers had changed, but no more than he had expected. Production increases hadn't been spectacular, but he had done better than his predecessor. He did, however, feel under pressure from above and from staff departments who interfered with the smooth running of his department. Riding herd on production seemed to take more and more of his time. There wasn't much, he concluded, to make him feel like a member of management. At least on his old job he knew who he was and where he stood.

"If only we could get him to see the whole job instead of just pushing production, we might still salvage him, Ray," Oscar Palmer stated in discussing the decision that must soon be made. Evidence of Burt's feeling that people were producers only was mounting up.

Once Burt's strengths (and they were substantial) and his limitations (also real) had been weighed, both men concluded that Burt Hall was too good a man to let go back to the ranks. He needed direction and guidance. They needed to know more about Burt.

1. What were Burt's strengths and limitations?
2. What is management looking for in a supervisor today?
3. What are the major responsibilities of a supervisor?
4. Is the supervisor really a member of management?

WHAT DOES TODAY'S SUPERVISOR NEED?

In considering the case of Burt Hall we see him in a situation that many supervisors have experienced or will experience—eager to do a job, not sure of where he fits in the scheme of things, and debating with himself the wisdom of his decision to become a supervisor. Until the doubts are resolved and new direction is established, Burt will flounder. His concern for production will deepen; his attitudes will harden; and his professional sense of balance will desert him. By a sense of balance we mean the ability to see the whole job in perspective. For this the integration of the company's philosophy and policies with personal goals and ambitions is essential. Recognition of the major responsibilities of a supervisor in addition to production must be clear. Overemphasis of one responsibility to the neglect of others has caused the downfall of many men with excellent supervisory potential.

For several years now in researching the problems a worker encounters in making the transition to supervisory work, the question has been asked, "What does today's supervisor need?" Contributions from thousands of foremen, plant managers, educators, authors, and consultants point to three major areas of need. First, a supervisor must be *management-minded*. Second, he needs the *skills of leadership*. Third, he must possess *job knowledge*.

Management-mindedness

Here, perhaps, is one of Burt's greatest shortcomings. The supervisor is the front-line of management. No matter how the company is organized, no matter what title is used, there is always that first-level management position that calls for the direction of the productive employee. Most men at this level are called foreman or supervisor, but whatever their titles, they are members of management. Identified in the minds of others as a manager, they should think like, act like, and perform like the management of their organization.

This involves knowing the firm's aims and what the firm stands for. It means understanding the goals and objectives of the entire organization as intimately as the supervisor knows the standards and quotas that exist in his own department. Working in harmony with management, the supervisor becomes a part of this philosophy in word and deed. J. Paul Sticht, when he was Vice-president of Campbell Soup

Company, wrote, "Whenever a man accepts a supervisory position he accepts with it the responsibility of supporting and advocating management philosophies, policies, and procedures—and can expect the full support of management in return." * It's safe to assume that the great majority of members of higher management share this view. Unfortunately much more is hoped for from supervisors than is actually expressed in orienting them for management positions. Many management-minded supervisors carry Mr. Sticht's thought one step further by saying that if a man cannot wholeheartedly dedicate himself to his management's philosophies and approaches, it would be better for him to resign his assignment.

Developing management-mindedness requires among other things adopting constant self-improvement as a way of life. The day when supervisors could sit back and coast is gone. There's no room for the "I've arrived" way of thinking. An effective supervisor personally identifies with the company's struggle for survival in a competitive world. Just as the company must constantly seek ways of improving its products and services, the supervisor must look for opportunities to increase his value to the organization. Technological improvement, expansion, reorganization—all spell out the fact that unlimited opportunities await the man who is keeping pace through self-improvement.

The supervisor must also recognize that he is the pacesetter for those who report to him. Setting the example is a powerful means of demonstrating that personal development is expected from subordinates. A supervisor who rests on his laurels after he's on the job and who does nothing to keep abreast of new developments is shortchanging his organization. The same can be said about a company which showed no interest in improving its products, expanding its markets, or updating its facilities.

To be able to understand the vital role supervisors play in communication is also a part of management-minded supervision. Communication is the nervous system of any business enterprise. We can easily see how effectiveness is impaired when the necessary information on which to base decisions isn't available. A manager must be in the know to function effectively. The smooth running of a department or an entire firm is directly proportionate to the communication ability of its management.

* *A.M.A. Encyclopedia of Supervisory Training,* Chapter 1, American Management Association, New York, 1961.

We can easily recognize that supervisors occupy a unique position as far as communication is concerned. Orders, rules, standards, policies, and attitudes must all be communicated to the production employee. Since supervisors have direct contact with employees, the burden falls on their shoulders to see that they understand what is expected of them. And it's not hard to see how much higher management must depend on the supervisor to communicate to its members the attitudes, feelings, and problems that exist in the departments. Management policies are formulated in the light of this information. The supervisor's job is to keep management informed.

One of the truly distressing elements of organizational communication is the clarity with which we can see the deficiencies of others. Supervisors and foremen from many companies often say that communication is a prime weakness in their firm. "This communication training is fine for me, but the man who really needs it is my boss," is heard repeatedly. Yet whenever higher-level managers plan supervisory development programs, communication is invariably identified as a high-priority need.

Awareness of the need to communicate is the first step in improving communication in an organization. The management-minded supervisor doesn't complain about the poor communication of others; he initiates steps to get the information he needs. He sees to it that those with whom he deals understand him. Most of us will find that when we do a good job of communicating with others, it makes others want to communicate well with us. Harmony and cooperation between individuals on a management team depend on communication. Communication between individuals who respect one another is spontaneous and creates mutual respect that continues to grow. All the communications principles and techniques in the world, however, won't help those who dislike each other. Every supervisor has the potential of being an excellent communicator, but first he must think like a manager.

The management-minded supervisor is enthusiastic about change and is skilled in initiating it. He feels that it is not enough to accept change but that he must be a part of it, find opportunities to make improvements, and implement with vigor the changes introduced by higher management. Here again Burt Hall gave his superiors reason to question his support of management's way of thinking. Unconsciously he was resisting change because it would interrupt the smooth operation of his assembly lines. Yet Burt would have been the first to deny that he was resistant to change or guilty of the kind of thinking expressed in these words: "We've been getting along fine with the present method. Why change now?"

The expectations of higher management were nicely summed up by Malcolm MacNaughton, President of Castle and Cooke, Inc., when he wrote this message to supervisors about their jobs and the future.

> In looking forward to what the future will bring, there is one factor in management I can feel sure about. That factor is change—change in products, change in methods, change in organization. At Castle and Cooke, Inc., change has been facing us continually and at an ever increasing rate. We feel that change is a necessity for growth, and we intend to grow. When I have meetings with our management personnel, I stress the need for change and growth because to survive we must change, and we must grow. If you, in your job, recognize that we are in a changing industrial world and we have to change and grow with it, then you will be able to continue to do your part effectively as a member of management.*

Leadership Skills

Volumes have been written about the supervisor as a leader. Social scientists have sought to identify qualities of leadership, in the hope that once they found the formula, a mold could be built and each of us pressed into it—to come out an ideal leader. This is nonsense.

Make no mistake about it. When we are placed in positions demanding leadership, as Burt Hall was, we will lead in different ways, according to the personalities we have been cultivating all our lives. Leadership is not coddling people, as some would have us believe; nor is it hitting people over the head to get what we want. Leadership is getting people to work to achieve the goals of the enterprise. It's giving people something to work for.

Burt Hall started out well enough, but as the months went by, a stronger and stronger orientation to the requirements of production put him in danger of losing sight of the requirements of people. He was beginning to see his people as tools—and this is a shortcut to failure. It's universally acknowledged that in any organization people are our most priceless asset. We've heard this so often that we risk

* "What's Ahead for Supervisors in 1966," Supervision, Vol. XXVIII, No. 1, January, 1966.

overlooking it. Production is a prime responsibility of supervision, but productivity depends on people. The intelligent and successful manager recognizes this. He can't afford to take the people who make up his work force for granted.

The management-minded supervisor, then, will know and understand his employees as individuals and treat them as such. He will realize that motivation is much more than money or a pat on the back and that some of the more commonly accepted incentives do almost nothing to stimulate a man to do his best.

To lead people, one must teach them. Any manager, from the top all the way down, accepts an obligation to train and coach those reporting to him. A job at the supervisory level is frequently bigger in this respect because a supervisor has so many more people under his direction. So many supervisors delegate this job to their better employees, yet they aren't satisfied with the results they get. Is it because they find it convenient to ignore the fact that a good operator doesn't necessarily make a good instructor? The management-minded supervisor recognizes that when he delegates the authority to train, he doesn't divorce himself from his responsibility to be sure that he has well-trained employees under him. A supervisor must train those who train others or at least should make provisions for their training so that his responsibility is effectively carried out.

Leadership skills not only call for skills in motivating and training; the management-minded approach also calls for creating a positive climate for discipline—training people to make punishment unnecessary. Many an enlightened foreman will quickly acknowledge that discipline should not be thought of as restrictive, or as a policing operation. Discipline has the ultimate goal of self-discipline. There is a great difference between the leadership approach and the "bull-of-the-woods" approach.

Job Knowledge

Many executives and educators have declared emphatically that job knowledge isn't a vital concern to them in placing men in supervisory positions. "Give me a supervisor who can lead men, and he can function in any department or any industry." There is an element of truth in that statement. We can add, however, that the new supervisor had better set about learning the methods, procedures, equipment, and machinery in his department if he's going to function very long. When a man starts supervising in a strange department he has the extra burden of learning as much as he can as quickly as he can about the work performed. A man will not gain his employees' respect until he demonstrates an understanding of the problems faced by the operator in performing his job.

As much as we hear about minimizing the importance of job knowledge in supervision, it is still the factor to which management gives the most weight in selecting men from the ranks for supervisory jobs. In a recent survey conducted by the University of Wisconsin's Management Institute, 225 plant managers were asked, "What are the most important considerations in selecting a production worker for the position of foreman?" Ranked number one in that survey was job or technical knowledge, and close behind in the number two position was ability to get along with people.

With automation and technological advancements becoming more and more a part of the industrial way of life, job knowledge is likely to remain an important attribute of the management-minded supervisor. The technical knowledge of the department's operations is, however, only a part of the job knowledge of the modern supervisor. Of primary importance is knowing how to manage. Precious few come to the supervisor's job with this knowledge. Production employees have their work planned for them; they are given orders; their work is supervised and inspected. Until they actually become supervisors, they have little opportunity to learn these management skills. In most cases no one knows how well they can perform the process of managing.

The process of management at any level consists of four functions: planning, organizing, motivating (or directing), and controlling. Degrees of difficulty and emphasis vary, of course, from one level of management to another. Top executives, for example, spend a great deal more time and effort planning and organizing. Although at the supervisory level these functions are not ignored, usually the primary emphasis is on motivating and giving orders and on controlling performance.

Inability to plan has put many supervisors behind the eight ball in their jobs. Standards, schedules, goals, quotas are all a part of the planning function. Determining when work is to be started, how long it should take, what materials and equipment are needed, who will do the work, how one job will coordinate with the next—this is planning. A supervisor who has a lack of skill in planning often complains that there isn't enough time to do everything expected of him. Burt Hall is beginning to reach this point in his career, and if he doesn't check this tendency, he will soon become a "crisis manager"—one who spends most of his time jumping from one crisis to another, constantly putting out fires. The planning of personal time on the job can be an extremely satisfying and rewarding first venture into organized planning. We'll discuss this in a later chapter on planning and organizing.

To narrow the gap between what he wants and what he gets when he gives an order, a supervisor should know what happens when he issues that order. Why do some orders produce an enthusiastic response, others the blank stares of confusion, and still others a grudging minimum compliance of questionable quality? Spending as much time as he does in directing the work of employees, the supervisor needs to be sensitive to how people react to him when he gives them orders.

Once the work of the department has been planned and organized, and the orders issued, the management-minded supervisor knows that jobs and activities must be followed up. Control is a key to effective managing. It is here that he matches performance against the goals and standards set forth in his plans. Modification may be necessary. The opportunity for recognizing a job well done becomes apparent. The control function is intimately related to the planning function. Most supervisors use many forms of control every day—production reports, attendance and time reports, cost and quality reports, progress checks, and performance appraisals. Of these the last is most difficult for many supervisors. To evaluate an employee's performance and periodically review that evaluation with the employee has for many supervisors produced negative rather than positive results. Instead of improving morale, it has lowered it. As a management control properly administered, the performance appraisal and review has the potential for substantially upgrading the performance of the entire department.

Job knowledge for the management-minded supervisor, then, consists of two major areas: the technical knowledge of methods and equipment and the knowledge of how to manage. The first is brought to the job by most supervisors. The second must be learned, for few have the opportunity to acquire it before accepting management positions. Part Three of this book will deal in more detail with this aspect of job knowledge. Interestingly enough the management process is very seldom covered in management development programs for the first-level supervisor.

IS THE SUPERVISOR REALLY CONSIDERED
A PART OF MANAGEMENT?

Perhaps in considering the case of Burt Hall, we have taken for granted that because Mr. Palmer and Ray Ford wanted Burt to become a member of management, managers in general prefer to promote supervisors from existing employees; and that because Burt himself had doubts as to where he stood, most supervisors feel they are not truly part of the management group. Is Burt's situation—being chosen from the ranks—typical? Let's consider the survey of 225 plant managers from companies employing over 9,000 supervisors to see, perhaps, how managers view the problem of management-mindedness at the first level.

The question was asked, Are foremen usually appointed from within your organization, or will you go outside the company to hire? Ninety-four percent said they follow the practice of promoting from within. However, there is an increasing emphasis on formal education. Two-thirds of the group considered a high school diploma a minimum educational requirement. More and more technologically advanced companies insist on college degrees for the first management level. An obligation to look first within the organization for those with the proper qualifications will be recognized for some years to come.

Ninety-seven percent said yes to the question, Do you consider your foremen a part of management? While in many companies the ability of higher management to create this feeling on the part of the supervisor is lacking, supervisors should not ignore the fact that the desire is there. One of the most exciting challenges for a supervisor, it seems, is to demonstrate his management-mindedness by taking the initiative rather than waiting to be initiated into the club. A company, like any organization, stands in need of men with management and leadership abilities. Sixty-two percent of the plant managers surveyed responded negatively when asked, Do you feel that the foreman in your plant adjusts easily to the management viewpoint as contrasted with what he felt as a worker? Plant managers recognize that the adjustment is difficult and want to see the adjustment made as quickly as possible.

Higher management, even though evidence sometimes points to the contrary, wants and expects the first-line supervisor to feel and act like a member of management. But how about the supervisor? How does he feel? In another survey 250 first-line supervisors were asked,

Do you feel in your present assignment that you are truly a member of management? Significantly, only 74 percent said yes. Those who felt they were members of management only sometimes accounted for 24 percent, and the remaining 2 percent flatly said no. Those who said no or sometimes gave as their reasons the failure of management to communicate with them and the lack of authority to make decisions in their own departments. Implied in the responses is the fact that supervisors, too, want to feel they are a part of management. Why then the concern?

It is expressed in the attitudes of those 225 plant managers toward their 9,000 foremen and the many others who at one time or another had come under their supervision. In two widely separated sections of the questionnaire, the plant managers were asked about the difficulties new foremen had in making the transition and the weaknesses the foremen most commonly displayed. Bear in mind that these were completely open-ended questions; there were no suggested answers. This makes the responses especially significant. The two questions appear below, with response indicated.

What do you feel are the three most common weaknesses foremen display in the performance of their job?

1. Poor attitude   56%
2. Poor management of their job   50%
3. Poor disciplining   22%
4. Poor communication   21%

What, according to your experience, are the most difficult problems faced by the newly appointed foreman?

1. Management (planning, organizing, etc.)   43%
2. Adopting a management attitude   42%
3. Human relations   25%
4. Discipline   22%

Now the reason for the concern becomes more obvious. Poor attitude—or a lack of a positive management-mindedness—is either first or second in the responses to both questions. The same is true for the management skills we discussed earlier—skills for which there has been so little training. What does today's supervisor need? The survey confirms it: (1) management-mindedness (an attitude); (2) leadership skills; (3) job knowledge (especially of the management process).

BUILDING A POSITIVE MANAGEMENT ATTITUDE

Management is many different things to many people. Here let us think of it in connection with the organization, the company. The excitement an employee felt at being selected for promotion to supervisor may have died quickly once he was burdened with the responsibilities of the job. The glamour of managing can fade rapidly into the headaches of personnel and production problems unless something is done to keep enthusiasm alive. The Reverend Norman Vincent Peale wrote of near miracles in transforming people's lives when they found and experienced "the power of positive thinking." Dr. John Schindler used much the same approach in his book *How to Live 365 Days a Year*. Both said in essence that how we think determines how we act. Psychologists stress the importance of participation in winning the cooperation of others. Participation as a part of the management team in the organization is the beginning. But how should a supervisor participate? How should he identify with his firm?

Part of the answer can be found in knowing just as much about his organization as he possibly can. The history of the company in which a man is building his career is often fascinating. Who were the founders, and what were their dreams? Many companies started with an invention—the product of one man's imagination. Others started with a needed service and then grew, expanded, and diversified until the original purpose was lost completely.

How much does a supervisor know of his company's total line of products or services? How does his department fit into the total scheme of things? A management-minded supervisor will have some knowledge of how his company is organized. He will know where its markets are and what is being done to expand those markets.

If a supervisor were to consider investing a few hundred dollars of his hard-earned cash in the common stock of a company, he would investigate the progress of that company, its earnings, its growth potential, its concern for research and development, its capitalization, the strength of its management, the diversification of its products, and so on. He is thinking now, however, of investing his lifetime, his career. Shouldn't he then know at least these things about his own firm? As a supervisor learns more about the company, he naturally builds a stronger identification with it. In fact, many supervisors testify to having drawn attention to themselves as potential supervisors when as production employees they demonstrated an interest in what was going on in departments other than their own.

The truly management-minded supervisor represents the company both inside and outside the plant. Among the many hats he wears is the hat of the public relations man. He is the representative of his firm wherever he goes—at professional meetings, in social groups, and in community activities.

MANAGEMENT RESPONSIBILITIES OF TODAY'S SUPERVISOR

Burt Hall was moderately concerned, when accepting his new job, about the tremendous responsibilities it entailed. Unlike most production workers, he was willing to shoulder these responsibilities perhaps without a clear-cut idea of what the responsibilities actually were. On the one hand, he used the word *tremendous*. On the other, he demonstrated a limited awareness of the scope of his responsibility when he concentrated his attention almost exclusively on production, costs, and quality, in that order.

A group of supervisors, when asked to enumerate the things they are responsible for, will contribute over one hundred if given enough time. Supervisors can generally reach agreement on seven basic supervisory responsibilities when their jobs are analyzed. These seven cannot be ignored. When one or more of them are overlooked, the supervisor's approach to his job is not balanced. The seven identified here are not in order of priority. At any given time, any one of them might merit a supervisor's prime concern. No one of them, however, can be set aside for very long.

Production

Broadly conceived, production is a major responsibility of every supervisor. Production might be a product; a service, such as maintenance; a subassembly; clerical work; or sales. The supervisor's job is to accomplish that production with the resources available.

Quality

In today's competitive economy, many salesmen hold that the quality of their products is all they have to sell. Quality is built in where the product or service is produced. The supervisor is the key man in stimulating quality-consciousness in the work force. The management-minded supervisor knows his company's policy on quality and accepts as a major responsibility the quality of work performed in his department.

Costs

Most of us work for profit-making organizations. Profit is the reason why people are in business. The profit motive has brought this country to its present economic level. The management-minded supervisor strives through cost control and cost reduction to contribute in any way he can to the profit of his firm. Further, he helps employees understand that they, too, have a responsibility to contribute to profit. In government and nonprofit organizations, the supervisor is still charged with the responsibility of seeing that the work of his department is accomplished with the lowest possible expenditure of funds.

Methods

Production, costs, and quality are all aided by using the most efficient methods. Management-minded supervision is continually seeking easier and better ways of doing work. Work methods which waste time, effort, supplies, materials, and tools should be analyzed and improved. Stimulating employee participation in improving work methods is the mark of an effective foreman.

Morale

Morale is people's collective attitude toward work, the company, management, their equipment, and their workplace. The responsibility for high morale and an enthusiastic work force lies essentially with the supervisor. Good morale doesn't happen by chance. It begins with a supervisor who is sensitive to the feelings of those whom he supervises. He is neither a coddler nor a slave driver. He brings out the best that his employees have to offer.

Training

Every responsibility we have mentioned is dependent on the employee's knowing what his job is and what's expected of him. Teaching the employee the requirements of his job is important. So is the development of positive attitudes toward quality, costs, housekeeping, and safety. A characteristic of any new employee is his eagerness to do a good job. With proper training, this eagerness can be cultivated and maintained.

Safety

Minimizing risks and hazards in work areas is the interest and desire of all management, but it falls to the first-level supervisor to see that the safest possible working conditions are maintained. Most industrial firms have safety departments charged with the responsibility of safeguarding the work force and protecting plant equipment. The safety director will be the first to admit that he depends almost completely on the foreman of the department to enforce safety regulations and to see that safe practices are followed by the work force.

As already mentioned, these seven basic responsibilities have not been listed in order of importance, and at any given time any one of them might demand special attention for prolonged periods of time. During a period of recession, for example, our primary concern is often cost reduction. A series of lost-time accidents might very well produce a concerted emphasis on safety. The announcement of a new product by a competitor frequently brings renewed concentration on quality improvement. Rapid expansion or the automating of production lines may make training the most important part of a supervisor's job. The temptation to let other responsibilities slide during these periods may throw a supervisor's view of his job out of perspective—when the need for a balanced approach is imperative. A balanced approach means a proportionate concern for each of the seven major areas.

Figure 1 shows the job of the management-minded supervisor diagrammatically. The supervisor brings his understanding of the functions of the management process to his job in order to carry out his major responsibilities. Inability to see both his people and the work in proper perspective can quickly lead to trouble. For example, a supervisor who can think only of the work to be done, or production, soon

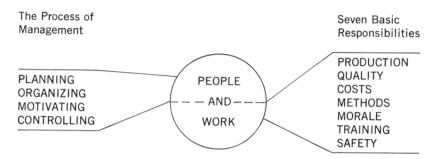

The Process of
Management

Seven Basic
Responsibilities

PLANNING
ORGANIZING
MOTIVATING
CONTROLLING

PEOPLE
— — AND — —
WORK

PRODUCTION
QUALITY
COSTS
METHODS
MORALE
TRAINING
SAFETY

Figure 1. The supervisor's management job

acquires the reputation of being a slave driver, a company man, or a bull of the woods. At the other extreme is the supervisor who puts personal popularity ahead of all other considerations. Nothing is more important to him than being a good guy, and he develops a wishy-washy approach to management. The need for some kind of balance again becomes quite apparent.

How can we describe the *real* management-minded supervisor? How does higher management regard him? Philip A. Coleman, President of Bristol Brass Corporation, expressed the answer to these questions quite well: "A real topflight foreman is the most maligned, most over-worked and most underpaid jewel in the corporate crown. He is, at the same time, a man of pride, with a deep sense of achievement who knows full well that he is a substantial contributor to the finest standard of living in the world—the American system of free enter-prise." *

HIGHLIGHTS

1. The three basic needs of today's management-minded supervisor are:
   a. To think and act like a full-fledged member of management
   b. To demonstrate leadership skills
   c. To possess job knowledge—both technical know-how and knowledge of the management process

* "What's Ahead for Supervisors in 1966," *Supervision,* Vol. XXVIII, No: 1, January, 1966.

2. Management-mindedness involves:
   a. Knowing and supporting management's philosophies, policies, and procedures
   b. Adopting constant self-improvement as a way of life
   c. Recognizing the vital role of communication in a smoothly functioning organization
   d. Being enthusiastic about change and skilled in initiating change
3. The management-minded supervisor recognizes that he needs to understand his people as individuals and that motivation is the key to effective leadership.
4. Most supervisors come to their job with the necessary technical knowledge but lack an appreciation of the management process, which involves:
   a. Planning
   b. Organizing
   c. Motivating (or directing)
   d. Controlling
5. Both higher management and most supervisors consider the foreman a member of management, but higher-level managers frequently feel that foremen lack the proper management attitudes.
6. The way we think determines the way we act. Supervisors need to know as much as possible about their organization, its history, its products, its markets, and the company's policies, goals, and objectives.
7. The supervisor's seven major responsibilities are:
   a. Production
   b. Quality
   c. Costs
   d. Methods
   e. Morale
   f. Training
   g. Safety
8. In viewing his major responsibilities, the employees, and the work to be done in a department, a supervisor must bring balance to his job.

DISCUSSION QUESTIONS

1. In your own words describe the management job of the supervisor.
2. What, in your opinion, are some of the primary reasons supervisors fail?
3. Does a supervisor find his freedom to express his personal opinions limited when he becomes a "member of management"? Explain why or why not.
4. Why does management put such heavy emphasis on job knowledge in selecting supervisors from the ranks of employees?
5. Do you consider the first-line supervisor a member of management? Why or why not?
6. Why do you think that in over 90 percent of the companies surveyed, supervisors were selected from within their employee groups?
7. Why should it be difficult for an employee to adjust to a management viewpoint when he is made a supervisor?
8. What do you think of using college graduates without work experience as production supervisors?
9. Why is a "balanced aproach" to the supervisor's seven major responsibilities so important?
10. Elaborate on Philip Coleman's statement that a topflight foreman is "the most maligned, most overworked, and most underpaid jewel in the corporate crown." Do you agree? Why or why not?

SUGGESTIONS FOR FURTHER STUDY

Bittel, Lester R.
What Every Supervisor Should Know, 2d ed.
Chapter 1, McGraw-Hill Book Company, New York, 1968

Ecker, Paul, John MacRae, Vernon Ouellette, and Charles Telford
Handbook for Supervisors,
Chapter 2, Prentice-Hall, Inc., Englewood Cliffs, N.J., 1959

Famularo, Joseph J.
Supervisors in Action
Chapter 2, McGraw-Hill Book Company, New York, 1961

Gardiner, Glenn, and Associates
Managerial Skills for Supervisors
Chapter 12, Elliott Service Company, Mount Vernon, N.Y., 1960

CHAPTER
TWO

CONTINUAL
SELF–DEVELOPMENT

THE CASE OF A PREDECESSOR'S ADVICE

Burt Hall had just finished going over the day's production reports and was getting ready to head for home when Ray Ford, assembly superintendent and Burt's immediate boss, walked into the office. Ray immediately came to the point of his visit. The company training director was starting a series of training sessions on improving communication skills. Ray thought Burt might like to attend them.

The questioning, almost hurt look on Burt's face told Ray further explanation was necessary. The series, he told Burt, had been offered last year; he himself had gotten a lot out of it, and he thought that Burt would find it well worth the time. Participation through workshop, rather than a lot of lectures, made the meetings very interesting and enjoyable, Ray assured Burt.

Asking for time to give it some thought, Burt volunteered the opinion that he thought his communication had been all right. Ray sensed that Burt had interpreted his suggestion as a criticism and hastened to explain that none had been intended. He tried to present the idea of Burt's attending as an opportunity to develop himself and broaden his understanding of communication, but there was still no change in Burt's expression. "Look, Burt," he said, "just the fact that I'm having trouble making you see that I have your interest in mind illustrates the kinds of problems we have in communicating. I know what I want to say, but you're getting a different picture. We discussed things like that when I took the course. If you take the course, you might use this conversation for a case problem."

Burt said he was sorry he misunderstood, but said it without much conviction, and promised to let Ray know in a day or so. He also apologized for being in a little bit of a hurry but Wednesday night was bowling night. After a little friendly kidding about bowling scores, Ray and Burt said their good nights and headed for the parking lot.

On the way home Burt argued with himself. On the one hand, he reasoned that if the boss wanted him to take some training that would help him in his job, he should be grateful. There wouldn't be another course like it very soon. On the other hand, he was having trouble enough getting everything done now without knocking an hour off every Wednesday afternoon. To top it off, it had to come on bowling night, which would mean he wouldn't have any time at all with the kids that night. The real hurt, though, was that Ray said he would get a lot out of it. He had always been very careful to keep Ray informed about what was going on, and now to be practically told he needed communication training made him wonder where he had failed. No matter how you add it up, he thought, a suggestion from the boss is the same as an order. If I know what's good for me, I'll take the course.

On the way to the cafeteria the next day, Burt met Harry Gates, the man whose place he had taken. Harry was a popular man whom Burt admired; Burt tried to pattern his own approach to the job after Harry's. Burt always felt that Harry was the one man most responsible for his promotion. It was he who broke the news to him and gave him the most encouragement. Burt was especially pleased to see Harry now. It would give him a chance to voice his concern about taking training to his friend. Harry welcomed Burt's invitation to lunch.

Harry laughed when Burt related his conversation with Ray and explained his concern. "Relax, fella," Harry said, "Ray's OK. He's not picking on you. He probably made the same suggestion to every assembly supervisor who reports to him. Just forget the whole thing." Burt said he couldn't forget it because he had promised Ray an answer soon.

Pushing his chair back and lighting his pipe, Harry said, "Look, Burt, let me give you some advice. A supervisor's got one job—get out production. You keep your nose clean, meet your production schedules, and you're all set. They can't ask any more of you. Now from what I hear you're doing just that—even doing better than I did. I like that. It makes my last recommendation a good one.

"Now, Ray and Oscar haven't been around as long as I have. They're from what you might call the new school—heads filled with a lot of this management development jazz. Somebody sold them a bill of goods—probably the new training guy who thinks he knows how to run the whole company after a couple of years here. Anyhow, they're both smart enough to know which side their bread is buttered on, and that's with the stuff that's coming off the end of the lines. You keep that coming the way you have been, and you're all right."

Burt asked Harry if his refusal to take the training might not be interpreted as a lack of interest in his job and the company. "I don't think so," Harry replied, "but what if it is? They still can't do anything to you as long as you're pushing out the stuff that brings in the money. You've got enough headaches and pressure keeping those lines producing without going to school. Don't stick your neck out any more than you have to. That's the way I operated for almost twenty years, and if it worked for me, it ought to work just as well for you. With all the new reports they get topside from the data processing guys, you just know they're interested in only three things—production, high quality, and low costs. No sir, if you ask me they can take all these highbrow training programs, throw them out the window, and never miss them."

Back on the job, Burt began the debate with himself all over again. He hadn't expected Harry to be quite so outspoken about personal development. He felt much the same way as Harry did. There's a limit to how much they can expect of a man. Yet Burt knew it wasn't that simple—not that clean-cut. He was bothered by what Harry had said, even though agreeing with him would make his decision easy. He knew there was more to his job than just production. Production is important, but it's not the whole job, he thought. It's fine for Harry to say what has worked for the past twenty years; but times change, and I've got the next twenty years to think about.

The whole problem suddenly loomed much larger than just the communication training program. He knew now that he would tell Ray he'd sit in on the program, but what next? He knew that there would be other requests. Was he opening the door to more of the same by saying yes this time? What would be expected of him in the future? Would raises and advancements be affected by his willingness or refusal to go along on training in the future?

"Ray is a guy you can level with," Burt said to himself. "Maybe I'll jot down a few things I can ask him." Here's what he wrote.

1. Is studying a part of the supervisor's job if he's getting out the production expected from his department?
2. Does management expect a man to put in his own time on self-development? If they want him to study, shouldn't they set it up all on company time?
3. When does this studying and going to training programs stop?
4. If management wanted to conduct training, why couldn't something be set up that would help him get out production?

THE NEED FOR CONTINUAL SELF–DEVELOPMENT

From any point of view self-development is a growing requirement of the supervisory job. It's not just something dreamed up by educators and training directors to make work for themselves. We said in Chapter 1 that continual self-development will be a way of life for the management-minded supervisor. Is this simply academic propaganda? No, it's just a cold fact of management life that is best illustrated by the feelings of a Chicago plant manager.

His firm employs nearly 5,000 people and has over 200 supervisors on the payroll. Electronic data processing had been introduced into manufacturing operations in the past year, they had just completed total automation of one production line, and they were planning the conversion of others to automated processing. His outlook was tough:

> Nearly one-third of our present supervisory force are going to be doing something different within the next year unless they decide to do something to prepare themselves to keep pace with the changes this company is undergoing. Many of them are mistakes we made years ago in selecting our supervisors. Some of the others have picked up the cockeyed idea that they have arrived—that they can just keep quiet and coast their way to retirement.
>
> The day has long passed when we can afford that kind of attitude. It used to take us six months to know what had happened in a department. Now we know every day at the end of the day what a supervisor has accomplished in his department. Our data processing unit is giving us information on the results we achieve daily. We're finding out who's doing a job for us and who isn't.
>
> The members of the group I'm talking about either don't give a thought to improving themselves or are sitting around waiting for us to spoon-feed it to them. Well, it's not going to happen. If they're going to be managers, they're going to have to act like managers. We'll give them all the help they want, but they're going to have to take some of the initiative. If they want to attend an institute at the university, they only have to ask. If a group wants technical courses set up in the plant, we'll set them up. We'll underwrite correspondence or night school courses, but we don't ram any of these things down their throats.
>
> We're moving ahead fast to stay in front of our competition. There's no other choice. I'm happy to say that most of our supervisors realize the part they have to play in keeping us and themselves ahead. Those who don't are unfortunately going to be eased into early retirement or fall by the wayside.

His attitude is tough but typical of the feeling of many managers who have been disturbed by what they say is the tendency of the younger generation of supervisors to sit and say, "Well, here I am—develop me." Every indication points to increasing technological advancement in both the office and the plant. With those changes will come increased demands for better management, particularly at the first level. The supervisor of today who is content with things as they are will soon find that things just don't stay that way.

Learning is a lifelong process. The challenge is how to direct and channel that learning in order to grow in a job. Formal education—high school or college—isn't enough to sustain a manager in his job very long. With today's knowledge explosion formal classroom education quickly becomes obsolete. The dean of a well-known engineering school, for instance, claims that in five to seven years the knowledge of a graduating engineer will be obsolete. A medical doctor who is not abreast of the latest developments in his field is cheating his patients. Supervisors have a similar responsibility to keep pace with technical advances in their chosen fields and to understand the new developments in the practice of management.

The West Coast branch manager of a farm-implement manufacturer underscored the concern of many high-level managers when he said while attending a seminar, "I expect my supervisors to have some self-development activity in process at all times. I'm particularly concerned that they read constantly, and I don't mean novels and murder mysteries. I mean a planned reading program geared to their jobs as managers. I expect them to keep me posted on what they're reading." This is an extreme attitude, perhaps, but it is indicative of the interest more and more managers have in seeing their subordinates direct their own development.

We seem to be almost completely out of the era when an organization accepts the total responsibility for the development of its people. Most companies recognize their obligation to make developmental opportunities available and to stimulate an interest in those opportunities. But they are at the same time supporting the principle that in the final analysis all development is self-development. In setting forth its philosophy on management development the Illinois Bell Company stated, "Formal development programs may have limited value unless the individual assumes a major share of the responsibility for training." In further explanation it stated, "The man must feel a strong personal responsibility to plan and direct his own program for self development." In these brief but comprehensive statements two facts emerge clearly:

(1) The company is vitally concerned with the development of management personnel. (2) Initiative for planning and directing self-development should come from the individual, not the company.

WHY SHOULD THE SUPERVISOR BE CONCERNED?

Since self-development requires a supervisor's own time and effort, he might take a rather selfish approach and ask, Should I be concerned? After all, as a member of management I have it made, haven't I? This, in essence, is what Burt Hall had in the back of his mind, and his thinking was reinforced by Harry Gates. It's also the type of thinking demonstrated by those 65 or so supervisors in the Chicago plant who were the concern of their plant manager. Aside from the high priority of management's expectations, there are three good, selfish reasons why a supervisor should be concerned. Let's look at them.

To Increase His Promotional Potential

Reading this book is one evidence of interest in advancement. In the great majority of plants, the supervisor's job is not a dead-end job. In a recent University of Wisconsin survey, for example, plant managers were asked whether foremen in their plants could advance to higher-level jobs, and 75 percent responded affirmatively.

Evidence of self-improvement activities will always be given consideration by companies when they search their ranks to promote from within. They want to know how well prepared a man is to take on higher responsibility. Common sense tells us that promotions will go to those who demonstrate that they are prepared for them. One sure way of showing interest in a better job is by doing more than is expected— that is, the job plus self-improvement activities.

Supervisors have set themselves apart from the great majority of the working population by accepting the supervisory jobs they now have. Surveys indicate that seven out of ten production-level employees have no interest in supervisory jobs because they don't want the responsibility that goes with them. Many organizations have difficulty finding qualified people to take on the responsibilities of supervision. Supervisors have already demonstrated a willingness to shoulder the extra burden and in all probability have an interest in the promotional ladder. If that is so, the potential for promotion will be enhanced by making self-improvement a way of life.

To Improve His Effectiveness in His Present Job

According to the late Moorhead Wright of the General Electric Company, "Primary emphasis must be on development in the present assignment rather than emphasis on the promotional ladder. . . . The development process should be integrated with the normal conduct of the business so that they work together instead of competing for the manager's time and energy. The manager's work is actually simplified, rather than being made more complex, by the development process." * Supervisors are all interested in how they can do today's job better today, and it stands to reason that the best criterion for promotion is performance on the present job.

Jobs are changing constantly. Approaches to management practices have undergone drastic changes in the past decade. For example, in evaluating management effectiveness the primary emphasis used to be on personal traits such as loyalty, judgment, and initiative. Now the emphasis is almost completely on the practice of appraising performance on the basis of results achieved. Those who have had the same job title for the past five years know very well that the job they have today isn't the same job they had five years ago. In a recent University of Wisconsin survey, 87 percent of the plant managers responding said that the foreman's job carries more responsibility today than it did five years ago. Certainly no one can dispute that conscientiously followed self-improvement activities pay off handsomely in meeting increasing responsibilities.

To Live a Fuller, Richer Life

To some this last reason may not seem valid, but the truth of it became quite apparent in the evaluation of a supervisory training program of a large Wisconsin paper mill. The program had been established for the usual reasons: to improve morale, to lower grievances, to improve productivity, and to lower costs. Over two hundred super-

* From an article entitled "How Do People Grow in a Business Organization?"

visors participated in the basic program that included discussions of the supervisor's job, human relations, motivation, discipline, job instruction, communication, and self-development over a two-year period. Follow-up interviews were conducted by a university professor with a cross section of about eighty supervisors. When he asked what they had gotten out of the program, he received answers like these: "I'm a better father than I used to be"; "I don't blow my stack as often or as quickly as I used to"; "I've learned there are two sides to any argument"; "I get along better with my wife"; "I enjoy working more than I used to"; "I've learned that my employees are human, too." When their comments were brought together, the great majority were saying that they were enjoying life more. At first glance this information might be totally unexpected, until we stop to consider that the function of all higher education is the enrichment of people's lives.

If broadening himself through self-development activities makes a supervisor approach his job with greater confidence and satisfaction, does he not have reason enough to begin a self-development program? People's lives are to a large extent what they make of them. We don't, of course, have control over everything that comes to us in life, but we do control what we put into life and especially into our working life. The more we put into life or the job, the more we are likely to get out of it.

CHANGING THINKING ABOUT DEVELOPMENT

Research done at the General Electric Company and reported by the late Moorhead Wright in the article entitled "How Do People Grow in a Business Organization?" contributed greatly to some significant shifts in emphasis in our thinking about management development. Past efforts, for example, to identify the traits of an ideal manager or leader and then to try to develop these traits in all managers were doomed to failure. Wright put it this way,

> The development of people cannot be based upon any set of ideal or specified personality characteristics or traits. . . . The truth is that there just *isn't* any standard pattern of personality traits that make a good manager. . . . So the focus is upon the work rather than the individual personality. . . . Work can be seen—identified —analyzed—measured. . . . This viewpoint provides a more logi-

cal, reasonable, and therefore reasonably secure framework upon which to base action, instead of 99 different ideas that somebody might have about what is important in managing.

People spend their whole lives developing their personalities. The chances of changing their personalities are rather remote by the time they are adults. What we should be concerned about is the skills and knowledge required to do our job. Education can contribute greatly to improving our skills or adding to our body of knowledge. Why shouldn't we, then, concentrate our efforts in those areas where we stand a reasonable chance of success and leave personality development to the charm schools?

A second significant change in thinking about development concerns the idea once commonly held that development takes place in the conference room or classroom. It was felt that managers or supervisors were not being developed unless they were attending in-house training programs, outside seminars, institutes, or evening courses, or completing correspondence courses. While these educational experiences can make substantial contributions toward adding to a body of knowledge and broadening viewpoints, we are becoming increasingly aware that most growth occurs on the job. The problem that faces the supervisor in on-the-job development is to see that he arranges for himself well-directed growth experiences and that he does not leave his development to chance.

Again the General Electric research touched on this point when Wright wrote, "A man's development is 90 percent the results of his experience in his day-to-day work. . . . Every man in the Company is having experience in his day-to-day work that tends to develop him or to retard his development. He is daily reacting to the climate in which he works and to his relationship with his immediate manager. And these appear to be more important factors in the developmental process." It's important to recognize from Wright's comments that day-to-day experience may either stimulate or retard development. A supervisor who uses his own initiative in cooperating with the boss will move toward positive development.

A third significant change in thinking about growth and development is evident in the shift of primary responsibility for planning and directing developmental activities from the company to the individual manager. The mark of a good manager is his demonstrated ability to take charge—to make things happen rather than to wait for things to happen. A management-minded supervisor will seize every opportunity he can to learn more about how he can do his job better. No one learns until he wants to learn. Over one hundred years ago, Abraham Lincoln observed, "You cannot help men permanently by doing for them what they could and should be doing for themselves." And even further back in history Galileo said, "You cannot teach a man anything. You can only help him to find it within himself." No matter how much or how little an organization provides in the way of growth experience, supervisors cannot escape their obligation to plan and implement a program of personal development.

THREE ESSENTIALS OF PERSONAL GROWTH

Development, we have observed, does not happen by accident. Well, then, how does it happen? Development is the supervisor's prime responsibility. But where do we go from here? Thousands of management-minded supervisors have found the answers to these two questions. They have found that there are three essential ingredients in cultivating their own growth as managers: an inventory, a plan, and follow-through. The presence of these essentials should assure some growth. but how much growth depends entirely on their quality. Fortunately for us, quality control is in the supervisor's hands. Let's take these points up one at a time.

Inventory

What's my status now? What do I need to perform my job the way management expects? How well am I doing my job now? In what areas will improvement activities help me most? A good personal inventory conscientiously conducted should answer these questions for the supervisor. A practical two-phase approach is needed. First, what skills, knowledge, and abilities are required by anyone to do my job today? Second, how well am I performing each of these?

There aren't many people who have a better idea of the requirements of the supervisor's job than the supervisor himself. Certainly no book could state with any validity what the supervisor's job is. We can recognize some skills and knowledge that are common to many jobs, but the final inventory form is something each supervisor must complete individually according to his own conception of his job. Here, then, are some common requirements for the first-level supervisor: job knowledge (for example, knowledge of chemistry, machinery, sanitation, law, building codes, systems programming, products being sold) and the ability to train employees, maintain discipline, improve work methods, plan and organize, delegate responsibility, communicate (in spoken, or written form), maintain quality standards, motivate employees, and control costs. Careful consideration will determine which of these and many others have the greatest priority in a supervisor's own job.

Some will find it easier to think of it this way: If the boss were to evaluate my performance, what would I want him to consider as a fair list of factors? Many times the form used in an organization's performance appraisal programs will provide a starting point for construcing such an inventory. Certainly, if a supervisor is being evaluated for purposes of salary increases or promotion potential, he will want to include the factors on which he will be evaluated in his inventory. He should be able to sift out the six, eight, or ten most important aspects of his job. Let this list comprise the first phase of the inventory.

The second phase of the inventory is obvious. A self-evaluation on how well a supervisor is performing in each of the areas contained in his inventory form is the critical step. A sample analysis form is shown in Figure 2. It shows five levels or grades (ranging from weak to excellent) on which performance can be rated.

Many supervisors ask whether a man can do an accurate job of evaluating his own performance. The answer must be an unqualified yes, provided that he is fair with himself. No one has a better knowledge about a supervisor's own performance than the supervisor— including the boss. The problem is most frequently one of honestly recognizing strengths and avoiding the tendency to let false modesty downgrade the whole appraisal process. No supervisor would be in a management position unless he rated excellent in at least some of the factors that make up a personal inventory. It is just as important for us to recognize strengths as it is to face up to limitations.

The Plan for Self-development

The first step in planning is a goal to give direction to the planning process. After completing the inventory, a supervisor should turn his

Self-analysis for Supervisors

Skills, knowledge, and abilities required on my job today	Weak	Below par	Satis-factory	Above average	Excel-lent

Figure 2.

attention to where he wants to go as a result of the self-analysis. Experience teaches that resolutions or vows to do a better job in general don't accomplish very much. The best method is to select one area of the inventory and concentrate improvement efforts on that one knowledge or skill. Since the time available for developmental activities is limited, concentrating efforts on one area yields much better results.

For a long time the selection of an area for concentration would have been automatic. Standard procedure specified selecting the weakest area. More recently we have begun to recognize that supervisors might do themselves more good by working on those areas where they are already strong. The theory here is that they are valuable on their jobs because of the strengths they possess and because their interest in the areas of their strengths is likely to be high. Interest and motivation are essential for continued developmental effort. Therefore, it would appear that supervisors are likely to help themselves more and to accomplish more by selecting an area of strength as a target for personal development.

Since development is a personal matter it deserves a more personal approach. What, the supervisor should ask, is likely to do me the most good? If I can help myself most by concentrating on something in which I have already demonstrated strength, then let me do so. On the other hand, if one particular skill is holding him back or handicapping him, then by all means he should take steps to upgrade himself in that area. It is important to identify the one ability he wants to improve as the basis for his planning.

Now whatever he has chosen, what can he do to help himself develop a higher degree of proficiency? What resources are available? Figure 3 is simply a form to help think through a variety of activities that would contribute to development. It calls for a general listing of possible activities and resources such as special job assignments, books, staff departments, training available inside or outside the company, analysis of current practices in the area selected, and consultation with the boss.

Figure 4 calls for the specifics of a real plan. Having completed the general list, he must now pin down the activities which will be most helpful to him. The first column requires a definition of specific, realistic activities which would be helpful to his growth. The second column allows the supervisor to detail how he's going to get started. Such details might include visiting the plant or city library, attending an institute away from the plant, or checking to see what material the training, production planning and control, or industrial engineering departments might have. Essential in the planning of self-development is to establish target dates for each activity. The dates provide a control against procrastination. He should set the dates realistically, keeping in mind the many other demands on his time.

Follow-through

The best plans for self-development are a complete waste of time until they are put into effect, and that's the hard part. Unless the supervisor has a real desire to improve, not much is likely to happen. Little can be done that hasn't already been done by management to

Personal Development Plan—Phase 1

To improve my ability to _____

Possible things I can do to develop this ability (for example, consider reference materials, job assignments, consulting those skilled in this area, staff assistance, internal and external training, trade publications and meetings, analysis of current practices):

1.

2.

3.

4.

5.

6.

7.

8.

9.

10.

Figure **3.**

give him the desire. Assuming that the supervisor has carefully defined his job in terms of the skills and knowledge it requires, that he has fairly appraised his own performance, that he has selected the area in which he wants to develop, and that he has made a realistic, workable plan, the rest depends on his own initiative. There are many people in an organization who are ready and willing to help, but they are resources the supervisor must cultivate. Job assignments which provide an opportunity for growth experience will more than likely

Personal Development Plan—Phase 2   **Be Specific—Be Realistic**

What to do	How to get started: Sources of help	Starting date	Completion date
1.			
2.			
3.			
4.			
5.			
6.			

Figure 4.

have to be asked for. Books and periodicals are waiting on the shelves for the chance to make their contributions.

Progress in self-development is measured in terms of the work the supervisor completes toward his goal. In terms of performance, did he do what he set out to accomplish? Once he has done everything spelled out in his plan, the inventory and appraisal might be repeated. Is further effort in this area indicated, or has the time come to channel his efforts into another area? Has his job changed in any way that would require special study? Short-range plans should be frequently evaluated and improved to suit current job requirements. Many supervisors find that they can take the boss into their confidence on self-development plans. He has a great interest in what the supervisor is doing and is in a position to give him invaluable guidance and assistance. Besides, it never hurts the supervisor to let the boss know that he is serious about making himself as effective in his job as possible.

A WAY OF LIFE

Self-improvement is more than developing a plan and following that plan. For the management-minded supervisor self-improvement is a way of life. He is constantly on the lookout for ways of broadening his knowledge and improving his value. Opportunities to do this occur almost daily and he can't afford to adopt the attitude of Burt Hall, who wondered when it would all stop. It never stops. It's part of the job. Let's take a look at some ways a supervisor can increase his value to his company.

Be Alert to the Boss's Needs

The supervisor's job is to make the boss look good and support him in any way he can. If the boss is working on special assignments or projects where the supervisor can make a contribution, the supervisor has a real opportunity to learn and to help him. Selfishly, the supervisor can recognize that if he helps his superior, he is more likely to help him when he wants assistance or approval to take some special training.

Read to Keep Abreast of Developments

Modern-day supervision requires extensive reading. More and more supervisors select periodicals for reading on a regular basis. The trade journals in a supervisor's field do an excellent job of keeping him posted on new developments and innovations. Many excellent supervisory publications provide valuable insight into the supervisory job. Reading a book on management techniques every year or every six months isn't too heavy a burden for most, and it can pay handsome dividends.

Be an Alert Listener

Listening is learning. The boss, staff personnel, subordinates, employees—all have ideas and communicate them in conversation. Suggestions for improvement in the department are frequently available just for the listening.

Be an Alert Observer

Without exception, supervisors who have participated in any of the variations of the DuPont Observation-Perception program report that they have observed things in their department that they never noticed before. The supervisor need only take a tour of the department for the sole purpose of looking for safety hazards to discover how much goes on right under his nose. The supervisor who is constantly observing the department will more than likely find many ways to make improvements.

Set up Targets

Constant improvement of departmental operations is dependent on the supervisor's having standards and meeting or exceeding those standards. Where he can measure results in such areas as production, quality, costs, and safety, he can set realistic improvement targets either monthly or quarterly and keep score. Every target reached is another step in making himself more valuable to his organization and is something he can regard with pride as a personal signpost of progress.

Perhaps a supervisor will never achieve everything he sets out to do in self-development, but he will find satisfaction in this approach to his job. So the words of Ben Franklin have real meaning for him, "I never arrived at the perfection I had been so ambitious of attaining, but fell short of it; yet I was by the endeavor a better and happier man than I otherwise would have been."

HIGHLIGHTS

1. Self-development is a growing requirement of the supervisor's job. The supervisor can no longer be satisfied with things as they are but must improve himself constantly to keep abreast of the changes in his organization.
2. Management expects the supervisor to take the initiative in planning his own development instead of the passive attitude "Here I am—develop me."
3. Three reasons why the supervisor should be concerned about his own development are:
   a. To increase his promotional potential
   b. To improve his effectiveness in his present job
   c. To live a fuller, richer life

4. Some significant changes in current thinking about supervisory development are:
   a. A switch from the emphasis on developing "ideal" traits to a concentration on the skill and knowledge required to do the supervisory job
   b. The recognition that most growth and development occurs on the job and not in the conference room
   c. The growing acceptance of the idea that primary responsibility for planning and directing development rest with the individual and not the company
5. Three essentials for the personal growth of the supervisor include:
   a. A careful inventory of the knowledge and skills required by his job coupled with a self-analysis of how well he is performing each
   b. A specific, realistic plan to give direction to his efforts
   c. The follow-through necessary to see that the plan is implemented
6. People act according to the way they think, and for the management-minded supervisor self-development is a way of life.

DISCUSSION QUESTIONS

1. Explain in your own words why today's supervisor must be concerned about self-development.
2. Why is the personal inventory so essential as a first step to self-development?
3. Is the trend toward putting the responsibility for planning his development on the shoulders of the supervisor sound from the company's point of view? From the supervisor's point of view? Explain your answers.
4. In your own words, evaluate the "traits" approach to self-development. What are its limitations?
5. What kind of on-the-job activities contribute to personal development?
6. Does management have a right to expect a supervisor to engage in self-development activities on his own time? Why or why not?
7. What are the advantages and disadvantages of consulting the boss about self-development plans?

SUGGESTIONS FOR FURTHER STUDY

Bittel, Lester R.
What Every Supervisor Should Know, 2d ed.
Chapter 35, McGraw-Hill Book Company, New York, 1968

Drucker, Peter F.
The Practice of Management
Chapter 29, Harper & Row, Publishers, Incorporated, New York, 1959

Gardiner, Glenn, and Associates
Managerial Skills for Supervisors
Chapter 12, Elliott Service Company, Mount Vernon, N.Y., 1960

Lateiner, Alfred R.
The Techniques of Supervision
Chapter 10, National Foremen's Institute, New London, Conn., 1954

THREE

MANAGEMENT COMMUNICATION

THE CASE OF THE CONFUSED COMMUNICATOR

Jack Holt, supervisor of final assembly, was sitting looking at the ceiling when Burt Hall stopped in on his way home for the day. Burt and Jack lived in the same neighborhood and shared rides on occasion. The new training sessions on communication prompted Burt to ask Jack if he were going to attend and if they might take turns driving those days.

"Are you kidding?" Jack blurted. "The lousy communication in this outfit has me ready to look for a new job. Life is too short to put up with what I've had to endure this past week. I can think of a hundred guys around here who could make my job easier if they knew how to communicate. Just once, I'd like to find out what they expect of me. How do they think I can do a job if no one tells me what's going on? I haven't got a crystal ball. If old man Palmer wants results, he's got to give me a little cooperation. This is no one-man show. I can't do it all alone."

"Hold on a minute, Jack," Burt kidded. "It can't be as bad as all that."

"You don't know the half of it," said Jack. "Let me tell you what happened just this morning. I was checking over the production reports from Friday and noticed the Acme job didn't go out when it was supposed to. So, I went to see Jake to find out why. He told me that Mr. Palmer had been down Friday morning and ordered him to move the Sampson Company job ahead of everything."

'What did you do?" Burt asked.

"I did what anybody else would do in my place," Jack replied. "I told Jake that from now on he takes orders from nobody but me and that I can't have every Tom, Dick, and Harry coming in here changing production schedules. Then when I calmed down, I went up to Oscar's office to tell him in a nice way that I'd appreciate his making changes through me. Well, I got a quick brush-off. He told me that I wasn't around and that the job had to get out—period. Now, how in blazes can you run a department with cooperation like that?"

Burt didn't try to answer because it was obvious that Jack had more to say.

"Friday afternoon is another good example. Boy, that was a beaut," Jack continued. "The word came down at noon that another job scheduled to be shipped this week would have to go before the week-end. That's not so bad. It happens every once in a while. I figure that if we all pitched in, we could handle it with about two and a half hours overtime. About 2:30 I started to make the rounds to tell everybody we'd have to work late, and you'd think I was asking them to work the whole weekend without pay. Grousing and griping was all I got from nearly everyone. Sure, a couple of meat hounds were happy, but I never heard so many excuses in all my life from the rest. I finally got so fed up with their unreasonable attitudes that I just told them to quit the damned griping and get the stuff out so we could all go home. You'd think that anyone with an ounce of brains would understand that you have to put up with a little inconvenience to take care of a good customer now and then. On top of all that, no one bothered to say anything to Shipping, and the stuff was still sitting down there this morning."

Burt could only ask, "Shouldn't you have followed up with Ship-ping?"

"Why should I? It's not my job. We got the stuff assembled and sent it down to them. That's where my responsibility ends. If they want to improve communications around here, why don't they start by seeing that everybody does his own job and set up some procedures? Then maybe people wouldn't go behind my back like last week." Jack con-tinued, "When the word got out that Stan Ames was going to be moved up, I got to thinking that Tony Puccia was ready to tackle a supervisory job and planned to talk to Ray about it. Before I even had the chance, Ray was down here saying that Tony had asked him for a crack at the job. Ray told me that he wouldn't make a move without my OK and wanted to know what I thought about trying Tony out. Well, I queered that deal in a hurry. I told Ray that Tony wasn't ready for supervision yet and that I couldn't get along without him while we're so busy. But just as soon as I got rid of Ray, I got Tony in here but quick and let him have it with both barrels.

"I asked him how come he didn't tell me he wanted to be a super-visor and how come he didn't come to me first instead of going over my head to Ray. Well, he looked kind of sheepish and said he thought he had a better chance with Ray, that he wasn't sure of where he stood with me. You know what I said? I said, 'You know now, because you're going to wait a long time before you get another chance.' He's been pouting ever since, but if he gets away with going over my head, pretty soon everybody will be trying it.

"And it's not just my guys that can't communicate. It works two ways, you know. When you're on the receiving end, you have to use your head a little, too. Last Wednesday one of my bellyachers complained that the night clean-up crew wasn't doing its job. It wasn't the first time he complained, so I wrote a memo to the crew leader and told him to get this place cleaned up because I didn't want any more complaints. The next morning you'd hardly recognize the place. It really looked nice. But then things started popping. It turned out that the crew spent the whole night in my department and never got around to the others."

"I know," said Burt, "they sure didn't get over into my area. When I called Barney, he said that you had something special on and had them tied up all that night. I just figured I'd keep quiet as long as it didn't happen again."

"You're probably the only one who did," Jack told Burt. "I had four calls that day from men Barney told the same thing to, so I waited for him to come in Thursday night. I wanted to know why he had the whole crew spend the entire night in my department. The dumb cluck said he assumed from my memo that top brass had been complaining and that I wanted a real spit-and-polish housecleaning. Man, I really told him off. I asked him who in hell gave him the right to assume anything and told him to ask if he didn't understand a simple written instruction. He just put his old tail between his legs and walked off. I'll bet it's the last time he pulls a stunt like that.

"You see what I mean, Burt. If everybody did their job the way they were supposed to, we wouldn't have any communications problems and we wouldn't be asked to waste our time going to any communication school. No sir, first I've got to see some evidence that it helps upstairs, and then we probably wouldn't need it."

Burt, without much enthusiasm, told Jack that he might be right, but as long as he had signed up for the program, he would go. Actually his conversation with Jack stimulated his interest in the program because he could see in Jack's attitude indications that Jack might be his own problem. Burt began to wonder whether attitudes would be discussed in the program, because they certainly seemed to have a lot to do with Jack's feelings about communication. In fact, the more he thought about it, the more he became convinced that Jack was in greater need of communication training than any of the people he had referred to as his problems.

By the time Burt arrived home, he decided that he wanted to plunge into the coming program with gusto. The best way to do that, he felt, was to write down some of the questions he would like answers to, if not in the first session, then in one of the later ones. By dinnertime here's what he had written.

1. What is the supervisor's responsibility for communication? Was something wrong with the way Jack was looking at communication when he said it stinks in this company?
2. Would more written communications have helped Jack? After all, there was that one situation with the instructions to Barney on the clean-up crew. What went wrong there?
3. How should Jack have handled the problem of the overtime work needed to get that job out Friday night?
4. Nobody likes to be bypassed, and it happened to Jack twice— once when Mr. Palmer changed the production schedules and again when Tony went to Ray Ford about a promotion. Didn't Jack have a right to be peeved? How should situations like that be handled?

COMMUNICATION: ATTITUDE OR METHOD?

Burt Hall was beginning to put his finger on one of the most frequently overlooked or misunderstood facets of the complex area of management communication—the tremendous importance that individual attitudes play in the effectiveness of an organization's communications. Without much hesitation most executives, educators, and consultants will acknowledge that communication stands today as management's number one problem. Yet each one of us has the potential to be an expert communicator. We have all the methods and procedures necessary to do an outstanding job. What most of us need is a full appreciation of what communication means, what prevents us from being as effective as we might be, and what we can do to build our communication skills. Once we have developed an understanding of how communication works, we don't need communication commandments.

For years we thought of communication in terms of the media by which we communicate. To the office manager communication meant teletype and letter writing; to the production manager it was blueprints, specifications, production orders, and reports; and to the executive it was policy statements, directives, and meetings. More recently we defined communication as the giving and receiving of the information needed for intelligent action and decisions. Intelligent action and decisions are expected of everyone in an organization from the messenger boy to the chief executive. Yet no one can do his job unless he knows what is expected of him and where he stands in relation to the people he must work with. Supervisors must recognize their need for information from their superiors, from other operating departments, from staff personnel, and from employees. Jack Holt's concept of communication was essentially limited to this one-way flow to himself. But supervisors have an equal and often greater obligation to give these same people the information they need to function intelligently. Jack never understood this side of the communication picture.

Today our concept of communication has an added dimension— the dimension of depth. Today we define communication as *the creation of understanding,* recognizing that whenever messages are transmitted from sender to receiver, the whole point and purpose of the communication is to create understanding between the two. What is transmitted may be words, actions, facial expressions, tone of voice, gestures, and even silence, but each contributes in some way to an understanding of what is wanted.

It has been reliably estimated that supervisors spend about 85 percent of their time communicating. Those who question this statement by claiming that they have too much work to do to spend that much time in communication, must ask themselves what they do that doesn't involve communication. Every time they instruct an employee or give him an order, they are communicating. Reading or creating reports, job tickets, specifications, time cards, letters, memos, or any other type of paper work is communication. Attending meetings, listening to employees' problems, complaints and ideas, listening to orders and requests from the boss, talking to customers and suppliers, telephoning maintenance and service personnel, and answering requests for information are all a part of daily communication. It is impossible to function as a supervisor without spending a major portion of the time communicating.

The effectiveness of supervisors and managers is directly proportionate to their skill as communicators. The management-minded supervisor has a keen awareness of the tremendous importance communication has in his day-to-day functioning. Each chapter in this book covers a facet of the supervisor's job that is wholly dependent on communication. Whether we're discussing appraising performance, motivating employees, training people, disciplining, giving orders, or initiating change, we're discussing supervisory skills that require the creation of understanding. As supervisors set personal goals in their department, whether they be production, quality, attendance, safety, or cost goals, they realize that effective communication is an absolute necessity in achieving those goals. In Chapter 1 we identified the major responsibility of a management-minded supervisor. We can easily see that the supervisor's skill in discharging those responsibilities is built on a foundation of effective communication. Management is communication.

Jack Holt personified an extremely short-sighted attitude that seems more and more to prevail in the area of communication. Increasingly, managers are developing a tendency to look outside themselves for the reason for communication failure. According to Jack Holt, Barney, Ray Ford, Oscar Palmer, and his whole department were the fault of the problems he was experiencing. Not once could he see himself as the problem or recognize that he had an opportunity to prevent each of his four problems. Actually any number of people could have eliminated those problems if they had felt it their personal responsibility to create understanding. For example, Barney might have read Jack's memo and questioned Jack about where the complaint had come from and how much extra cleaning was needed. Jack, of course, could have reread his memo and decided that a spoken explanation of what he wanted would have been better. Jack may have been right when he said it wasn't his job to tell Shipping about the rush job coming down Friday night. But suppose he had thought, "This job must be pretty important to keep my whole department on overtime. Just to play it safe, I'd better give Shipping a call to tell them when they can expect it." Not his job? No, but it would have resulted in far better customer and internal relations.

Cooperation and communication in an organization go hand in hand. When two people have mutual respect for one another, it isn't necessary to spell out rules and procedures for communicating. They'll take care of their communication very nicely and without help. But when two people deal at arm's length out of mutual disrespect, then all the principles and procedures in the world won't help. They'll misunderstand, forget, and accuse each other of poor communication without regard to their own responsibility.

How often have we heard complaints about what a poor job management does of communicating? "If only we had a procedure covering that." "Why didn't they tell me so I'd have it before the union?" "How can I interpret policy when I don't know what policy is?" These are complaints we've all heard from time to time. Management is not "they" but "we," and the supervisor can usually have the information he needs if he asks for it. When our friends have information useful to us, we ask them for it. We don't complain because they're sitting on it. The same holds true for the supervisor in his relations with his boss. The management-minded supervisor recognizes his responsibility to get what he needs in order to function effectively and to give what is needed by others to do their jobs.

Supervisors should also recognize the responsibility they have to make the boss look good. Keeping him informed of everything he needs to know about departmental operations is a vital part of the supervisor's job. What the boss wants to know may include changes in personnel requirements, problems in the department that will affect other departments or that will reach higher levels, changes that the supervisor has had to make, disciplinary actions he has taken, progress on jobs or projects in which the boss is interested, delays in receiving materials or services, suggestions for improving operations, or anything the boss will need to know in working with his superiors. Supervisors should be sure that he never has occasion to learn from someone else what he should have learned from them.

Some supervisors have observed that by being precise in communicating with the boss, they have trained the boss to communicate better with them. If setting the example is a good way of training subordinates, why shouldn't it be just as effective in training the boss? As he discovers that the supervisor is concerned with keeping him posted, he begins to appreciate the imporance of good communication. Then no one needs to tell him how to communicate. He does it naturally. Improvement in communication between the supervisor and his boss begins when someone becomes aware that improvement is needed and decides to do something about it. Cooperation begets cooperation, and cooperation is born out of good communication relationships.

Effectiveness in communicating is much more the result of attitudes

than of methods or procedures. The moment we begin to blame communication failures on particular people, we intensify the misunderstanding. We put people on the defensive and cause them to say things
they don't mean which builds greater barriers to understanding. The
management-minded supervisor takes an entirely different attitude
toward communication. First, he recognizes that communication does
in fact mean the creation of understanding. Second, he constantly
looks for ways to create better understanding. For example, when a
problem arises, he asks himself how can he get it straightened out
and keep it from happening again; he doesn't waste his time trying to
blame it on someone. Interestingly enough, the helpful, positive attitude in communicating causes others to respond in kind. And since
everything he does depends on communication, a healthy attitude
toward communication can be a great asset in meeting management
responsibilities.

BARRIERS AND BRIDGES

In any communication there is generally a transmitter and a receiver. A supervisor giving an order, for example, functions as a transmitter, and the employee who is to carry out the order is the receiver.
Later, as the employee explains a problem to his supervisor, the
employee becomes the transmitter, and the supervisor the receiver.
Between the transmitter and the receiver we encounter barriers that
prevent us from creating the understanding that is the goal of all
communication. Countless barriers have been identified by experts in
communication, but our purposes will be well served here if we identify
five of the more important ones and then examine ways of eliminating
them through bridges of understanding.

The Listening Barrier

Day in and day out most of the supervisor's communicating is done
in face-to-face situations calling for explanations, orders, and descrip-
tions. If the receiver is to respond, he must not only hear, but he must
understand. This distinction between hearing and understanding is
important because the assumption that listening is the same as hearing is dangerous. We hear with our ears, but we listen with the mind.
It is entirely possible to hear every word a person says but to have

none of it register. It's like the husband who comes home tired from a day's work and wants nothing more than to kick his shoes off and have some time to himself with the evening newspaper. His wife, who has been alone or with small children all day, wants to talk, and talk she will. Her husband hears her voice, but her words don't take on meaning for him until in exasperation she says, "You're not listening to me."

According to Dr. Ralph Nichols of the University of Minnesota, the average person speaks at a rate of about 125 words per minute.* Yet most of us are able to listen, allowing for individual differences, at rates varying between 400 and 600 words per minute. This spare listening or thinking capacity we have gives us time to get ahead of the speaker or to leave him completely while our minds dwell on other topics.

Most of us have probably experienced this type of mental departure from someone who is speaking to us. Sunday morning church services provide an excellent opportunity to check this phenomenon. We go to church with the very best intention of listening carefully to the twenty-minute sermon. Few of us are able to focus all our attention on that message and resist the temptation to turn our thoughts to the activities of the night before, the plans for Sunday afternoon, or any of the other problems we're facing on the job or at home.

One of the characteristics of the poor listener is that he is usually a good bluffer. Seldom willing to admit that he hasn't listened, he will fake understanding and take a chance—often with disastrous consequences. When confronted with his mistakes, he will counter with, "But I thought you said . . ." Unless a person has truly listened to another, there is little chance of creating real understanding, which is the sole purpose of the communication.

Who, we might ask, has the responsibility for listening—the transmitter or the receiver? The obvious answer is that they both do, but let's make it a little more specific and say that individual supervisors have the responsibility for listening in any communication situation. Communication, we said, will be improved by the person who is aware that improvement is necessary. Certainly we can't afford to adopt the attitude that if our explanation is clear, the responsibility for understanding rests with the receiver, any more than we can say, "If he wants

* From "Listening Is a Ten-Part Skill," *Nation's Business,* July, 1957.

me to listen, he'll have to find ways of holding my attention." Whether sending or receiving, we must accept our responsibility to see that understanding results. Working to achieve understanding is the job of the management-minded supervisor who is aware of his communication responsibility.

The Feedback Bridge

In any face-to-face communication the receiver is constantly feeding back reactions (either knowingly or subconsciously) to what is being said. For example, we have all observed that glassy, "I don't know what you're talking about" look on the face of a person to whom we are giving directions. He broadcasts without saying a word the fact that he isn't listening. The receiver is constantly sending out signals that tell us whether or not he's listening. These signals may be in his posture, in his attitude of attention or inattention, or in the nature of his questions or responses. As we learn to watch for these signs and to interpret them, we develop greater skill in getting our message across. It isn't necessary to accuse a person of poor listening when we see his attention wander. We simply say, "Let me see if I can put it another way." Our object is only to ensure that our message is understood. When we blame the failure to listen on the receiver, he simply becomes defensive and listening becomes even more difficult. As emotions cloud the mental processes, listening with true understanding becomes almost impossible.

Up to this point we've discussed only the reading of natural feedback. When we're not sure how to read the feedback we're getting, it's advisable to build more in. This can be done by asking questions. For example, we might ask a person to repeat key points in an instruction, or to explain what he feels might be the logic for following a certain procedure, or to ask for an evaluation of an idea presented. As the listener's responses are fed back, we can determine whether it's safe to proceed or whether we should repeat the explanation. In a lengthy spoken communication the supervisor should build in several deliberate feedback requirements in addition to attempting to read the natural reactions of the listener.

Nichols points out that we can improve our ability to listen by using our extra listening speed to better advantage. He suggests that these four steps be developed into a definite pattern of thought when listening: (1) Try to anticipate what a person is going to talk about or what points he's trying to make. (2) Mentally summarize what he has been saying or what points he has made so far. (3) Weigh the person's evidence by mentally questioning it—Is he accurate? What are his sources? (4) Listen between the lines to what he is really saying with his tone of voice, facial expressions, and body movements. Nichols writes, "Not capitalizing on thought speed is our greatest single handicap. The differential between thought speed and speech speed breeds false feelings of security and mental tangents. Yet, through listening training, this same differential can be readily converted into our greatest asset."

The Semantics Barrier

Semantics is the science that deals with the meaning of words. Meanings of words vary according to the people using them. Many communication experts claim that meanings are in people, not in words. We select the words we choose to communicate with because they convey a picture that we have in our minds. Having come from a different environment, the listener may get an entirely different picture because our words have a different meaning for him. For example, the word *policy* to an executive is a broad general statement or a guideline. To an employee a policy may mean a very specific rule that prevents him from doing something he would like to do. The word *profit* has vastly different meanings to the stockholder and the union official. Our past training, our needs, and our interests give meaning to the words we use.

A classic illustration of the semantics problem is the word *fast*. One expert says it has over eighty different meanings. Let's just look at a few more contradictory meanings. By using the word *fast* to describe a horse, we mean that horse is quick—he can run. The same word used to describe the color in a fabric indicates that the color won't run. Or if the horse is tied fast to a stake, it means he can't run. When fast is used as a religious term, it means to abstain, but a fast woman proves to be one who won't abstain from anything. Or as one wag put it, she won't run from anything. What, then, is an employee to think when he is told make something fast?

Every business has a jargon that is peculiar to that business. Consider the difficulties experienced by a new employee who is being trained by an old-timer who is insensitive to the semantics barrier and who subconsciously uses all the jargon in his vocabulary to demonstrate how much he knows.

The semantics barrier can create problems even within a company in communication between departments. Specialists in accounting, production, research, sales, and finance are all equally adept at speaking a language all their own. It's not improbable that the head of research would have difficulty in making himself understood when communicating with a production foreman or that a production foreman might have a little difficulty in understanding or making himself understood by the computer programmer. For example, the word *hardware* means something different in different departments.

The Bridge of Gearing to the Receiver

Once we are aware of the problem of misunderstanding that can be created by the semantics barrier, we naturally turn our attention to what can be done to remove it. A two-part approach to this problem has proved helpful to many supervisors. First, and most obvious, we need to gear our communications to the vocabulary of the receiver. For example, a man has a great deal more latitude in discussing a production problem with one of the old-timers in the department than in giving directions to a new employee. When we have used words that people don't understand, feedback in the form of facial expression will usually indicate that further explanation is necessary. Special caution is needed when using terms that have obvious common meanings apart from specialized usage. Dr. Berlo of Michigan State University cites the example of the manager who gave his new secretary the only copy of a specification sheet and told her to "burn" it. Burning had come to mean make a copy or burn a copy. Imagine his dismay on learning she had touched a match to that precious piece of paper and tossed the ashes into the wastebasket.

Second, we need to swallow our pride and admit when we're not sure of the meaning of words spoken or written to us. We, too, tend to gamble when we're not sure. The price of pride is frequently too high to pay. We strengthen our standing with people when we seek clarification. Most of us would have far more respect for someone who asks us to be more specific when we request a job "as soon as possible" or "at your earliest convenience." To ask a transmitter exactly what he means by a word or term not clear to us is not only evidence of our interest in serving him but also alerts him to his need to clarify his language.

The Self-interest Barrier

Personal interests act as filters through which communications are received. We listen to what we want to hear, shutting out what we don't want to hear. Our personal desires can very easily color or exaggerate the meaning of what we hear or read. An excellent example of this barrier was introduced in a recent Institute discussion of communication problems. One of the participating supervisors asked the group, "Did you ever hear of a man who got mad when you gave him a raise?" He went on to explain that an employee under his supervision had just finished his probationary period. The supervisor called the man in to tell him that he was extremely pleased with his work, that beginning the following Monday he would go on permanent status, and that beginning the following Monday he would be getting 10 cents an hour more. The employee thanked his supervisor and went back to his job apparently elated. Ten minutes later he was back. He angrily accused his supervisor of trying to pull the wool over his eyes because he found out that the increase was a general one and that every one in the department was getting that 10-cent raise. The institute group tended to agree with the employee and said, "Well, weren't you trying to pull the wool over his eyes?"

"Look at it from my point of view," the supervisor said. "I was pleased with his work, and I told him so. I was putting him on permanent status, and I told him that. Now, we've just had this general increase, and I told him he'd be getting more money. What's wrong with that?"

Most of us would agree that from the supervisor's point of view there was nothing wrong with what he did. However, from the employee's point of view, there was an obvious connection between his excellent work and the raise. Finding out that everyone else was getting a similar raise was a blow to his ego. From a purely logical point of view, the employee was just praised by his boss for good work, put on permanent status, and given a nice increase. Why should there have been a problem?

If we stand back and take an analytical view, we see that both the supervisor and the employee contributed to the misunderstanding. The supervisor was at fault because he was willing to let the employee think that the raise was a reward for good work which as his boss he had recommended. The employee was at fault because his desire for a feeling of importance colored what his supervisor had in fact told him.

Jealousy and personal interests can play havoc in communication between departments especially where rivalry for the boss's favor exists. If management puts more emphasis on results without empha- sizing a real understanding of the total approach at the department level, employees will often put department or personal goals ahead of the welfare of the whole organization. When personal interests become all important and communication takes place on an emotional level, real understanding is nearly impossible. An empire builder in a firm is not likely to add much, if any, substance to the realm of another.

The Empathy Bridge

The importance of empathy for proper supervision will be mentioned several times in this book. By "empathy" I mean simply the ability to put yourself in another person's shoes and see things from his point of view. To develop empathy is to develop a sensitivity to the feelings and needs of those with whom we deal. In the chapter on self-development we recognized that the "ideal" manager cannot be defined in terms of personal qualities and that supervisors will be better off if they con- centrate their developmental efforts on skills and knowledge. The most prominent exception to that principle is need to improve the ability to empathize in working with and in communicating with people at all levels.

Building the empathy bridge over the self-interest barrier requires us to analyze our communications from the standpoint of the other party. When we listen, for example, can we ask ourselves, Why is he saying that? Why does he feel that way? What would make him ask that? In responding negatively to an employee's request, can we couch our response in terms that will help him understand why the answer must be no and perhaps suggest alternatives that will demonstrate that we have given serious consideration to his needs? When personal interests have clouded the true meaning of a communication, the person capable of empathy stands a much better chance of contributing to real understanding. When we *try* to understand a person or a situation, we usually succeed. We reap the additional benefit of encouraging others by our example to try to understand our viewpoint.

The Planning Barrier

We might more appropriately label this the *lack of planning* barrier. Spending as much time as he does in communicating, would it not be logical for the supervisor to devote considerable effort in planning his major communications? When he is scheduled to discuss a change in job assignments with an employee, does he stop and ask himself how he can explain it in such a way as to be sure the employee will understand? When a complex project must be assigned to a subordinate, does the supervisor sit down beforehand and outline the points he must cover to give a complete picture? If an employee asks for an opportunity to discuss a personal problem, what does the supervisor do to ensure his having his full and undivided attention? If the supervisor must make a report either spoken or in writing, does he outline it with the objectives, needs, and interests of the receiver in mind?

Examples of poor planning of communications are endless. Consider what Bill Powers might have achieved in building morale when he called Orv Lane in to discuss a change in jobs. Bill had singled Orv out because he had a talent for the type of work involved. Bill regarded it as a promotion for Orv, but he was so anxious to have Orv accept that he made it sound too easy. Orv got the impression that he was being asked to do kid's work and turned Bill down, insulted by the request.

A paper-mill supervisor confessed, while attending an institute, that he had muffed a real chance to help an employee. The wife of one of his back-tenders in the mill was going to return home from a mental institution. He wanted to discuss the problems of bringing her back into normal family and social life in addition to asking for time off to make the adjustments. Obviously nervous in discussing so personal a matter, the employee became increasingly annoyed with one interruption after another—first by phone, then by other workers' questions about production matters, then by the phone again, and so on. Finally, in exasperation the employee walked out and put his request for time off in writing. A little planning in these situations could contribute greatly to building a bridge of understanding between supervisor and employee.

The Planning Bridge

Planning more important communications is usually not very complicated or time consuming. It comes almost naturally to the supervisor who is aware of his responsibility to create understanding. Most communication planning can be achieved by mentally answering the six planning questions that follow. *What* am I trying to get across—understanding of a transfer, action on a grievance, praise for good work, a suggestion for improvement, a report of progress on a project, or acceptance of an idea? *Who* am I communicating with—a stubborn employee, a worried person, a boss in a hurry, an aggressive union steward, a loud mouth, a shy individual, an impatient customer, a delinquent supplier, or an unconcerned maintenance man? *When* is the best time to communicate—now, after I've cooled off, at the end of the shift, during the lunch break, when the project is completed, or the next time he has a similar problem? *Where* is the place to communicate—in my office, at his machine, in the cafeteria, in the conference room, or away from the plant? *How* should I communicate—face to face, in a meeting, with a memo, over the phone, in a letter, by telegram, over the P.A. system, on the bulletin board, or through the suggestion system? *Why* am I communicating—to inform, to persuade, to sell, to publicize, to listen, to solve a problem, to discuss, to instruct, to give an order, or to report?

In any given communication situation, we can see how quickly the answers to these planning questions can be pinpointed. And yet it becomes obvious even to the most inexperienced how these questions lead naturally to planning a communication which is likely to lead to understanding. It's not a major job, but rather common sense applied to management's number one problem.

The Barrier of Failure to See the Need

All too often communication problems are the result of sins of omission rather than sins of commission. To many authorities the failure to see the need to communicate is the greatest barrier of all. It isn't that we communicate so poorly, but that we don't communicate at all. How often have we said or have we heard others say, "I didn't think it was necessary to tell him"; or, "I assumed she would know that"; or, "Can't they draw their own conclusions?" Almost daily we are made aware of our dependence on good communication in order to do our jobs well, but for many supervisors that's where the awareness ends. Like Jack Holt, many supervisors are keenly sensitive to the responsibility of others to keep them informed and will look anywhere outside themselves for the cause of failures.

For example, a farm-implement dealer in the Middle West telephoned a rush order for a tractor to his branch office. He was quite specific in identifying the attachments and options he wanted. But when the tractor arrived in his yard, he was on the phone protesting that he couldn't deliver it to the farmer because it didn't have a hydraulic transmission. "You didn't order it," said the branch manager. "You know damn well that I always want the automatic transmission in my area," retorted the dealer. And where does it go from there? Both are right. Both are wrong. Either could have avoided the misunderstanding if he had been a little more aware of his communication responsibility. It's easy to see now that when ordering a special tractor, the dealer should have specified the automatic transmission along with the other options or that the branch manager, in taking the order, should have clarified this vital feature rather than assume a standard transmission when the automatic was not mentioned.

The "failure to see the need" barrier provides fertile ground for the grapevine. In the absence of accurate information, rumors start and spread like wildfire. Contrary to what many writers say, the grapevine is not a good means of communication. Feeding the grapevine accurate information does not ensure clear communication. Everyone can without much effort think of several examples of rumors spread through the grapevine that grew out of all proportion simply because some one didn't see the need to give the correct information through official channels.

The Awareness Bridge

Most of the problems created by poor communication can be quickly solved by a person with average intelligence. As we have already mentioned, we all have the potential to be expert communicators. The moment we become aware that the possibility of misunderstanding exists, our common sense will dictate what steps are necessary to prevent that misunderstanding.

One example of developing that all-important awareness comes in the realization that putting everything in writing is not the answer to most of our communication difficulties. We have seen over the years an outcropping of memo pads suggesting that we avoid spoken orders. All too often this approach is the result of defensive communication attitudes designed to establish the blame for communication failures. The whole approach fails to recognize the superiority of face-to-face communication over the written. We have already recognized that we communicate with facial expression, tone of voice, pauses, gestures, and posture. These supplement oral communication and are completely lost in written communication.

By and large it is much more difficult to create understanding in writing because all we have to convey meaning are words recorded on paper. The opportunity for instantaneous feedback is lost. Every opportunity for creating misunderstanding is present. Jack Holt's memo to Barney on the clean-up crew is a case in point. Or consider the reactions caused by the office manager who used a memo to announce the creation of a central stenographic pool. He wrote, "All men in the office who do not have private secretaries can now take advantage of the girls in the stenographic pool." Enough said?

The truly management-minded supervisor is aware of his responsibility to communicate completely. He knows that the methods and procedures by which we communicate are only aids to help him create understanding and that his own attitude is the real key to communication effectiveness. How do we develop that vital awareness? Here are three suggestions.

Strive continually for understanding

As we consider the hundreds of communication situations we face, the ultimate goal of creating understanding should be a part of our thinking. How often, when we have written a memo, do we check it for the possibility that the receiver might misunderstand what we have intended? Do we recognize the responsibility we have to be sure our subordinates have all the information they need to perform their jobs? Are we aware of what the boss needs from us in order to make the decisions he faces? Do we work at listening to others, knowing that unless we do, we are short-circuiting communication and preventing understanding? When uncertainty clouds our communication, do we build in the feedback necessary to clear the atmosphere? The way we think determines the way we act. We can be the instrument by which communication improvement is achieved, or we can be a Jack Holt, condemning everyone and everything for the communication failures around us.

Put communication on a positive basis

Here's a real test for the person who would be a management-minded supervisor. When problems arise, as they inevitably will, are we big enough to concern ourselves with how to prevent their happening again rather than finding someone to crucify for the failure? Jack Holt was primarily interested in finding scapegoats for the situations he himself helped create. Certainly the most unsophisticated observer could see how Jack could have put every one of his complaints on a positive basis and contributed to harmony and cooperation in his department rather than sowing the seeds of dissension. Burt Hall, as inexperienced as he is, sensed immediately that Jack's negative attitude was largely responsible for his difficulties.

Accept the personal challenge of communication

If communication is management's number one problem, we might very well ask, "What can I do about it? If it's a worldwide problem, I'm only one man. It's too big for me." Many supervisors have recognized that their world is the people around them with whom they have day-to-day contact. Certainly it's not hard to see that Jack Holt's world is made up of people like Ray Ford, Burt Hall, Barney, Tony Puccia, and those people in his department who pitched in to get that rush job out on Friday night. With this perception of our world, the critical question is, Are we creating the communication problems in our world, or are we devoting our energy to their solution? The management-minded supervisor is determined to be a part of the solution rather than a part of the problem.

Communication, whether intra- or interdepartmental, is a matter of creating understanding between people. Improvements will be made, not by programs and techniques, but by the supervisor who senses that he alone can do something about better communications in his world.

Improvement doesn't begin somewhere up or down the line; it starts with our own awareness and our willingness to take a look at our own communication attitudes.

HIGHLIGHTS

1. Communication is the creation of understanding, and effectiveness in communicating is dependent on the supervisor's attitude much more than on the methods and procedures used to communicate.
2. Management is communication, and a manager's effectiveness is directly proportionate to his skill in communicating.
3. There is a disturbing tendency, when communication problems arise, to look outside ourselves for the cause rather than to concern ourselves with what we might do to help create the necessary understanding.
4. Harmony and cooperation in an organization are totally dependent on good communication.
5. The management-minded supervisor has a very clear-cut responsibility to keep his boss informed, to make him look good, and to see that he is never surprised by learning from others what he should have learned from him.
6. When we communicate we are likely to encounter barriers to the creation of understanding. These barriers can and must be bridged. The following barriers and bridges are recognized:

Barrier	Bridge
a. Poor listening	Feedback
b. Semantics	Gear to the receiver
c. Self-interest	Empathy
d. Poor planning	Answer planning questions
e. Failure to see the need	Develop awareness

7. The key to improving communication is the development of an awareness of the importance of communication in performing our jobs. Suggestions for developing that individual awareness are:
   a. Strive continually for understanding.

b. Put communication on a positive basis.

c. Accept the personal challenge of communication.

DISCUSSION QUESTIONS

1. How many ways does a supervisor communicate in a day? List as many as you can.
2. Cite three examples of problems you have experienced because of poor communication—at home or on the job.
3. Explain in your own words why the supervisor's effectiveness as a manager is directly proportionate to his skill as a communicator.
4. Why are harmony and cooperation in an organization totally dependent on good communication?
5. How can you explain the tendency of people to blame someone else when communication problems develop?
6. Five common barriers to communication were identified in this chapter. How many others can you list?
7. Discuss what should have been done to avoid the problems you described in question 2.
8. The responsibility for listening is defined as our own whether we are sending or receiving. Do you agree or disagree? Why?
9. Identify five words or phrases from your own work situation that would likely be misunderstood by an outsider.
10. It is more difficult to communicate in writing. What situations call for written communication?

SUGGESTIONS FOR FURTHER STUDY

Black, James M., and Guy B. Ford
Front-line Management
McGraw-Hill Book Company, New York, 1963

Bittel, Lester R.
What Every Supervisor Should Know, 2d ed.
Chapter 5, McGraw-Hill Book Company, New York, 1968

Famularo, Joseph J.
Supervisors in Action
Chapter 1, McGraw-Hill Book Company, New York, 1961

Gardiner, Glenn, and Associates
Managerial Skills for Supervisors
Chapters 4 and 6, Elliott Service Company, Mount Vernon, N.Y.. 1960

Wiksell, Wesley
Do They Understand You?
The Macmillan Company, New York, 1960

FOUR

MANAGEMENT
OF
CHANGE

THE CASE OF THE CHALLENGE OF CHANGE

Demands for more production had been increasing almost weekly. Burt Hall was diligently staying on top of the situation but looking forward to leveling off so he could relax the pressure he was putting on his people. They were cooperating beautifully. Burt was proud of the results they had achieved but knew full well that he was now getting the maximum he could expect from them. Both Oscar Palmer and Ray Ford had indicated their pleasure with the response of Burt's department. Recently they had promised Burt some relief if pressure for more production continued.

During the past week Burt noticed a couple of methods engineers looking around the department, but he was too busy to bother much with them. He was satisfied with their explanation that they were just making a few observations. He didn't particularly care much for the methods boys, and since he didn't know these two, he was satisfied to let them go their own way. As long as they didn't get in anyone's way, Burt ignored them.

Burt was visibly upset, then, when Ray told him that two new contracts would mean another 15 percent increase in production requirements and that some changes would have to be made in his department. The change would involve breaking up the jobs done now by two five-man groups and introducing two new people to each group. By reducing the number of operations each assembler or adjuster performed and rebalancing the sequence over seven stations rather than five, the necessary production volume could be achieved—at least that's what the methods engineers using predetermined time standards had predicted. They had it all worked out into a neatly packaged system: layout, instructions, standards—the works.

Some new testing equipment would have to be installed at the end of the line to handle the added volume, four new people brought in and trained, and ten present employees trained to do jobs requiring fewer operations on many more assemblies. Burt, to put it mildly, didn't like it. He saw two smoothly operating groups disrupted, changeover delays, resistance from the crews and the union, and a lot of extra work for himself. "It looks fine on paper," he mumbled, "but wait until you try to fit people who have been busting their guts for us into those new jobs."

Burt suggested handling the increase, which he felt was only temporary, with overtime. And if it continued, a second shift could be added. He was assured by Ray that all forecasts pointed to further increased requirements. The contracts which prompted the change were only the beginning of a potential long-range arrangement. Ray explained that overtime was too costly except for very short-range emergency situations. The added costs of second-shift operation could not be justified until such time as more departments would also have to add second shifts. Ray said that Personnel was already interviewing people to find the four new assemblers they would need.

After giving every possible reason to keep the present system and still being told by Ray that the change would be put into effect, Burt grudgingly started to prepare for the initiation of the new system. First he called in Greg Archer, the union steward. Greg listened to Burt's almost apologetic description of the proposed changes. In conclusion, Burt mentioned to Greg that he assumed they would get a lot of objections from the union. Greg said he didn't see why they should. There would be four new members and a couple of the present jobs would be upgraded. Greg said that looked pretty good to him. Burt asked if they weren't concerned about the overtime they would lose out on. "Overtime is fine," replied Greg, "but the union is interested in more steady jobs. Give us reasonable allowances for adjusting to the new setup, and you won't hear any squawks from us."

So far so good. He still didn't like the change, but not having to fight the union helped. Burt took the same apologetic approach in explaining the plan to the employees in his department. He stressed the fact that it wasn't his idea, that he didn't like it, but that it would have to be done. As might be expected, Burt started to get the resistance he was looking for. Several didn't like the idea of changing the makeup of the crews by adding new people. They were working like a team, they said. The new ones might not fit in. Burt just shrugged his shoulders and said that they would have to hope for the best. There were complaints that the new jobs would be more monotonous, with fewer operations to perform. Burt said, "I know it, but what can I do?"

Somebody said he ought to go to bat for them. That hurt Burt. He told them that they didn't have any idea how hard he fought the new setup.

Later on that day Norm Wiley, his best assembler, and Dave Bangs, his best adjuster, asked Burt for a chance to talk with him. They all agreed to get together at the end of the shift. Both Norm and Dave were loaded with questions, many of which had never occurred to Burt. Would the present members be given any preference on the jobs they wanted? Would seniority govern? How many more units were they expected to assemble? Who was going to train the new people? Would the five people on the present crew have to stay together, or would two experienced people go to one of the crews? That would put four new people on one crew, but give you one crew of experienced people to set the pace. What kind of wage adjustments would be made, since a couple of jobs would be upgraded? Would all the jobs be restudied, since both new methods and new testing equipment would be installed? Had arrangements been made to move the completed units away from the end of the line? Would quality standards be just as high? New people and more people working on a unit would make it more difficult to maintain quality. Was there any possibility of a special crew to rework rejects instead of sending them back through? Could something be done to improve the finish on the parts they were getting? There would be less time for an operator to stop and deburr or polish parts during assembly.

An impartial observer listening to their conversation would have said that Norm and Dave were simply seeking straightforward answers to previously unanswered questions. He might also have observed that some of their questions were actually well-intended suggestions on how the change might be implemented more smoothly. Burt didn't see it that way. He regarded their questions as more of the resistance he had been anticipating. In the beginning he answered to the best of his ability, without any show of emotion. As time went on, however, he became more and more defensive. He began to show annoyance. When they seemed not to agree with him, he said they were resisting change. He lectured them briefly on the fact that their security was wrapped up in the company's being able to satisfy its customers.

While no arguments developed, the usual friendly relationship between Burt and these two men was missing. Burt concluded by telling Norm and Dave that he had given them all the information he could. He said that if they had any more objections, they had his permission to take them to Ray Ford. "I just don't like being the middleman, taking a beating from both sides," he told them.

The next day Burt related to Ray Ford as accurately as his bias would let him the reactions he had from those involved in the change. He gave Ray an almost word-for-word playback of his conversation with Norm and Dave. He commented that resistance to change was going to make it a lot tougher than he thought to get things rolling smoothly again. It was a real surprise, he told Ray, that two of his best men objected the most. "You'd expect it from some of the girls and the old people," Burt said, "but not from Norm and Dave. I figured they would provide me with my biggest support."

Ray replied, "They still might, although it sounds as if you gave them a rough time. I'll back you all the way, Burt, but if they do give you trouble, come to me. At the moment, though, I'm more concerned with your analysis of Norm and Dave. It doesn't sound to me as if they were resisting. If anything, they were trying to be helpful. They had a couple of ideas there that we should check into."

"For instance?" asked Burt.

"Well, clearing up that bottleneck at the end of the line, for one. I didn't know you were having a problem there. Why, neither one of us was aware that the assemblers were having to deburr and polish some of the stuff they were getting. I'll check with Fred Jones on that right away and see that what you get is top quality.

"Look, Burt," Ray counseled. "Step back and take another look at this whole thing. We've got to expect some resistance to any change as big as this. A lot of people are involved. But is it possible you're seeing resistance where there really isn't any? Questions about a change don't necessarily mean resistance. It's so easy to see resistance in other people, but so hard to see it in ourselves. Think about it, Burt. I've got to go down and see Fred."

He left Burt sitting there wondering:

1. Can a person be guilty of resistance to change without ever realizing it?
2. What should a supervisor's role be when confronted by a change like this?
3. If resistance to change is inevitable, what can be done to minimize or to overcome it?
4. What was Ray's real opinion about how I handled things? What made him ask me to think about it again?

THE NEED FOR CHANGE

American business is in a period of change, progress, and growth that dwarfs anything we have known in all history. Change is more frequent. Progress is more dramatic. Growth is unparalleled, and it certainly won't stop in the foreseeable future. So dynamic is the period in which we live that many top executives, in viewing the future, have remarked that the only constant today is change.

Competition, of course, stimulates much change. Every day businesses fail because their management does not know how to keep pace in our dynamic economy. It is no longer uncommon to read of well-known, once successful companies being absorbed by more progressive firms. Occasionally we witness a once-flourishing industry dwindling to nothing because the need for its products ceased to exist.

Competition on a price and quality basis from companies producing similar products and services is now a commonplace. New materials have made serious inroads into markets that once were exclusive. Consider, for example, how paper has moved into areas which were once the exclusive domains of lumber, glass, and textiles. Paper pallets have replaced wood pallets. Paper boxes have made wooden fruit boxes a thing of the past. Paper containers have almost eliminated the glass milk bottle. Paper clothing, household draperies, and toweling have had an impact on textiles. On the other hand, disposable plastic drinking cups are replacing paper cups. Growing emphasis on research and development can only mean intensified competition for the consumer's dollar.

The need for change, progress, and growth stimulated by domestic competition is easily recognized. Often overlooked is the fact that worldwide trading will intensify that need. Europe, Asia, and South America are increasing their impact on our domestic economy. In time Africa, too, will have to be reckoned with as a serious competitor. World trade, of course, offers unlimited opportunity to expand the markets for our products. To compete we must constantly be improving our methods, technology, and productivity.

Let's identify just a few of the common changes. Automation and technological improvements have become almost a way of life—tape-controlled machines, automatic handling and processing, and mechanical packaging, to name just a few. Nearly all technological improvements involve the learning of new skills. In many cases it means the wholesale transfer of employees to new jobs. Demands for increased production and lower costs have resulted in a mushrooming of methods-improvement activity. As we seek to improve methods, we search for mechanical means of replacing costly human effort. Introduction of new methods and equipment is frequently followed by new standards of costs, quality, and performance. Incentives and pay scales are revised. Entire departments are reorganized. In some cases, a department is eliminated in the search for more efficient production methods. Computers have brought new ways of processing and analyzing data, setting standards, measuring performance, allocating materials, controlling inventories, dispatching finished products, making decisions, keeping records and accounts, and so on. Staff specialists in methods, engineering, quality control, maintenance, production control, and personnel are constantly seeking ways to upgrade efficiency and are constantly making changes. Firms with unionized labor experience continual pressure to change conditions of employment. Changing concepts of management have resulted in new approaches to handling people. Expansion creates new jobs, both in production and in management. As new supervisory vacancies are filled, employees must adjust to the new boss. Over all this, customers' demands for better quality products and improved service require new and higher standards of performance. Supervisors in dynamic, growing organizations live in a world where nothing is so certain as change.

THE SUPERVISOR'S ROLE IN CHANGE

Burt Hall is in most respects a good supervisor. All too often a supervisor feels, like Burt, that he's the man in the middle—presented by higher management with the job of initiating their changes and at the same time resisted by the employees under him and the union who use him as the target for their objections. It's a feeling the management-minded supervisor can't afford to harbor. They aren't management's changes; they are the supervisor's changes.

The plant manager of a large printing company in the Middle West was recently reviewing a proposed supervisory training program developed by his training director and an outside consultant. The program was very comprehensive. It was the result of much study and analysis of the needs of the firm's supervisory force. After carefully considering the course outline, the plant manager put it on his desk, looked up and said, "Not bad! But unless you build in something I don't see here, it will never get off the ground—not with my approval. Somewhere, you have got to teach our foremen that they can't stand in the way of the changes we have to make to stay in business."

He went on to explain that when new presses and new equipment were introduced, it was their foremen who resisted most strongly—not the employees, not their unions. He said that he wanted something in that training program that would open their minds, something that would help them see how change was a part of staying alive in their highly competitive industry and that would convince them that their job was to implement change, not block it. "Now," he said, "you bring me a program that will do that in addition to all these other things, and I'll give it my blessing."

Essentially what he was saying was, "Get these foremen to act like managers." Supervisors are not the middlemen in the matter of implementing change. They are clearly and unmistakably on the side of management. Upon accepting a supervisory position, a man becomes a part of his management's philosophy and practices. The progress, the growth, and the changes are his to support with enthusiasm if he is to consider himself a member of management. In spite of an outstanding production record, it was his attitude toward change that caused Oscar Palmer and Ray Ford to question Burt Hall's management potential—and with good reason. He was reluctant to make the change from the very beginning. Much of the resistance he encountered was of his own creation. The employees under him were in many cases reflecting Burt's attitude. They simply took his lead.

Many new supervisors are slow to realize that they have an unquestioned obligation to support management's changes. Perhaps this is because so few new supervisors are told in so many words what is expected of them. It is assumed that having become members of management, they are sympathetic to all changes proposed. Unless his responsibility to implement change is made absolutely clear, the new supervisor striving to stay on top of production is likely to regard changes as a deterrent rather than a help or a necessity.

Half the battle in initiating changes in a department is developing the proper attitude toward change. So often those who have the most difficulty in introducing change are the ones who subconsciously resist it themselves. As an example of the importance of attitude let us consider the case of a young professor at the University of Wisconsin. Working in adult education with foremen and supervisors, several years ago, he had become quite proficient as an instructor in the techniques of work simplification. He was quick to recognize the importance of the human element in improving methods and devoted much of his study and teaching to ways of overcoming resistance to change. Within a relatively short period of time he was asked to talk at many management meetings on overcoming resistance. He became an expert on eliminating resistance to change. Imagine the shock, then, when the director of his department told him that he was the first to throw cold water on new ideas in their weekly staff meetings. The director cited five or six specific instances where the "expert" had reacted to new ideas with, "It won't work"; "It will cost too much"; "Our customers won't buy it"; "We've been doing it this way for ten years, why change now?" and "Let's sleep on it for a couple of months." Was it possible for him to tell others how to overcome resistance to change and not realize that he was the world's worst example? It was.

Of course, the most important thing to the professor and the director was the question of how to remedy the situation. After much discussion, one simple step was agreed upon. Our young professor agreed that before he reacted negatively to any ideas in the future, he would first ask himself, "What's good about it?" The result was almost a transformation. Negative thinking was replaced with suggestions for improvement. He became an idea man rather than a "no-man." Nothing had really changed but his attitude. At last he saw himself as the personification of the very thing he was working against, and he was determined that good ideas were not going to die at his hands.

How many supervisors could benefit by the same approach? As they look at the changes that they are charged with implementing, can they ask themselves what's good about them? It's really the first step toward developing the personal enthusiasm that higher management expects supervisors to have. It's the attitude that stimulates enthusiasm for change rather than the typical resistance.

Resistance to Change

People do resist change. To claim that they don't would be to close our eyes to the facts of life. However, it would be equally unrealistic to state that resistance to change is either automatic or universal. It is encouraging that employees' reactions to change so often depend upon how the change is presented to them. And how that change is presented to them is completely under the supervisor's control.

One of the first steps in overcoming resistance to change is to understand what the reasons for its existence are. As so many supervisors who have stopped to analyze the problem have observed, we can't overcome it until we know what it is and why it is there. Let's look, then, at some reasons for resisting change—some of them very real and some imaginary.

Personal economic loss is certainly a good reason for resisting change. Potential loss of job, downgrading, transfer to other departments requiring lower skill, loss of overtime—all pose threats to a feeling of economic security. Where these threats do in fact exist, we can naturally expect a marked lack of cooperation and even concentrated resistance to any change that would bring them about. Our experience shows, however, that management has done an outstanding job of minimizing and eliminating such an economic loss. For example, when seeking ideas for methods improvement, a company usually tries to ensure that people will not lose their jobs as a result of any improvements actually installed. Pay rates are frequently guaranteed until the employees affected can be placed in positions requiring commensurate skill. Much concern over economic loss, then, is imagined by anxiety-ridden employees. This concern generally occurs when changes are not fully explained and sold to the employee.

Implied in many changes is a criticism of the way things have been done in the past, and it's fairly safe to assume that no one likes criticism. Burt Hall, for example, was strongly oriented to production and rightfully proud of his department's achievements. We can easily see how he might mistakenly interpret the changes he was asked to make as a criticism of his ability to meet the new demands. His resistance took the form of suggesting the alternative of overtime to increase output.

Most of us have at one time or another asked for criticism because we know that it's good for us and that it helps us grow. Yet we hope that nothing in our behavior justifies criticism—we're only human. That's why, in implementing change, we need to be especially careful to assure people that the change is not a criticism of them or of the methods they have been using.

Unfortunate experiences with changes of a similar nature in the past have a tendency to make some employees distrustful, suspicious, and even angry. Frequently this is a condition over which a supervisor has no control because the bad experiences happened before he came onto the scene. An alert supervisor, however, will quickly recognize when his people have been so conditioned. He must then make an effort to prepare his people for the change by helping them understand how it will affect them individually and by showing them both the short- and long-range benefits of the change. He will want to stress that he is anxious and willing to help make any adjustments to facilitate the change. By doing this, he demonstrates his awareness of their needs and feelings and makes his own job infinitely easier.

The human ego sometimes creates an almost impenetrable barrier to the implementation of change. Many people are afraid of losing status because a new job doesn't seem as demanding as the old one. The concern that once-valuable skills are no longer needed disturbs those who felt pride in those skills. Others dislike seeing younger people move ahead of them. Countless other emotional reactions make the initiation of change difficult. We all have a need to feel important. That need is frustrated when people are not consulted on changes concerning their jobs. Much of Burt Hall's resistance might be traced to this cause. His pride in his ability to get out production was dealt a blow when the methods engineers and higher management worked out a new method and handed it to Burt without consulting him. Subconsciously he fought back by dragging his feet.

But the human ego can also be important in facilitating change. People are far less likely to resist change if they are given the chance to participate in it. Burt would have liked to be in on the formulating of the change. Denied this chance, he radiated his own lack of enthusiasm. He thus missed the golden opportunity to involve his people in the implementation of the change. Stan and Dave opened the door for a constructive approach, but Burt was too much on the defensive to recognize the opportunity.

Age is another commonly cited reason for resistance. We acknowledge that the older people get, the more they resist change, and the more set in their ways they become. Even Burt Hall said he expected the greatest resistance to come from his older people. Yet age, by itself, has little to do with how well we learn or how much we resist change. If age is a factor at all, it tends to be a positive rather than a negative influence. There is much evidence to show interest in improvement, inventiveness, and creativity at very advanced ages.

Mr. Ben Miller, writing in the American Management Association's Research Study Number 44 (1960), "Gaining Acceptance for Major Methods Changes," contradicts the commonly accepted preconceptions we have about age and change. He states that, in the six companies studied, there was evidence that older people are more willing to accept change than others. Here are two of the reasons he gives for this unexpected finding. First, older people tend to have a stronger identification with the company or the department they've known for years. This identification develops an interest in seeing the company grow and prosper. It's natural that they should want to associate themselves with changes that will cause that growth. Secure in their jobs, they can perhaps see their own security enhanced rather than threatened by change. Second, a long background of experience enables older employees to understand the change—a key factor in cooperation. Cooperation results when people have a clear understanding of why cooperation is needed.

Many supervisors wouldn't be in the job they hold unless they were very much open-minded. Most of them will admit that they are more open-minded today than they were ten years ago. To remain effective, they can't afford to resist change. Yet they assume that the older other people get, the more they resist change. Either they do not see themselves in the same light as they see others, or they do not give other older employees their due. Mr. Miller is suggesting that we take another look at age and resistance to change.

Burt Hall's reaction to his conversation with Stan and Dave prompts us to recognize one last cause of resistance to change. He interpreted their questions as resistance. Ray Ford cautioned him to take a more objective look at their questions. Ray might have followed his comment with an explanation pointing out that questions might very well be evidence of interest in the job and of a very healthy, positive attitude. Actually Stan and Dave were indirectly making some very sound suggestions. As members of management, supervisors should interpret questions concerning changes as a desire for information and not as resistance to change.

Having to deal as often as he does with the implementation of change in his department, it's especially important for the management-minded supervisor to take a healthy, positive, supportive attitude toward change. He starts by recognizing that it's just as natural for people to want to improve as it is for them to resist change. The problem is both to stimulate the desire to improve and to suppress the tendency to resist change. Resistance is easy to detect or suspect in others, but seldom do we recognize ourselves as the boss who never wants to listen to a new idea or as the subordinate who stands in the way of progress.

Creating a Climate for Change

How people react to proposed changes is greatly influenced by the kind of climate for change that the supervisor has created in his department. Burt Hall is a perfect example of what should not be done. Now, how is the right kind of climate created?

It begins, of course, by having the enthusiasm for progress and change which builds a healthy climate. Supervisors are first, last, and always members of management. A dynamic organization will be constantly seeking and introducing new methods, new equipment, new people, new standards, and new internal organizational structure. The enthusiastic support of these changes is the obligation of management-minded supervisors. Employees are quick to sense that a supervisor is dragging his feet, and they will play it safe. Why should they stick their necks out until they know where the boss stands? Management expects and assumes that its front line is in complete harmony with its decisions. It has every right to make such assumptions.

Creating the right climate is more than just passing changes on. It involves encouraging employees to seek ways of improving their jobs. Seeking suggestions and ideas from employees requires that a supervisor listen and seriously consider suggestions. It's easy to see that there's a great deal of ego involvement in coming forth with an idea for improvement. Employees can quickly develop a sour attitude when their ideas are ignored or ridiculed. Change can become a way of life— exciting and dynamic. The leadership supervisors provide determines the climate in which they initiate change.

How to Initiate Change

Often it is easier to carry out a job if there is a specific plan to follow. When major changes are to be installed, careful planning and preparation are necessary for success. Here, then, are six steps that many management-minded supervisors have found helpful in initiating major changes.

1. Get ready to sell

Much of the difficulty a supervisor encounters in getting cooperation stems from the employees' lack of understanding of how the change will affect them. With a little effort he can find most of the answers to employees' questions before they are even asked. Burt Hall, with a little empathy, could have anticipated most of the questions Stan and Dave asked him. What is the reason for the change? Whom will it benefit and how? Will it inconvenience anyone and for how long? Will training or retraining be necessary? How will the training be carried out? Will earnings be affected? When does it go into effect? Will there be a transition period when adjustments can be made? Armed with the answers to these questions, a supervisor can head off many objections and can develop a plan to present the change.

2. Identify sources of help

Why should a supervisor shoulder the burden alone? Staff people can frequently be a great help in preparing to sell a change by explaining technical aspects and demonstrating new techniques. Instead of fighting them, as Burt Hall was unconsciously doing, wouldn't it be smarter to recognize the potential staff specialists have for helping initiate a change? After all, the long-range responsibility of staff specialists is also to promote a progressive, productive, profitable company.

One of the most overlooked sources of help in introducing changes are the informal leaders in the work group. With their help the job becomes easier. Giving recognition to the leader puts him in a cooperative frame of mind and on management's side. He maintains and strengthens his leadership. Stan and Dave were demonstrating their leadership in coming to Burt. Instead of welcoming their help, he showed annoyance and sent them to Ray Ford. Bypassing the informal leader caused him to demonstrate his leadership by organizing the resistance. Since the union steward in a department is often the informal leader, his cooperation ought to be solicited. His backing makes the job easier. This is not to say, however, that management's position on the change can or should be compromised.

Older employees should also be seriously considered as a potential source of help in selling changes. Frequently younger employees will take their cue from the response of the old-timers. Whenever a supervisor can identify opinion leaders, his first approach should be through them.

3. Anticipate objections

Changes that upset routine, require new knowledge or skills, or inconvenience people are bound to meet with some objection or resistance. Looking at a change from the employees' point of view will usually be enough to help determine what their objections are likely to be. Knowing the objections, we can, with a little creative thought, turn these objections into advantages. For example, when Stan and Dave raised questions about the extra work involved in adjusting to the change, Burt had a perfect opportunity to tell his leaders how much he was counting on them to sell the necessary adjustments to others. He could have at that moment turned two potential objectors into real allies. It really doesn't matter how much authority a supervisor has or thinks he has; he should recognize that he can't force people to his way of thinking. If he wants cooperation, not just grudging compliance, he has to win it. Snowing a man with reasons or logic won't do the job. People are going to have to be made to feel that the change is really best for them, and that won't happen until their objections are seriously dealt with.

4. Sell benefits

Everyone is concerned with, "What's in it for me?" "Will the change mean more satisfying work, greater security, opportunity to show what I can do, more responsibility, more pay, less fatigue, less confusion, greater independence?" The benefits used to try to motivate people to cooperate should be put on as personal a level as possible. It would be dishonest, however, not to recognize any disadvantages that a change may bring. These can usually be countered with long-range benefits.

5. Listen in depth

Employees have a right to be heard. Their questions may be their way of demonstrating interest in their jobs, or as in the case of Stan and Dave, a means of making suggestions which would facilitate the change. Burt was hearing their questions, but a little in-depth listening would have helped him tremendously. If an employee is treated with respect, like an equal, he probably will respond in kind. He'll feel better, too, if he knows his concerns have been considered. What he says doesn't always echo what he feels. It's possible, we know, to resist change without verbalizing objections. In the same vein, it is possible to challenge without being uncooperative.

6. Follow up

It is easy to resent the salesman who loses complete interest in us just as soon as the sale is finalized. After having conscientiously sold the benefits of a change, isn't it of tremendous long-range importance for a supervisor to see that his promises have materialized? Did any difficulties develop that he hadn't anticipated? Are adjustments necessary to realize the full potential benefit of the change? A sincere interest in how the change has affected the employee and a willingness to make adjustments help build the climate in which future changes will be initiated.

Now, and in the years to come, a supervisor's effectiveness as a member of management will be measured in large part by his skill in initiating change. In an era when change is the only constant, a supervisor demonstrates his management-mindedness by answering the challenge that change presents with enthusiastic support.

HIGHLIGHTS

1. We are in an era of unprecedented change in business and industry. The foreseeable future will bring more and more change, and the supervisor is the key man in initiating change at the production level.
2. Supervisors' own attitudes are the key to how effective they are at initiating change. As members of management they have an obligation to support change with enthusiasm. Management-mindedness is measured by willingness to accept change and by skill in initiating it.
3. People do resist change, but not automatically or universally. It is just as natural to want to improve as it is to resist change. Many times the difference between the two depends on whether or not the employee is involved in the implementation of the change.

4. The reasons why people resist change include the following:
   a. They fear economic loss.
   b. They fear the unknown.
   c. They fear loss of status.
   d. They feel that criticism is implied.
   e. They have had unfortunate experiences with change.
   f. Damage to the ego may be brought by the process of change.
5. Older employees are more likely to accept changes than to resist changes.
6. Setting the example with an enthusiastic attitude toward change is important in creating a climate for change. Also important is the ability to develop mental flexibility—"the ability to meet new problems with new solutions."
7. There are six steps for initiating change. The supervisor must
   a. Get ready to sell
   b. Identify sources of help
   c. Anticipate objections
   d. Sell benefits
   e. Listen in depth
   f. Follow up

DISCUSSION QUESTIONS

1. Identify and discuss three changes that have taken place in your work situation in recent years.
2. Do you agree or disagree with the proposition that the supervisor is the key man in initiating change at the employee or production level? Discuss the reasons for your position.
3. Describe a time when someone you know resisted a change. Why did he resist?
4. In this chapter a claim was made that older employees are more likely to accept change than resist it. Do you agree or disagree? Discuss your answer.
5. Can you cite an example of an instance when an employee over fifty years of age accepted a change more readily than younger coworkers?
6. Discuss the statement that it is just as natural for people to want to improve as it is for them to resist change.

7. If you had to sell employees on a new method using mechanical conveyors for small-part assembly work instead of benchwork and tote boxes, what questions would you want answers to before presenting the change? Where would you expect to get the answers?

SUGGESTIONS FOR FURTHER STUDY

Batten, J. D.
Tough-minded Management
Chapter 15, American Management Association, New York, 1963

Gardiner, Glenn, and Associates
Managerial Skills for Supervisors
Chapter 8, Elliott Service Company, Mount Vernon, N.Y., 1960

PART
TWO

LEADERSHIP SKILLS

The true genius that conducts
a state is he, who doing nothing himself, causes everything
to be done; he contrives, he
invents, he foresees the future;
he reflects on what is past; he
distributes and proportions
things; he makes early preparations; he incessantly arms
himself to struggle against for-
tune, as a swimmer against a
rapid stream of water; he is
attentive day and night, that he
may leave nothing to chance.
FRANCIS DE S. FENELON
(1651–1715)

CHAPTER
FIVE

UNDERSTANDING
THE
INDIVIDUAL
EMPLOYEE

THE CASE OF FEARLESS FRANK CONNORS

"Just give him a little more time. He'll have you tearing your hair out too," Frank Connors, supervisor of the toolroom, was saying to Burt Hall. "He's just a stubborn kraut. Thinks he's smart, but he hasn't got enough sense to come in out of the rain. They're all alike. The only muscles he uses are in his mouth."

The object of Frank's tirade was Eric Mader, who had worked in the toolroom until about a month ago, when he had requested and secured a transfer to Burt's assembly department. Frank said he had been impressed with Eric when he first hired him as a helper in the toolroom. Eric dispensed tools, stored them, and kept records. There was plenty of activity to keep him busy. What caused Eric and Frank to be at odds with one another was that Eric constantly looked for shortcuts and tried to improve on systems that had been serving the toolroom well for many years. Frank had caught Eric a couple of times making small changes on his own—changes that Frank had previously vetoed when Eric first suggested them.

"When I clamped down on him, he got sullen. But people can't keep going behind your back and disobeying orders," Frank told Burt. "He's there to do a job—to do what he's told. What difference does it make to him how the work is done as long as he's well paid for the time he puts in?" Frank went on to explain that he didn't talk to Eric any more than he had to and that Eric didn't do any more work than was absolutely necessary to keep Frank off his back. When Frank did criticize, Eric was always ready with alibis. "I honestly don't know how a guy so dumb could come up with some of the stories he did. It didn't even sink into his thick skull when I refused his merit increase. Instead of straightening out, he got worse. That guy is a professional gold-bricker," Frank said shaking his head. "You're welcome to him, Burt, and don't say I didn't give you fair warning."

Burt had found Eric to be a hard worker with an unusual interest in doing his job well. Eric's dedication had attracted Burt to him very soon after he had OK'd the transfer. Eric had been born in Germany but had come over at the age of five with his parents just before the Second World War. The war years and early postwar years were difficult for him because he was never sure that people trusted him. Close friendships were a luxury he never enjoyed. His father taught him respect for work and set an example for him in finding satisfaction in producing more than was expected of him. Eric found that satisfaction in the jobs he held until he came to work for Frank. He felt that Frank just wasn't interested in seeing him do a good job. Bitter feelings developed after Frank called him a "crazy kraut." Eric wanted to work for the company but confided in Burt that he would have quit if the transfer hadn't been approved. He said he couldn't work for a boss he couldn't respect.

Burt reflected, after Frank had left, that he had almost muffed the ball with Eric himself. After about a week on the job, Eric came to Burt with an idea for a bench fixture that he said he could knock out himself after hours. The fixture would save several motions and enable Eric to get more work out. Almost automatically, Burt started to reject the idea by telling Eric to get a little more experience before starting to change methods that were doing the job. By the time Eric finished his explanation, however, Burt could see the possibilities and gave him the green light.

A significant increase in Eric's output excited Burt and two other assemblers doing similar work. With Eric's proud permission, Burt had two more fixtures made and installed for the other two assemblers. Eric not only got his pat on the back from Burt but was recognized by several fellow employees who admired his idea. Ray Ford stopped by to observe the fixture. Burt had asked Ray to do this. Ray was so impressed that he sent Eric a commendatory letter the next day. Eric was beaming when he showed his letter to Burt. Watching Eric work, Burt wondered how Frank Connors could be so wrong about Eric. He was everything you could ask for in a production employee if you treated him right.

Maybe that last thought was what got Burt to thinking about Larry James again. Larry and Burt certainly weren't tuned in on the same wavelength this past week. Something had happened to Larry's attitude, but Burt couldn't put his finger on it. He had just about decided he'd call Larry in next week to get things out in the open.

Larry James was very quiet and serious, and a steady worker. His steadiness, general reliability, and quiet manner made it easy to overlook him or take him for granted. Burt, for this reason, hardly knew Larry. For example, he didn't know that Larry was very sensitive about never having finished high school. As a matter of fact, Burt didn't even know that Larry didn't have his high school diploma. He didn't know either that Larry was anxious to advance and worried a great deal about the handicap his lack of education posed. Burt did know that Larry was inclined to be slow because everything had to be just right. Burt couldn't remember a single instance of any rejects or mistakes in Larry's work. Burt couldn't have known, then, that Larry had just made a personal decision to start going to night school to get his high school diploma. He couldn't have known because Larry didn't want to broadcast his deficiency by letting people know he was going back to school.

It was the very morning after he made the decision that getting ahead required his going back to school that Burt stopped by his workplace. Larry had just finished a job, and the inspector had OK'd it as Burt walked up. "That's the way, Larry, slow but sure," Burt said to him, intending the remark as a compliment to Larry's consistently high-quality work.

Larry, however, flushed and said, "Well, I do the best I can."

Burt responded with a smile and the comment, "That's what I mean. You're OK—keep it up." Burt didn't see the disappointment register on Larry's face as he walked away. He felt that Larry had the recognition coming and that he really should show more of his appreciation of Larry's work on an informal basis.

To Larry the props had just been cut out from under him. He interpreted Burt's comments as a double-barreled criticism of his work and wondered how much his limited education had to do with it. He knew how concerned Burt had been about production. It hurt, then, to have Burt tell him that he was slow. When anyone tried as hard as he had, Larry felt, just being told "You're OK" was a big letdown. Since he had been giving his best to the job, Larry began to think maybe he should look for a job where he could show up a little better. This concern, this worry, was reflected in Larry's attitude in the days that followed Burt's brief conversation with Larry.

There weren't any problems, any arguments, any changes in his output, but Burt could see and feel that something was bothering Larry. It was especially puzzling to Burt since the change came about right after he had taken the trouble to give Larry a pat on the back.

Burt thought his comment had been a compliment. He was telling Larry that quality was just as important to him as quantity. To Burt, telling a man that he was OK was about as personal as you could get without getting sloppy. At least that was the way Burt felt. Burt never dreamed that their conversation had anything to do with whatever was bothering Larry. But he thought he still had better have a talk with Larry. "Funny," he said to himself, "how different two people can be. Paul Botts is almost the complete opposite of Larry."

Paul was a good employee, a worrier, and a talker. Paul's wife had for some time been having problems "with her female organs," as Paul put it. Just this past week the decision had been made that surgery was the only course left. Naturally Paul was concerned about his wife even though their doctor had assured them there was nothing to worry about. Another problem Paul had was how to take care of their three elementary school children during his wife's hospitalization. He told Burt that he had found a woman who could come when the kids got home for lunch and stay through the supper hour. He didn't think he could find or afford another woman to come in during the morning to help them dress and get their breakfast. The kids usually weren't up yet when Paul left for work at 6:30 A.M.

Burt had suggested that they work out a schedule for Paul whereby he would come at 8:30 A.M. and work the extra hour and a half at the end of the shift. Then the woman who was helping out would be there when the kids got home, and Paul wouldn't lose any money when he needed it most. Paul said that he appreciated Burt's thoughtfulness but didn't think Burt should make so much of an exception.

"If you do it for me, you'd have to do it for everybody, and I don't want to make problems for you," he told Burt.

"Look, Paul," Burt replied, "right now it's important to both of us that your family is taken care of and that your wife goes to the hospital without any worries about the kids or your job. If adjusting your schedule for a couple of weeks will do that, I'm glad I can help. Everyone in the department knows we have to keep regular working hours, so I don't think we're going to get any wholesale requests to change working hours. You're going to have your hands full with the job, keeping things going at home, and visiting your wife, so don't worry about my justifying an exception in your working hours. If there's any worry on that score let me do it. You just take care of mamma and the kids."

Tears came to Paul's eyes as he thanked Burt and told him a guy couldn't have a better boss. It made Burt feel good. He hoped that he wouldn't get any objections from Ray Ford and the personnel department when he told them what he had done. He knew that if he had been in Paul's shoes, he would have appreciated the same consideration.

As he thought about how Frank Connors had handled Eric Mader, how he himself had nearly muffed the chance he had to let Eric show his stuff, how Larry was behaving since he complimented him, and how Paul Botts thought he couldn't have a better boss, Burt mentally conceded that understanding people was certainly a challenge for a supervisor. There just didn't seem to be any rules for handling people. But a man sure did have to think about his responsibilities for directing the people who worked for him.

1. How should a supervisor develop a personal philosophy for handling the people in his department?
2. Should a supervisor have to get involved in the personal lives and problems of his people?
3. Obviously all people can't be treated alike, but what guidelines can members of management use in working with people?
4. What put Frank Connors, an experienced supervisor, so completely at odds with Eric Mader, who turned out to be a topnotch worker in Burt's department?
5. How should a good supervisor handle the problem Burt will face in calling Larry James in to clear the air?
6. How should we evaluate Burt's handling of Paul Botts?
7. What happens if we ignore our responsibility to treat people as individuals?

THE MANAGEMENT ATTITUDE TOWARD HUMAN RELATIONS

Many new supervisors are puzzled today at what their attitude toward human relations should be. We are confronted with a range of conflicting philosophies. At one extreme is the idea that people are our greatest asset and are to be treated with the utmost kindness and respect. At the other extreme is the idea that people are paid well to do a job and therefore should simply do what they are told. The situation is further confused because some managers give lip service to one philosophy and practice another.

Historically we have seen marked changes in management's approaches to human relations. Only a few decades ago, in the 1930s, the "bull of the woods" philosophy prevailed. A foreman was usually the toughest man available. He was able to handle anyone who got out of line, and he gave orders with a "do it or else." An employee who questioned his approach was quickly informed that if he didn't like the way things were being run, there was always someone waiting to take his place. The labor market was a buyer's market, and employees couldn't afford to question anything. The foreman of that era certainly didn't have to worry about human relations. The words weren't even in his vocabulary.

In the late thirties and in the forties a number of things happened to shape a new way of thinking about the role of the individual in industry. The impact of the first significant social research at Western Electric's Hawthorne plant was making itself felt. The discovery, for example, that such changes as breaks in the workday could contribute to increased production opened many eyes. Further, it was found that recognizing people as individuals and that separating groups for special study also contributed to healthier attitudes toward work.

The growth of unions put a few dents in the armor of the bull of the woods. The enabling legislation of the Wagner Act meant that employees' organizations became more and more a force to be reckoned with. Autocratic foremen saw their authority diluted and found that unfair treatment of employees resulted in costly grievances. The pressure of unions forced a reevaluation of our human relations practices.

The Second World War added still another dimension to our thinking and our management practices. With most able-bodied men in military service, we found our plants populated by housewives, young people of high school age, retired people, and men with physical limitations who were moved into more essential occupations. These people needed and usually received consideration of their individual problems in adjusting to the war effort. When "Johnny came marching home," more adjustments were needed—both on his part and on the part of those who were directing his work life.

Adding all these factors together, with the psychologists and human relations experts leading the way, the pendulum had swung completely away from the bull-of-the-woods philosophy to the other extreme. By 1950 the best label wo could give to our thinking about human relations was "the era of sweetness and light." This was the period in which an employee could do no wrong. The objective of a supervisor was to keep people happy. Seldom did he ever say no to an employee's request. This attitude permeated top-management thinking as well. It wasn't uncommon for an executive to state that the primary objective of his company was to be a good corporate citizen, to provide employment, to provide a fair day's pay for a fair day's work, and to provide the best possible working conditions. These are admirable goals, but hardly the objective for being in business; the primary objective that we generally and honestly recognize today is to make a profit. In the long run all the goals mentioned above are possible only when the enterprise is making a profit and can support the best in personnel programs.

Today we are experiencing the return swing of the pendulum to a philosophy somewhere between the two extremes. We now openly recognize the profit motive for being in business. Managers clearly see their profit responsibilities not only to the stockholder but to the employee and community as well. The long-range welfare of the employee requires a growing profitable organization. The job of a supervisor is to contribute to profits and to help employees understand that they, too, have a responsibility to contribute to the profit picture.

This healthy concern for profit does not mean a return to the bull-of-the-woods philosophy. We haven't come all this way with our knowledge of what makes people work only to chuck it out the window in a program of cracking down on them. A truly management-minded supervisor will recognize the tremendous investment his company has in its work force and will treat his subordinates with respect and dignity. He will also expect adherence to rules and established standards of performance. He cannot put being a good guy ahead of all other considerations.

An example of how easily the middle-of-the-road approach to human relations can be misunderstood occurred in a plant in New York. An outside consultant was conducting a series of training sessions for supervisors in a small plant. The leader had spelled out essentially the same points made in the introduction to this chapter. He concluded the first session by stressing the supervisor's responsibility to enforce plant rules and to see that standards of quality production were met. The next morning the plant manager was waiting for his training specialist with the question, "What in heaven's name did you say to George yesterday? He's turned into a tiger. Before the day ended I had two of his people in my office complaining about the unmerciful chewing-out he had given them without checking the facts or listening to explanations." George had interpreted the consultant's remark as the beginning of a new "get tough" policy and went at the job with gusto. He was determined that no one would brand him a wishy-washy supervisor. His impulsive behavior and lack of judgment had already been noticed. This most recent incident simply made it clear that George should not have been a supervisor, and he was eased out of his job within a month.

A part of the confusion about how to approach the human relations aspect of the supervisor's job stems from the fact that there is so much inconsistency in practice all around us. There are those who give lip service to considering individual problems and feelings while practicing the bull-of-the-woods approach. Others advocate the get-tough theory but never take a firm stand on anything. Almost any organization has its tyrants as well as those who just let things run themselves hoping it will all work out in the end. Most supervisors who are serious about wanting to do the best possible job as members of management eventually come to the realization that they must develop a personal philosophy about handling their people. When supervisors stop to think about their jobs and their people, they can generally agree on a number of approaches—approaches which should help fashion a philosophy.

1. The job of a manager is to get things done through people. He no longer produces but has his own effectiveness measured in terms of what his subordinates produce.
2. People are a very tangible asset in any organization and should be treated with consideration.
3. Most employees expect to work, want to work, and are most satisfied in a department where they are producing. High production and high morale usually go hand in hand.
4. To settle for less than an employee is capable of giving is a failure to respect him as an individual.
5. Employees look to a supervisor for direction, knowing full well that they must live as good citizens—adhering to rules and performing up to standards. Failure to get such direction can only result in a lack of respect for supervision.
6. Employees by and large would rather please their boss than they would displease him.
7. For most people work is one of the most meaningful aspects of their lives. They can find in work both dignity and personal satisfaction depending upon how the supervisor presents it to them.
8. The individual can control how hard he will work—indeed whether he will work at all. This raises the question of who really

is the boss. The challenge facing supervisors is to create a climate in which a man will want to continue to give his best.

Now the logic of the middle-of-the-road approach emerges more clearly. To spite the individual needs of people, to treat them as tools, and to follow a drivership policy makes employees resist proper standards of performance through lack of interest, uncooperative attitudes, tardiness, and absenteeism. To ignore the human side of supervision, to pay no attention to human feelings, and to fail to provide direction and leadership will frustrate employees as well as negate the responsibilities accepted by managers.

Understanding Others Starts with Understanding Yourself

Not long ago a supervisor who was highly regarded by his employees confided to a friend, "Every time I'm tempted to criticize the work of someone else, I ask myself if I have done anything to help create the situation that needs correcting. More often than not, it changes my whole approach to a more considerate one than I would otherwise have used. Even when I have done nothing wrong, I have started to see the situation from the viewpoint of the other person, and I force myself to treat him as a human being with feelings like my own." The thought expressed here brings to mind something many psychologists have stressed in trying to help managers understand people: To understand others we must first try to understand ourselves. Perhaps what tempered this supervisor's criticisms most was giving thought to how he might receive such criticism himself. By identifying his own feelings, he forced himself to consider the feelings of others.

Gaining insight into our own behavior is commonly cited as a primary objective of any seminar or institute on understanding people. We acknowledge the value that comes in taking a good hard look at ourselves. How, for example, are we as supervisors regarded by the employees working under us? If they think highly of us, what have we done to earn their respect? If we seem only to be tolerated, what in our behavior has created such indifference? If they are outright antagonistic, can we find in our own attitudes and actions any cause for such feelings? Perhaps all three conditions exist with different individuals in the department. Can we then find reasons for the varying reactions to our supervision? Such questions are not meant to suggest that the fault for every problem lies within ourselves. Common sense dictates, however, that if it does, we are better equipped to deal intelligently with problems when we understand our own role in relation to them.

To recognize that we have definite attitudes about work, about supervision, about responsibility, and about praise and criticism is the first step in recognizing that all members of the organization have definite attitudes about the same things, although certainly not the same attitudes. We work toward the realization of our goals and ambitions just as everyone else does. The vigor with which we pursue our goals and the methods we use to pursue them will differ.

We should know our strengths and where we contribute most to the organization. Equally important is the need we have to take stock of our shortcomings and any limitations that might handicap our ability to supervise people. Are we particularly quick to lash out at one violation of rules and turn our back on another? Are we keenly sensitive to feelings of others, or are we inclined to expect people to do their work and leave their feelings at home? Do we have any bias or prejudice against nationality or racial groups, female employees, some political persuasions, religious sects, union activities, boisterous behavior, or gossip? Before any such limiting bias can be removed, it must first be recognized.

Most of us will acknowledge that a mark of a mature supervisor is the ability to adjust to difficult or unexpected situations—to make decisions without displays of irritation or temper. How well are we able to roll with the punches? What kind of a leadership do we provide when the going gets rough? A part of understanding ourselves is gaining the insight which allows us to put our finger on the things that prevent us from using our better judgment. Again, if we can recognize these weaknesses in ourselves, we can better understand how others can be victims of similar emotional reactions. It's not hard to see, then, that a supervisor who controls his temper is better equipped to control problem situations. Most of us can think of a situation in which one party to a disagreement lost his temper while the other party controlled his. We know immediately that the person who controlled his temper also controlled the situation. At all times we have need as managers to be in control of ourselves whether we are dealing with people above or below us in the organizational hierarchy.

The late Dr. John Schindler of Monroe, Wisconsin, spent much of the later years of his life speaking to a wide variety of groups and individuals on how to live a fuller, richer life. Contained in his talks was some homely advice on how to achieve emotional maturity—advice that any of us who accept the responsibility for directing the work lives of others can benefit from. One of the things Dr. Schindler always started with was the suggestion that a necessary part of growing up emotionally was the development of an ability to assume responsibility independently of those around us. Our great need to develop a management-mindedness rests in part with this ability to develop a sense of independent responsibility—to view our jobs in terms of what we control.

Dr. Schindler also stressed that hostility, anger, belligerence, and aggressiveness are signs of weakness. How often have we seen people deluding themselves by shouting and displaying their temper as a means of showing who's boss. Dr. Schindler counseled that gentleness and kindness are our real strengths.

He frequently pointed out that maturity is in part the ability to distinguish fact from fancy. Every day we are challenged to exercise this ability—by rumors spread by the grapevine, by the feeling that persons are out to get us, by the temptation to worry about things that may never happen. He said that another quality of the mature person is his flexibility and adaptability—he can find and use the best solution in a problem situation. A simple system for doing this, he advised, was not to look back after a catastrophe, but to look ahead in order to decide how much good can be introduced into the future.

Many supervisors who have either heard Dr. Schindler speak or read his book say that what has helped them most in handling people was his statement that a mature person had a *giving* rather than a *receiving* attitude in his relations with people. We have all read of man's needs to be loved, accepted, recognized, and respected. The immature person is constantly concerned with how he will find satisfaction for these needs. The mature person, on the other hand, recognizes these needs in others and concerns himself with what he can do to satisfy them. The beauty of this philosophy is that it frees us from worry about how we're treated. A man finds that his needs are automatically satisfied by those who regard him as a good man to work for. A supervisor interested in improving his ability to understand others and in deepening his understanding of himself would find Dr. Schindler's book *How to Live 365 Days a Year* * well worth reading.

Individual Differences

"Treat them all alike"—impossible, ridiculous, we say. No two people are ever exactly alike. They differ in thousands of ways. Twenty people working under us will have twenty different personalities—each requiring a different approach. Most of us will quickly acknowledge the truth of that statement, but how easy it is to forget it in the search for some quick and easy formula that will guide us through every situation. People are basically and irrevocably individualists at heart. A management-minded supervisor accepts the idea that the better he knows his people as individuals, the better equipped he is to deal with them.

One of the real pitfalls we face is to engage in "either-or" thinking about our people—the tendency to classify them in one of two extremes. For example, we might say that Bill is either smart or stupid; if he's not fast, he's slow; if he's not lazy, he's a hard worker; if he's not pleasant, he's a grouch. Frank Connors operated this way. He saw his people in terms of such extremes. Eric Mader was at various times in Frank's eyes lazy, stupid, stubborn, and a loudmouth. In some respects it's the easy way. People are automatically classified and pigeonholed. There's no problem trying to understand them—just one quick judgment and they're either for us or against us.

Burt, on the other hand, was showing some early signs of developing the awareness of people as individuals which will mark him as an understanding boss. He wondered why Eric Mader was so different from Frank's picture of him; he was puzzled by Larry's behavior; and he recognized that Paul Botts deserved special consideration. Recognizing that people are not all alike, that each has his own strengths and abilities, his own limitations and weaknesses, is the first step in understanding people. Burt's wondering why his people behaved the way they did put him on the threshold of seeing that personality is a reflection of all that person has been, all that he is, and all that he ever will be. Personality simply means the total person. How he reacts today is the result of everything that has ever happened to him. Our own personalities, for example, have been shaped over a lifetime by our parents, our teachers, clergymen, friends, groups we've been a part of,

* Published by Prentice-Hall, Inc., Englewood Cliffs, N.J., 1954.

our bosses—a combination of experiences that has been uniquely our own.

Our particular concern is to recognize that an individual's set of values is the result of situations, training, and associations in which we have had no part. Why should Paul Botts have worried because Burt stuck his neck out to change his work schedule? It was no skin off his nose. What made Larry put a reverse interpretation on Burt's compliment? What made Eric a top producer for Burt and a goof-off for Frank Connors? To be effective in dealing with these three, Burt needed to know something about them as individuals. Paul Botts made this easy. He was a talker. Larry, on the other hand, was quiet. Burt was the first to admit that he didn't know what made Larry tick. He really hadn't given him much thought at all. Larry was a stranger to Burt. Unless Burt gets to know Larry better—his hopes, his worries, his special problems—he will probably continue to misunderstand him.

Failure to know the men under us as individuals forces us into the position of having to base work assignments and personnel decisions on generalizations about people which are rarely valid. When we hire, we hire the whole man. His dreams, his family, his interests, his problems, his values, his abilities, and his goals are all a part of the individual we place on the job. It is obvious that the better we are able to match his abilities and interests to the requirements of the job, the more productive he's likely to be. But too often that's where we stop. What do we know of where he wants to be in five years, of what hopes he has for his children, of what values he has that have been shaped by his parents, his church, and other supervisors he's had? Until we know and understand some of these, we don't really know the man.

Perception and Supervision

By perception we mean the meaning or interpretations we attach to the people and situations we face. We look at others in terms of our own values. We see the world in the light of our own needs and interests—our likes and dislikes. No two people see things exactly the same way. Again, for example, we have seen Eric Mader through the eyes of Frank Connors as a loud, lazy, troublemaker. From Burt's point of view, Eric was eager, hard-working, enthusiastic, and pleasant. The same man was perceived in entirely different ways by different supervisors. Larry and Paul certainly didn't see Burt in the same light.

Before we can understand the interpretations others place on our actions, we must first understand how we arrive at our own interpretations. As managers we have a reasonably clear understanding of the need for quality production and profit. We have accepted these management objectives as our own. If anything interferes with the realization of those goals, how are we to interpret it? How, for example, do we view a methods engineer who wants to disrupt a production sequence to try out a new idea? How about a key employee who stays home with a cold? How about a grievance which gets everybody talking? Certainly our own needs will color our evaluation of such incidents. We can be just as certain, however, that the other party in each situation will have his perceptions similarly influenced by his needs. Unless we recognize how such attitudes are developed in others, dealing with the dynamics of human relations can be extremely frustrating. A lack of sensitivity to the feelings of others results in snap judgments and inconsiderate treatment.

We have all known people who bragged about their ability to size up a person in a hurry. "Just give me a minute with him, and I'll have him pegged," they'll say. Anyone with an ounce of common sense will know that this is impossible, but we are frequently confused when these people say they have an almost perfect batting average. The fact we overlook is that people who make such boasts usually have the means to make them come true. Once a job candidate is sized up as just what we've been looking for, it's easy to overlook his mistakes to substantiate our judgment. On the other hand, when we have pegged a man as no good from the start, he has an uphill battle because we can so easily find fault. One of the real dangers in making snap judgments is that those same judgments tend to make us inflexible in handling people. We can so easily see in the behavior of others what we want to see.

Out of this tendency to look for what we want to see grows the temptation to look for our own image in people. Managers have frequently been accused of promoting those who operate the way they do. A biographical article on a major college's football coach illustrated the point. In the article his days as a high school and college player were described in terms of personal hardship—his father died at an early age; he was partly responsible for supporting his mother and family; he had a tough time making ends meet, etc. Because a prime responsibility of a big-time coach is recruiting, the interviewer asked his subject what he looked for in boys when he was considering them. The coach responded, "I look for a boy who's had a tough time, who hasn't had things handed to him all his life. I look for a kid who's hungry." He might just as well have said that he wanted boys who grew up the way he did because they make better players.

Above all we should be aware of the need for caution in judging people and their actions. It's important that we recognize the dreams, ideals, values, and feelings of others in directing their work lives and interpreting their behavior. The best route we can follow in exercising this caution is to develop what many successful and management-minded supervisors regard as the single most important trait of a manager—empathy.

Empathy in Supervision

In previous chapters we accepted as a definition of empathy the ability to put ourselves in the other person's shoes and see things from his point of view. We should recognize that empathy does not mean giving in to people or using a wishy-washy approach to management. To understand the reason why a person takes a stand does not necessarily mean that we agree with that stand, but it does equip us to deal more effectively with a person even though we may disagree with him. Empathy enables us to consider feelings and viewpoints other than our own.

In working with people who are bothered by personal problems, the ability to empathize is of special value to the supervisor. I am using "empathy" to mean an ability to appreciate the feelings and the needs of others without becoming emotionally involved yourself. It is not exactly a sharing of the feelings of a troubled person; for sharing feelings may color our judgment. I am thinking of a somewhat more detached attitude an attitude that says, "I know how you feel; I know why you feel. I understand."

The ability to empathize can be particularly helpful to the supervisor in areas of discipline, labor relations, and grievance handling. All too often emotion-laden charges and countercharges fly back and forth. If we can see the reason behind the charges, understand the feelings, and proceed along a reasonable course which keeps us in command, we are in a stronger position. Most of us would agree that this approach is better than trying to shout an adversary down or squelch him with the arbitrary use of authority. When one party can empathize, more often than not an effective compromise can be reached without injury to the feelings of either.

A supervisor attending a human relations institute related an incident which demonstrated how his boss was able to empathize without ever knowing the meaning of the word. The supervisor had only been in the position for five or six months. He was uncertain of how much he could open up with the boss. So he stewed and fretted a couple of weeks about a problem he had until he got up enough nerve to have it out with "the old man." Then one morning, with knees knocking, he stood in the doorway to the boss's office and asked for a few minutes to discuss a problem. The boss looked up, invited the young supervisor in, and got out of his chair to meet him. As they met in front of the desk, the boss pointed to his own chair and motioned the supervisor to sit down saying, "Tell me about it, but I want you to see it from that side of the desk." While the new supervisor was trying to recover and collect his thoughts, the boss plunked down in his visitor's chair, saying, "And I'll try to see it from your point of view." Relating the incident to the institute group, the supervisor said that the action completely took the wind out of his sails, that the problem totally resolved itself, and that the boss was a man he highly respected from that point on. "It's one thing" he said, "to have your head screwed around 180 degrees, but the real thing was to know he was willing to try to see my side of the problem. You can't help respecting a man like that."

During a plant supervisory training series that met once a week, the subject of empathy was introduced and discussed. The conference leader sensed that the concept had been taken to heart, but he didn't realize how much with one supervisor until the following week. Ten minutes before the meeting was to start, he sauntered into the conference room and said to the instructor, "Hey, Jim, you remember talking about empathy last week? Well, I went home and tried it on my wife. It works!" Of course it works. It works anywhere, anytime. It's simply a matter of giving consideration to others. Who among us doesn't respond positively to having his feelings and viewpoints being given consideration? That's why we find this ability to empathize important not only to supervisors, but to husbands, fathers, salesmen, executives, teachers, and clergymen. Wherever we find ourselves in contact with others, the need for empathy exists.

Psychologists tell us there is a reason for all behavior—not always a rational, recognizable reason, but a reason. The challenge facing us as supervisors is to try to understand the reason why our people behave the way they do instead of to label their actions as unreasonable. Actually, when we stop to think about it, anytime we say a person is unreasonable, we are confessing our inability to see the reason for his acts or statements. Has any of us ever done anything unreasonable in his life? Of course not. We have done things we have been sorry for. We have made mistakes. But seldom, if ever, have we done anything without reason. Unreasonableness is always from the standpoint of the observer. Other people are unreasonable—not me! Empathy challenges us to look for the reasons why people do and say the things they do. Had Frank Connors been able to empathize with Eric Mader, he might have gotten some insight into Eric's wish to improve the work methods he was using and thus have found himself with a crackerjack employee.

As supervisors, we can empathize, or we wouldn't hold the positions we do. We can't be managers and be completely insensitive to the feelings of others. We practice empathy as naturally as we smile or shake the hand of a new acquaintance. The real test is to practice empathy deliberately, knowingly. When we get upset with a person's behavior, can we ask ourselves what's the reason for such behavior? If someone makes an unreasonable demand of us, can we find their reason? Doing so may help us sell him our reasons for having to refuse. It's amazing what we can discover about people if we make ourselves sensitive to their feelings, their attitudes, their needs.

Empathy can make our lives fuller and richer by showing us where we can make contributions to those around us. To be able to settle an argument rather than prolong it, to be able to shed light on a perplexing problem, to be able to prevent a grievance, to be able to recognize special effort—these are the rewards of conscientiously doing our best to empathize. As Burt Hall did when he adjusted Paul Botts's work schedule, empathizing is managing with a heart.

WHAT SHOULD SUPERVISORS KNOW ABOUT EMPLOYEES?

We can see that it is easier to practice empathy with those we know best. Or as we have observed before, the better we know people as individuals, the better we are able to deal with them. But what, we might ask, is it important for me to know about my employees? Leaving out all the sentimental details and getting down to practical every-day worthwhile information, what should we know? This question is asked of about fifteen supervisory institute groups a year at the University of Wisconsin. The response of hundreds of successful supervisors who have given very serious thought to this question make up the following list of things we would do well to know about each of our people.

Family

A man is his family. Geographical separation of the man at work does not remove him in his thinking from his family. With most men one of the easiest ways to hit a responsive chord in opening up a conversation is talk about his wife or children. Let's think for a moment about some of the men who work for us. How many of them would show greater pride in the accomplishments of their children than in their own performance? To know something about a man's family is to know a great deal about the man. Is he married? How many children does he have? What are their names and ages? What schools do they attend? What things does the family enjoy doing together? The number of employees working under each of us would naturally limit how much information we could profitably gather and keep, but just raising the questions suggests to us how much better we could get to know our people.

Education

With the increasing emphasis being placed on education today, we find it more and more important to know something about a man's educational accomplishments. This emphasis is certain to increase in the years to come. Matching a man's training to his work is only one reason for our concern. If a man is taking night school or vocational courses while on the job, that may well indicate his interest in a better job and his willingness to work at improving his worth. Most companies now require at least a high school diploma before they will consider a man for a supervisory position. In many cases a college degree is a necessity for promotion. In guiding and counseling employees on their careers with the company it is necessary to know their educational backgrounds. What a mistake it would be, for example, to encourage a man's supervisory aspirations without telling him of the company's educational requirements. To overlook the technical education of people in our department when better jobs open up is shortsighted. Many of us consider it an obligation to encourage additional training for those who seem in other ways to have the potential for higher-rated, more responsible jobs.

Work experience

Where have our people worked previously? What skills and abilities do we have in our work group that might be more profitably utilized? Are job training plans geared to the previous experience of the trainee? What does the pattern of previous employment tell us? Is his performance good? Is he a job-hopper or a troublemaker?

Outside interests

We often find a clue to understanding a person better in knowing the things that interest him off the job. If nothing else, knowing an employee's interests may help us establish a communication bridge with him. Is he an avid baseball, football, hockey, or golf fan? Is he a spectator, a participator, or both? Undoubtedly there are a number of do-it-yourself handymen just looking for the opportunity to discuss their latest project with us. The person who takes his family camping during vacations and weekends wants to talk about it. Often these conversations give us insight into what kind of people are working for us. In addition to letting us learn more about individuals, our willingness to listen shows that we have an interest in them as more than just a means to get out production.

Goals and ambitions

How much do we really know about what our people want out of life? Do they want just steady jobs with no worries? Do they want to move into more highly skilled work? Do they want supervisory or higher-management positions? We really don't know a man until we know what he wants to do with his life—what he wants to be. One of the most satisfying aspects of our job can be the encouragement, the stimulation, and the coaching we give to a man who wants to carve out a career in our firm.

Other information

Individual supervisors may disagree at this point about how much more we should be expected to know about individuals in order to understand them. Each of us in the long run will have to determine what we think we must know about those who work for us. But we might consider what other supervisors have indicated they want to know. Here are some of them: birthdays; anniversary dates of employment or promotions; financial status; religious beliefs and affiliations; community activities; personal problems; politics; hobbies; union loyalties; personal habits; attitudes toward company, work, and supervision; nationality; and countless other things that make a person an individual. Many of us will recognize that we're beginning to touch on some extremely sensitive areas. In fact, some state laws forbid asking about such things as religious affiliation. On the other hand, knowing that a man's religious affiliation affects his attitudes toward profanity in the shop is helpful. Occasional profanity may be a part of our vocabulary, but few of us would use it in talking to a person who might take offense. It isn't the possession of such information that can create problems, but the unwise or prejudicial use of it or reaction to it.

An example of how seemingly unimportant facts about a person can help a supervisor appeared in an evaluation of a supervisory training program in a Wisconsin paper mill. One supervisor was relating applications he had made of material discussed in the meetings, and he said that he had made good use of the idea of recognizing the birthdays of his employees. His department was the wood yard. Whenever one of the men had a birthday, the supervisor walked out to see him and wished him well. His approach was tuned to the personalities of the men working for him. He might walk up to one man and say, "Hey, Jughead, how does it feel to be another year older?" He might say to another, "You know, Smokey, I'd like to give you the day off, but I can't, so happy birthday anyhow." The point is, he wasn't corny about it, and he did get a positive response from even the toughest of the gang.

Another supervisor attending the same meetings reported that he had nearly stopped attending when it was suggested that supervisors recognize employees individually on their birthdays. "How stupid can you get?" he asked. "I'll be damned if I'm going to go out and wish my guys a happy birthday."

In order to empathize deliberately and knowingly, we need to know as much about a person as we can. His attitudes, his needs, his feelings, his behavior are the dynamic expression of his personality, and his personality is the product of everything that has ever happened to him. We can never begin to know everything there is to know about a person, but the more we know, the better we are able to empathize.

Many supervisors have found it helpful and revealing to take inventory of what they really do know about their people. Taking inventory is quite simple and not very time-consuming. The first step is to make a list of those things we feel it's important to know about the people working for us. Then we might use a roster of names of those who work for us, and fill in as many "must know" items as possible. Some of us may find that we know our people better than we realize. Others may find that we have strangers working for us; but in this situation we have already given ourselves some direction in getting to know our people better.

Using a System

It helps to have some kind of system to keep the desirable information about employees where we can get at it quickly. The form of the system isn't really as important as having some organized way of recording pertinent information about people. Some supervisors have used an index card for each person, keeping on it the vital statistics for quick handy reference. Some use a looseleaf notebook for the same purpose. The blank departmental roster shown in Figure 5 is another example of how important personal details can be recorded. Whenever a useful bit of information is picked up in conversation, the supervisor makes a note of it as soon as he can.

The information kept in such a record is not "black book" information that we might not want anyone to see. It is, rather, facts which will be helpful to us in future contacts with employees. Some of us may be inclined to think of such a record as a lot of unnecessary paper work, but consider the value it would have at a time when discussions of a personal nature with an employee are necessary—as in reviewing per-

Department Roster

Name	Birth-day	Family and dependents	Education	Work experience	Outside interests and goals	Miscel-laneous

Figure **5.**

formance, discussing transfers or promotion, counseling on a personal problem, assigning special projects, or disciplining. If reviewing the record just before such a discussion did no more than start us thinking of that employee as an individual with feelings, dreams, and desires, the record would have served its purpose.

We should consider how to gather information for such a record. Obviously it's not a good idea to take a blank departmental roster out on the floor and start interviewing employees, explaining to them that you read in a book that it was a good idea to get such information. What we need can be gathered from a number of sources over a long period of time.

Listening to employees is probably the best single source of information about their family, their interests, their ambitions. Just a few minutes of listening to a man talk about his family can be tremendously revealing. Provide the opportunity for listening, then. In addition to providing information, listening to a man shows respect for him as an individual.

Personnel department records provide another valuable source of such information as dependents' names and ages, home ownership, educational background, previous work experience, wage adjustments, hobbies, and memberships in lodges. The personnel department has proved to many supervisors to be an ideal place for starting such a system because it has so much information immediately available.

Performance reviews with employees are another excellent means of learning more about them, especially if they are encouraged to speak out. Many of us know supervisors who feel that the performance review is their show and that they must do all the talking. Yet we can't learn while we're doing all the talking. Finding out how an employee feels about his supervisor, his job, and his future with the company might very well be an added objective of a periodic performance review. This should be a time when the employee can get things off his chest and plan with his supervisor how he is to conduct himself in the months to come.

Company-sponsored social and recreational activities provide an opportunity to see the employee outside the work setting. Bowling, golf, softball, and dartball leagues are examples. Picnics and Christmas parties give us the chance to meet the wives and children of our employees and—perhaps more important—gives them the chance to meet us.

Supervisors living in small and medium-sized communities have yet another valuable source of information—the daily newspaper. One burly foreman volunteered in a seminar discussion that he regularly read the society page in the paper first. To look at him, most of us would have guessed the society page to be the last thing he would ever read. Coming from a community with a population of 15,000, he said that hardly a week went by that he didn't read that an employee's wife or child had gotten some honor, served on a committee, or taken part in a community or social event. He said he always made it a point to see that person the next day and talk to him briefly. He found the sport page similarly helpful.

In summary, the management-minded supervisor should recognize the responsibility he has to represent the company to its employees. He certainly knows how he wants the company to treat him. Each employee has the right to expect the same from the supervisor. Employee relations, after all, are just another way of finding out how employees feel toward management. Members of management have an obligation to understand and treat their people as individuals, according them the respect which is their due. Certainly, higher management expects no less of the management-minded supervisor.

HIGHLIGHTS

1. Management attitudes and philosophies on human relations have changed from the bull-of-the-woods approach to the era of sweetness and light, and then to a middle-of-the-road approach which recognizes the employee as a valuable asset who is to be treated with respect but who is expected to contribute to a profitable enterprise.
2. Understanding people in the organization begins with self-understanding. When we begin to recognize our own feelings and attitudes and how we got them, we can move to an awareness of the impact of feelings on the behavior of others.
3. Emotional maturity or stability, according to Dr. John Schindler, is a matter of
   a. Developing a sense of independent responsibility
   b. Recognizing that anger and hostility are signs of personal weakness
   c. Being able to distinguish fact from fancy
   d. Developing a giving rather than a receiving attitude toward life and toward others
4. Failure to know employees as individuals forces us into the position of having to base work assignments and personnel decisions on generalizations about people which are rarely valid.
5. Empathy, the ability to put ourselves in another's place and see things from his point of view, is regarded by many as the single most important trait of a management-minded supervisor. Most of us empathize without thinking about it. Its tougher, but more important, to empathize knowingly and deliberately when faced with difficult situations.
6. To understand employees better as individuals, we should know something about
   a. Their family life
   b. Their education
   c. Their past work experience

d. Their outside interests

e. Their goals and ambitions

7. It's a good idea to use some kind of system, such as a departmental roster, to record information which will be helpful in getting to know employees better. Information for such records can be gleaned from:

a. Listening to people

b. Personnel records

c. Personal observation

d. Performance reviews

e. Local newspapers

DISCUSSION QUESTIONS

1. Is there a bull of the woods in your organization today? Without naming him, describe some of the attitudes that make him a bull of the woods.

2. Which demands more knowledge of human relations—the bull-of-the-woods approach, sweetness-and-light approach, or middle-of-the-road approach? Explain your answer.

3. Explain this statement in your own words: "To settle for less than an employee is capable of giving is a failure to respect him as an individual."

4. Describe a supervisor you know or have known who practiced empathy. Cite some examples.

5. Discuss why a supervisor should know something about his department's employees' families, children, hobbies, goals, ambitions, and outside interests in order to work more effectively with them.

6. List what you feel that a supervisor should know about people. Then take the names of six employees you know (your own, if you're supervising now) and take inventory. How many of the things you said it is important to know do you actually know about those six? How about your whole department?

7. Set up a departmental roster similar to the one shown in Figure 5. List five employees, and compile the desired information either by talking with each employee or by consulting records, or do both. Next, list your whole department, and do the same thing.

SUGGESTIONS FOR FURTHER STUDY

Bittel, Lester R.
What Every Supervisor Should Know, 2d ed.
Chapter 2, McGraw-Hill Book Company, New York, 1968

Drucker, Peter F.
The Practice of Management
Chapter 20, Harper & Row, Publishers, Incorporated, New York, 1954

Ecker, Paul, John MacRae, Vernon Ouellette, and Charles Telford
Handbook for Supervisors
Chapter 6, Prentice-Hall, Inc., Englewood Cliffs, N.J., 1959

Lateiner, Alfred R.
The Techniques of Supervision
Chapter 1, National Foremen's Institute, New London, Conn., 1954

Schindler, John A.
How to Live 365 Days a Year
Prentice-Hall, Inc., Englewood Cliffs, N.J., 1954

CHAPTER
SIX

MOTIVATING
IMPROVED
PERFORMANCE

THE CASE OF MOTIVATING MIKE MORAN

Mike Moran had Burt Hall baffled. How can you accuse one of your better producers of loafing on the job? Yet that's what Burt had to do. Ever since taking over Assembly Department B Burt had had his eye on Mike. In fact, long before he became a supervisor, Burt had noticed the way Mike worked—and didn't work.

An exceptionally friendly and talkative man, Mike bothered Burt by his frequent practice of stopping his whole crew to tell them a joke or a story. It didn't bother Mike that it was during working hours or that anybody might be watching. He just seemed to enjoy telling stories and being the center of attention. The trouble was that the rest of his gang enjoyed him, too. That's what made it tough to clamp down—there was no chance of using group pressure on him, for Burt had tried that with a marked lack of success.

Soon after he took over the department, Burt was determined to straighten that crew out, but he waited a couple of months before moving in. Because Mike was such a friendly guy, Burt was sure that he'd have no problem motivating him to get on the ball. The crew was on a group incentive. It shouldn't be hard, Burt thought at the time, to get them to see how much they were losing by standing around and talking. He waited for an opportune time to launch his campaign. One afternoon Burt heard the whole crew burst out laughing while he was standing nearby checking a job. As Burt walked over, Mike was holding the floor, telling of one of his escapades. Mike held the complete attention of the crew—all were enjoying his performance. No one seemed to mind that Burt had joined the group. Mike acknowledged Burt's arrival with a smile and a nod, but continued with his story. Burt interrupted by asking if anything was wrong.

Mike caught the inference in Burt's question. Speaking for the crew, he assured Burt nothing was wrong and explained that he was just telling them about his last date. Sensing that Burt was annoyed, he also added that it could wait and that they would get busy. Mike, without question, was the informal leader of the crew. He had no official designation as leader, but the crew followed him just as surely as if he carried the plant manager's title.

Mike's crew produced extremely well. When they worked—and that certainly was most of the time—they couldn't be equaled in their output. Burt had no quarrel with their total production: they were comfortably ahead of the other crews doing the same work. But the frequent nonscheduled breaks for storytelling did bother Burt. He reasoned that their production could be even better if they would stick to business. Their nonproductive time could be converted into badly needed production. Further, if they kept busy, they wouldn't be setting a poor example for the other crews and the rest of the department. Mike was the pacesetter for the crew, so Burt decided to start on him. The next morning he asked Mike to stop by the office during the break.

Burt started out by explaining that he wanted to talk about idle time. No sooner were the words out of his mouth than Mike asked if their production record was slipping. Burt had to acknowledge that it wasn't, but he said, "Mike, think of the money you could be making if you'd cut out the storytelling and keep that crew busy."

"What good is money if you can't enjoy it?" Mike asked. "I've seen too many people, my old man included, sweat their whole life away to rake in money. When they finish, what have they got?—A lot of miserable years and no way of knowing how to enjoy what's left. No sir, Burt, life is too short to spend every minute of it trying to make more dough. I want to enjoy myself. Now—while I can. Tomorrow will take care of itself. We'll keep up our end of production, but don't ask me to go around with a long face trying to squeeze out that last drop of blood. We've got a good producing crew. We'll see you get a fair day's output."

"I didn't mean for you to drive them," Burt apologized. "I just meant that the time you spend horsing around could be put to better use. You could be making more money without working any harder—just steadier. You can still enjoy working, but you'll never get ahead if you don't take things more seriously. We're all here to produce. It looks like hell to have your crew sitting around gabbing when they should be working."

"OK, Burt," Mike said. "We'll quiet down. If we aren't keeping up our end of production, you let us know."

The conversation hadn't gone exactly the way Burt wanted it to. He didn't anticipate that Mike would react the way he did to the chance of making more money. Things did improve for a while, but in a week or so the old pattern was right back where it had been. Burt decided that if he couldn't get to Mike, he would work around him. One at a time, he arranged to talk to Dave Bangs, Gladys Reed, and Manny Hill. The fifth member of the crew, Jane Shands, was relatively new, and Burt didn't think he should involve her.

The reactions of Dave, Gladys, and Manny were the same. They all felt that it would be nice to be making more money. On the other hand, their incentive earnings were pretty good—better than those of the other crews. Besides, it was a lot of fun working with Mike. Each said they would try to buckle down and cut down on the talking. But the pattern of response repeated itself—first some improvement would be made, and then they gradually went back to their old habits. Burt was convinced that it wasn't malicious. They were doing a fine job on production. It was frustrating, though, to keep knocking your head against a wall without getting any results.

As much as anything, Burt was worried about the appearance of things. He often wondered how he would explain how the crew could sit around laughing and talking if Oscar Palmer should happen to walk through while Mike was spinning one of his yarns. Even if they were producing well, it would be hard to justify a party on the job. It might be even worse if some other high-ranking executive walked through at the wrong time.

Burt was puzzled by his failure to motivate any of the crew. Why didn't they respond to the carrot he held out for them? Isn't everybody interested in more money? He remembered how he worked to make out and how it paid off. He remembered, too, how pleased his wife was with the increase he got when he was made supervisor. Yet Mike showed no interest at all, and the rest of them were interested but apparently not enough to put any pressure on Mike to stop horsing around. If a supervisor couldn't motivate his people with money, what in heaven's name was left?

Since it was obvious to Burt that he couldn't solve his problem by holding out the financial incentive to Mike and that his chance of forcing the issue with disciplinary action was not good, he searched his brains for alternatives. The only thing he could come up with was the possibility of using Mike as a utility man—transferring him to other crews. Maybe he could use Mike to spark higher productivity on other crews. There was no denying that Mike was a leader and that when he worked, he took everyone with him. The trouble with that approach was the risk of having Mike spread his practice of playing around. At least the way it was now, Mike only infected one crew. Perhaps containment was a wiser policy. But if Mike could stimulate higher production, it would really help. "With Mike's seniority, he couldn't be forced into a utility position," Burt thought. "You'd have to motivate him, and I'm right back where I started. It's a puzzlement."

Mike Moran had Burt Hall baffled!

1. How can we justify Burt's concern about Mike Moran—did he really have a problem?
2. What might be some of the reasons Burt failed to motivate Mike to buckle down?
3. If the rest of the crew really wanted more money, why didn't they keep things going when Mike stopped to tell his stories?
4. Burt felt that if a supervisor couldn't motivate his people with money, there wasn't much left. What does a supervisor have to motivate his employees with?

THE MANAGEMENT–MINDED SUPERVISOR AND MOTIVATION

Several of the conclusions reached in previous chapters point up the need for skill in motivating employees to improve their performance. First, supervisors have accepted the responsibility for high-quality production at the lowest possible cost. We have agreed also that their effectiveness as supervisors is measured not in terms of what they produce but in terms of what others produce. We know that the management process requires skill in planning, organizing, motivating, controlling, and innovating. Thus we can see that the ability to motivate is a key skill for a supervisor. In fact, that's really what this whole book is about. In succeeding chapters we'll consider such areas as training employees, using discipline, handling grievances, giving orders, and innovating. Behind each of these subjects is the challenge of getting people to do what we want them to do, and that's what we mean by motivation.

Having been placed in the management position that is in direct contact with the production employee, the supervisor is strategically situated to use motivational practices which will have the greatest pay-off. No one is in a better position than he to create a climate conducive to high worker production. Without fear of exaggeration we can say that the supervisor has greater control over the factors that motivate employees than any single management group. This control is both a promise and a demanding challenge. Certainly, we can recognize that a supervisor who can motivate effectively will not only advance in his organization, but will advance the organization itself.

The supervisor's responsibility for motivating employees is shared with higher management. Supervisors have no control over policies in the areas of wages, labor relations, expenditures for physical working conditions, and long-range planning. It cannot be denied that these policies do influence the motivational climate in which the supervisor works. But, as we shall see, their effect on employees is limited when it comes to stimulating an attitude of dedication to the job. The factors that supervisors alone control through day-to-day contact have much more far-reaching effects on the striving of an individual to give his best to his job. Higher management has the obligation to provide a base of fair wages and working conditions, stable employment, and competitive fringe-benefit programs. Above that base, supervisors continue to fashion the environment in which people work. They carry their management's desire to provide a healthy climate in which to work to the place where the work is done. To be truly management-minded, supervisors need to understand the motivational factors that they control. This we shall try to do through an examination of common-sense experiences and the latest research on employee motivation.

Let's begin with a definition of motivation. We might say that to motivate means to move. Management, however, is concerned with the direction of that movement. We can motivate negative as well as positive behavior. The dictionary says that to motivate is to provide with a motive. That definition, too, is lacking for our purposes, since we might say that salary does that. Dwight Eisenhower was credited with saying that, "Leadership is the ability to get a person to do what you want him to do, when you want it done, in a way you want it done, because he wants to do it." Here, it seems, we come much closer to defining the challenge that motivation poses for us.

First we should pay attention to the words "what we want him to do." There is no suggestion here of a supervisor's abandoning his responsibilities to management. His responsibilities are to direct the work of the department and to insist on adherence to standards of performance. To be able to do this in such a way that individual employees want to achieve the same results is the really tough part of his job. He needs to know the wants of the employee in the work situation, the skill of communicating the objectives or goals of the organization to him, and the ability to make him accept those goals as his own. Making employees want to do the job the way we want it done will serve as a definition for what we mean by motivation.

If we accept that definition of motivation, we establish a need to know what the employee wants from his job—his life. Or, to put it another way, we need to know what will make him want to do his best work with a minimum of supervision. For every generalization we make about people, any of us can cite a number of exceptions. But we will have to make some general statements, and each of us will have to determine for himself to whom they do not apply and why.

By and large, people want to work. Working gives meaning to their lives and satisfies their need to accomplish something of worth. It is unfortunate when people can't find this satisfaction in their work because they will then seek it in other areas of their lives. People want to be respected for what they know and for what they feel as well as for what they do. The bull of the woods usually fails to recognize this. Most people who accept the goals and objectives of the organization will control their own performance with very little supervision. Part of the skill of motivating employees, then, is skill in selling departmental goals to the individual. Many employees who fully understand their roles in the success of an enterprise will seek responsibility rather than run from it. The supervisor's job becomes, essentially, one of trying to mesh the individual's needs with the goals of the department and the overall organization. To the extent that he can demonstrate to the employee (notice we said *demonstrate,* not *tell*) that what he wants most from his job will be realized through excellent performance, he will be successful in motivating him.

We took note in the previous chapter of the fact that most employees would rather please their boss than displease him. Most of us have had occasion to doubt that statement, but a few moments of careful reflection convinces us of its truth. For example, Burt Hall may have felt that Mike Moran and the rest of his crew didn't give two hoots about his feelings. Yet, who for a moment would attribute to likable Mike a desire to displease Burt? How many of us, for that matter, believe that supervisors have any desire to displease any of their workers or make them unhappy? Knowing an employee's desire to do work of which he can be proud and his desire to please his boss, we can look toward the problem of what he wants from his job.

The Motivational Drives of Employees

Most, if not all, of our behavior is directed toward satisfying some need or want. Such needs change and vary in intensity. They can be very small, such as stopping at a water fountain when we happen to pass one. We don't think in that situation, "I am thirsty. I must have a drink of water." We are barely conscious of the desire for water. It is there. We help ourselves. Yet we can easily see that the longer we are denied the satisfaction of our thirst drive, the stronger that drive becomes, to the point where it dominates all our behavior. The principle of motivation illustrated here should be highlighted because it is so basic to our understanding. Our drives remain relatively quiet in us as long as they are satisfied; but deny or withhold the satisfaction of any drive, and it will dominate our behavior. It's very easy to see this principle at work in such physiological areas as hunger, thirst, rest, and breathing. But we often forget that the same principle operates with respect to our social and psychological drives. It's a point we'll want to remember as we consider other aspects of employees' behavior and motivation.

The striving for the things we want and need is what the psychologist means by motivation. So we see that motivation is within the individual. It is a highly personal matter. Because motivation is within the individual, we do not control an employee's motivation. A man's needs are his own, and the values and priorities of one need over the other are his own. We can find patterns on which to make generalizations, but we cannot successfully substitute generalizations for a genuine understanding of the individual. As Burt should have seen, Mike Moran did not respond to the incentive of money beyond a certain point. Other members of that crew attached more importance to money, but not enough to disturb the group relationship that they were enjoying. The attitudes of the entire crew must be examined in the light of the fact that they were earning a better wage than the other crews doing similar work. Unless we recognize the principle that a person attaches greatest importance to things he's not getting, we might conclude that money is not important. Everyone knows that it is one of the prime reasons why people work.

If motivation is within the individual and if we have no control over others' motivation, where do supervisors come into the picture? Their control or their influence on behavior comes in the area of incentives —the satisfaction of drives. Behavior is the result of an individual's striving to satisfy his needs. We might express it as a formula:

Motivating drive + incentive (satisfaction) = behavior

In terms of supervisory responsibility, behavior is what the supervisor wants to influence. This can be done by providing or denying the satisfactions an employee is seeking. The influence on behavior can be positive (motivating) or negative (frustrating). A pat on the back for a job well done may very well be all an employee needs to continue his excellent work or to strive to improve it. Inadvertently overlooking the good work or simply accepting it as something for which the employee is well paid might result in a lack of interest in work. Although supervisors do not control what the employee wants, in most cases they do determine whether or not he gets what he wants on the job.

There are almost as many ways of classifying and labeling human drives as there are psychologists. In the long run the classification systems aren't nearly as important as the principles on which they operate. We should, however, have some base from which we can depart in our discussion of the incentives supervisors control and the influence they have on employees' behavior. The following list of needs represents a fair cross section of what we read and accept.

Physiological drives

We are born with needs that are common to all life. These are the drives that concern the requirements of the body. Typical examples of the physiological drives are hunger, thirst, shelter, breathing, elimination, and reproduction. The physiological drives are the most basic of our drives and must be satisfied before our behavior is directed toward satisfying higher-level drives. These drives remain relatively quiet in us as long as they are satisfied, but they will completely dominate behavior if unsatisfied. Supervisors are really not involved with these needs in their employees. In our economy employees are well clothed, well fed, and well housed. We should not lose sight of the fact, however, that the money a man earns on his job buys the satisfaction for his physiological needs. Money, therefore, is the means of satisfying man's most basic drives.

Security drives

We all need freedom from worry about our future welfare. Normally we think of this need in terms of job security. Employees want to feel that their jobs are secure—that they will have a job and income until they retire. Security needs, by and large, are extremely well satisfied by the company, the government, and the individual on his own initiative. Examples of how security drives of employees are fulfilled would include unemployment compensation, guaranteed annual wage plans, social security, medical plans, hospitalization insurance, life insurance, and retirement programs. The insurance industry is founded on the needs of the individual for a feeling of security. The ability to satisfy these needs is again out of the supervisors' hands. The fringe-benefit program in a company (amounting in many cases to 25 percent of the payroll) is determined by top management. We can observe the effects on behavior of the desire for security during periods of recession when layoffs threaten a segment of the work force. The union recognizes this need by selling its members and potential members guarantees that it will fight for their security.

Social drives

Everyone wants to feel that he belongs to the group in which he finds himself. This urge is the social drive. Wherever we find ourselves in groups—the family, community or social activities, our church, fraternal organizations, and, most important to us, the work group— we want to feel that other group members like to have us around. Inability to satisfy this need for belonging will usually cause a man to quit the group if he can. We probably will never have accurate statistics on how many people leave their jobs because of a feeling that they don't belong. There is enough evidence to show that this is a prime reason for turnover during periods of high employment when other jobs can be obtained.

A company in Milwaukee failed for several years to find the reason for its unusually high turnover rates. In exit interviews, people mentioned better jobs or higher pay as the prime reasons for quitting. A new executive vice-president with an outstanding reputation in the field of employee relations put his finger on the real cause of their problem soon after he joined the firm. He discovered that most of the people leaving were new employees who felt no identity with the firm. A number of abuses in the personnel department and in the employees' own departments broke down the employees' feeling of belonging. Initiation of an employee orientation program and a supervisory human relations training program reduced turnover the first year to a tenth of what it had been.

The management-minded supervisor exercises a very high degree of control over satisfying his workers' need for a feeling of belonging. Actually no one person in the organization is in as good a position as the first-line supervisor to make the employee feel that he is a part of the work group, the department, the total organization. The supervisor, too, has this drive; he really wants to feel that he is a member of management. The new supervisor who has just moved up from the ranks starts acting more like a manager as he feels his identity with the management team grow.

Psychological drives

The individual needs to feel that he is important. Each of us, wherever we go, whatever we do, wants to feel that he is making a worthwhile contribution to the activities in which he engages. This is true both at home and at work. We usually recognize the importance of this drive at work, but frequently fail to remember that our wives and children are human enough to have similar drives. Keeping an orderly, well-run home is just as much a job as running an automatic screw machine, typing invoices, or assembling relays. Recognition of achievements is just as important to the homemaker as to the machinist. Satisfactions for the psychological needs of employees are many and varied. They include such things as: praise for a job well done, additional responsibility, promotion, pay increases, listening to ideas, just listening, delegation, challenging work assignments, and opportunities to participate in the decisions that affect the job. Many supervisors have experienced the effectiveness of an occasional written word of praise to an employee. If done judiciously and when deserved, a written commendation has special significance to the average employee. For the satisfaction of his need to feel important on the job, an employee must depend almost entirely on his supervisor. Supervisors are in complete control of the recognition incentive. Management must depend on its supervisors to satisfy this vital and personal need of the employee. The supervisors shoulder management responsibility to satisfy the psychological drive. The payoff is the employee's enthusiasm for improving performance and, in the long run, for working toward a more profitable operation.

Self-esteem drives

A person has a deep-seated need to respect himself—to feel that he is accomplishing what he was put on this earth to do. Each of us wants to reach as near our full potential as possible. All the praise and acceptance of an individual may go for naught if he feels that he is doing less than he is capable of doing. Some of the more recent research by M. Scott Myers of Texas Instruments, Inc., has pointed to a breakthrough in employee motivation by capitalizing on the self-esteem drive. His findings suggest that we can benefit by allowing much greater employee participation in the setting of production goals and standards.*

Supervisors should recognize their responsibility to match the skills and abilities of employees working under them to the requirements of the job. Further, they need to guard against any actions which might prevent an employee from making his best contribution. The most common example of such restrictive actions is the failure to listen to an employee's ideas for improvement of his job methods. We need only recall the success Burt Hall had with Eric Mader in the previous chapter when he allowed Eric to try his idea for a new fixture. We also remember that Frank Connors squelched both Eric's ideas and Eric's desire to work.

To summarize briefly, we see that the employee's needs are met by the organization (higher management) and his supervisor. Company programs and policies meet employees' needs in part. But they are not within the supervisor's control and are usually economic in character. Supervisors have a great deal of control over the motivational factors that concern an employee's need to feel that he is important, his need to feel that he belongs, and his need to respect himself. We'll come back to what we do and do not control later when we discuss some of the research done by Frederick Herzberg and M. Scott Myers.

* "Who Are Your Motivated Workers?" *Harvard Business Review*, January–February, 1964.

Frustration in Employees' Behavior

Motivation, we said, is the striving for the things we want and need in life. But what happens when we can't achieve or realize the things for which we strive? Frustration. Whenever we are prevented from achieving what we want, we experience frustration. Any barrier that stands in the way of our satisfying our desires creates frustrated behavior. Just as it is important for us to recognize motivated (positive) behavior, it is important that we learn to recognize the symptoms of frustrated (negative) behavior.

An example can again be found in the previous chapter. Larry James, we will recall, wanted to get ahead. He worried about his lack of education and the degree to which it might prevent him from achieving a better job. We can say that Larry was frustrated. He didn't have the education needed to achieve a promotion. To his credit, he had decided that going to night school would remove that barrier.

Characteristic of frustrated behavior is its emotional nature. Larry was extremely sensitive to whatever was said that might hurt his chances to advance. He reacted emotionally to Burt's comments, which had been intended as compliments, interpreting them as attacks on his work. His failure to respond to Burt thereafter was the result of his frustration. It was Larry's mild-mannered way of exhibiting the aggressive tendencies of frustration.

Behavior, we have said, is caused. It has a reason. When an employee takes an "I don't give a damn" attitude toward the quality of his work, what is the reason? Could it be that something he needs very badly, perhaps subconsciously, is missing from the job? Other forms of negative behavior that we might encounter could be excessive absenteeism, careless handling of equipment, frequent complaining and griping, horseplay, slowdowns, argumentative behavior, and sometimes resistance to change. All too often we are inclined to dismiss such behavior as unreasonable, without any attempt to try to understand what is causing it. Identifying the symptoms of frustrated behavior many times produces opportunities to change conditions to the satisfaction of the employee.

Common sense demands that we use caution in analyzing negative behavior by making the effort to determine whether the behavior is due to frustration or whether there might be a real cause for dissatisfaction. An undesirable working condition such as poor lighting may be a genuine cause for dissatisfaction and may be very easily corrected.

On the other hand, if the negative behavior is due to frustration, the cause may be much more difficult to determine. There is, as we've said before, no substitute for knowing as much as possible about the individual's background, interests, and ambitions. Empathizing has helped many supervisors determine the causes of frustrated behavior.

Deep-seated or long-standing frustration may require professional help. If consideration and fair treatment does not produce a desired change in behavior, supervisors should not hesitate to discuss the advisability of professional help with higher management or the personnel director. Unless the cause of frustration is determined and corrected, the frustrated behavior will continue and in all probability worsen.

What People Want from Their Work

Having discussed motivating drives, we have already gained a good deal of insight into what people want from their jobs. But let's be more specific. Employees spend at least one third of all their time in the work environment. They spend more of their alert waking hours on the job than they do with their families or in any other single activity. What do they expect from this occupation which consumes the major portion of their adult years? What they feel toward their work—frustration or satisfaction—cannot help but affect the relationships they experience outside the work environment. A genuine understanding of what employees want from their jobs sometimes eludes the supervisor who is wrapped up in reaching departmental production, cost, and quality goals.

Numerous surveys have been conducted seeking to find what employees want from their jobs. These surveys have almost no value to the supervisor in understanding what his own people want at a given time because changes in economic conditions, working conditions, and management affect responses. Whenever people are asked to rank what they want to get out of their jobs in order of importance, it is essential to understand that they tend to rank highest those things which they are not getting or which might be threatened. This tendency stems from the fact that an unsatisfied drive dominates behavior.

What we can learn from such surveys is the relationship that exists between supervisory and employee thinking. These surveys also help us remember that people want more from their jobs and from the

Employees' Ranking	Job Factors	Supervisors' Ranking
1	Full appreciation of work done	8
2	Feeling of being in on things	10
3	Sympathetic help on personal problems	9
4	Job security	2
5	Good wages	1
6	Interesting work	5
7	Promotion and growth in the company	3
8	Personal loyalty to employees	6
9	Good working conditions	4
10	Tactful disciplining	7

Figure **6.**

supervisor than a boost in pay or a pat on the back. One of the most widely quoted of such surveys was published in *Foreman Facts* by the Labor Relations Institute of New York in 1946. Ten thousand employees from a cross section of industries were asked to rank ten factors in the order of importance to them on the job. At the same time, the supervisors of the respondents were asked to rank the items as they thought their employees would rank them—in other words, they were asked to empathize a little. Let's look carefully at the results of their responses (Figure 6).

Most managers explode when shown the results of this study in conferences or seminars. Some accuse the employees of being hypocritical. Others claim that it doesn't check out with their experience. Employees' complaints, they say, are usually about wages, seniority (security), and working conditions, and these things show relatively low ranking in the study.

Now let's take a more objective view. First it's important to understand that these results were published in 1946 and do not apply to conditions today. Wages were going up after the removal of wartime controls, and employment was at a very high level. It's not difficult, then, to see why security and wages did not at that particular time concern employees as much as some noneconomic factors. However, we should not lose sight of the fact that the supervisors responded to the survey at the same time that their employees did.

It's of particular interest to observe that the supervisors gave the bottom three rankings to those factors which the employees had said were most important to them. Do we not have cause to question how much the supervisors were able to empathize? Of even greater significance, we see that the supervisors ranked first, second, and third those factors over which they had almost no control. Wages, job security, and promotions are factors determined at higher levels, frequently in negotiation with a union. Can we therefore draw the conclusion that supervisors were throwing in the towel on motivation by saying, in effect, "What employees want most is what we can't give them"?

Whether we agree with the employees' responses or not, it's interesting to observe that their top three rankings went to noneconomic factors which are completely within the control of their supervisors. We have already agreed that recognition for good work is an obligation which is almost exclusively the supervisors'. None of us would deny that showing appreciation for good work and making an employee feel that he belongs falls fully within the scope of the supervisors' responsibilities. A number of supervisors, however, do take exception to the employees' third ranking item—sympathetic help on personal problems.

Many supervisors state that they feel they have no business poking their noses into the personal lives of the employees under them. We should recognize, however, that there's a vast difference between poking our noses into their personal lives and creating the kind of climate in which an employee with a problem feels he can discuss it with his boss. A person with a problem often needs to share it with someone. Often it's only a case of listening. Other times it's best to help the troubled person find qualified guidance from a priest, minister, doctor, lawyer, psychologist, or family counselor. An employee's loyalty goes to that person or organization which demonstrates the greatest interest in helping him. How often have we seen workers' loyalty won over by the union steward who says, "Bring your problems to me. I'll see that they're heard. That's my job." At the same time the supervisor is saying, "Don't bring your problems to me. They're none of my business." Again it's completely within the supervisor's control to create the kind of climate he wants to exist in his department.

It is also important to recognize in examining this survey that employees look for *all ten* factors from their jobs. Management's job in trying to motivate improved performance is to see that none of the factors is neglected, or else conditions for frustrated or negative behavior will be created. Needs, in life, are continually developing and demanding satisfaction. Satisfaction frequently is only temporary, and the need arises again and again—or one need arises, and then another. Creating an environment in which all wants and needs of employees are satisfied borders on the impossible. Conscientiously striving, however, to develop a sensitivity to people's needs can't help but improve the supervisor's batting average and elevate his stature as a member of management.

New Insights Into Motivating Employees

Some of the most significant and practical research into the problems of motivating employees has been done by Frederick Herzberg of Western Reserve University * and M. Scott Myers of Texas Instruments, Inc.† Herzberg found that levels of job satisfaction and productivity in engineering and accounting groups were closely related to two sets of factors—"dissatisfiers" and "motivators." Myers carried on his investigation of these factors with technical personnel, supervisors, and production employees.

Both found that many of the factors we have considered as incentives or motivators for some time have greater capacity for dissatisfying employees than they have for motivating them. The dissatisfiers are essentially peripheral to the job and include such things as pay, physical working conditions, fringe benefits, job titles and classifications, orientation to the job, work rules, seniority rights, and grievance procedures. It is essential that these factors be maintained at an acceptable level because dissatisfaction can quickly arise where deficiencies exist. These factors have, however, relatively little value in stimulating high achievement or extra effort.

The second classification, the motivators, according to Myers and Herzberg, includes such factors as growth, achievement, delegation, freedom to act, recognition of work done, participation, goal setting, responsibility, and performance appraisal. Myers found that these motivators were primarily associated with the self-actualization of the

* Frederick Herzberg, *Motivation to Work,* John Wiley & Sons, New York, 1959.
† "Who Are Your Motivated Workers?", mentioned earlier.

individual on the job. He stressed that job satisfaction and high production were most often associated with the motivators and that disappointments and ineffectiveness were most often associated with the dissatisfiers.

Of particular interest to first-level supervisors is the fact that research now confirms the key role the motivators play in producing high levels of performance and job satisfaction. Here is proof that the supervisor can't wash his hands of the responsibility for motivation simply because he has no control over wages and job security. To be sure, the organization must maintain fair wages, assure job security, provide decent working conditions, and offer competitive fringe benefit programs to prevent widespread dissatisfaction—which is a complicated and expensive responsibility for any employer. But for the most part, the motivators are under the supervisor's control. Management must depend on its front-line for the creation of a motivational climate.

Nonfinancial Incentives for Improving Performance

Good work, extra effort, and motivated behavior occur when a supervisor supplies something outside the employee (an incentive), thereby satisfying something inside the employee (a motive). In carrying out his job of motivating people, he is likely to be most effective when he selects and tailors incentives to meet the workers' individual needs. Burt Hall neglected to give consideration to Mike Moran's individual needs, assuming instead that Mike was primarily interested in financial reward. Since we have established that the supervisor's control is essentially over the nonfinancial motivators, let's identify some specifics which he can use in motivating his people. Here are some suggestions that many successful supervisors have found helpful.

1. Treat employees as individuals

"Show a personal interest in them," many supervisors have said. The supervisor gets so wrapped up in his own problems that he forgets that the employee is an individual with feelings and opinions needing the opportunity for expression. Most employees would like the chance to express their opinions, ideas, and feelings to the one man who more than any other is management to them—their supervisor. Remembering that all men want to feel important, the management-minded supervisor finds two easy and natural ways to satisfy that need. First, he talks with them—listens to them. Most employees like to be able to go home to their wives and say, "I was talking with the boss today, and I told him . . ." Generally speaking, we find that the chance to identify with leadership in the department goes a long way toward satisfying the employee's need to feel important. Second, the supervisor has the opportunity, particularly with new employees, to show them the importance of their jobs to the overall operation. They do make a distinct contribution, or they wouldn't be employed. The easiest, most natural thing in the world is to show them the importance of their job.

2. Offer sincere praise and recognition

The key to giving praise is the word *sincere*. No one wants praise given "by the numbers." We want to feel that we have earned it and that the boss means it. Praise, we know, ought to be specific. For example, if the quality of a man's work was particularly outstanding, it should be recognized; if finishing a job ahead of deadline was accomplished because of extra effort, praise should include a recognition of the difficulties overcome. Lavish or undeserved praise can have a negative effect and do more harm in the long run than no praise. Many supervisors have found it easier for themselves and for their employees to praise indirectly—that is, to praise the work rather than the individual. Instead of saying, "Joe, you're a topnotch worker. I couldn't get along without you," many supervisors make it more palatable by saying, "Joe, that job you turned in yesterday was really top-grade. It's work like that that makes us all look good. Keep it up."

Listening to employees is an easy, natural way to recognize them. Promotion, increased responsibility, and written commendations are also effective means of giving recognition when they are timely and deserved.

3. Provide growth opportunities through delegation

Many managers regard this suggestion as a way of killing three birds with one stone. Delegation demonstrates confidence in the employee, thus satisfying, in part at least, his drive for self-esteem. Delegation gives him a chance to show what he can do. And the increased responsibility he assumes gives him the opportunity to make a greater contribution to the work of the department and increases his feeling of personal worth.

Delegation also provides the supervisor with the chance to strengthen his departmental team by creating growth opportunities for individuals. As the members of a department grow, so does their supervisor. We identified in the first chapter the supervisor's responsibility for the training and development of employees. Delegation is one of the most practical ways of developing people if it is properly handled. It is not without risk—but then what worthwhile things are ever accomplished without some risk? The risk of sharing in a subordinate's mistakes, for example, causes many supervisors to shy away from delegation, saying, "It's easier to do it myself."

The third benefit is the time supervisors can save. Supervisors who will study the activities they engage in and the decisions they make will find many that subordinates can do. This not only makes jobs more meaningful for subordinates but frees the supervisor to do more of the things he can't find the time to do. One of the more satisfying aspects of supervision is having subordinates come to supervisors with the solutions to problems they have carefully thought through. When supervisors encourage thinking and problem-solving at the lowest possible level, they are motivating the employees in their departments.

4. Review their performance

Many supervisors say that supervisors should let their people know where they stand. People want to do a good job and would rather please than displease. Common sense should tell us, then, that they need to know how the supervisor thinks they're doing. Imagine the frustration of an employee who really tries to do his best day in and day out and never hears a word of evaluation, never has a chance to discuss his accomplishments. Most of us know supervisors who operate on the theory that "You're doing all right as long as you don't hear from me." Yet we recognize immediately that anyone concerned about motivating better performance can't afford to operate that way. Some of us have heard supervisors say they can't evaluate or review performance because the company doesn't have a program for review. Few, if any, supervisors would ever be denied the right to sit down informally with an employee and let him know what they think are the strengths in his performance and discuss with him how that performance might be improved. Such reviews are just one more way of recognizing individuals and the contributions they make to successful operations.

5. Provide for participation

When we discussed resistance to change in a previous chapter, we noted that one of the best ways to overcome resistance was to provide for opportunities to participate in the formulation of the change. Proper motivation of employees is best encouraged when a supervisor can involve the employee in improving his performance. Many companies are now experimenting with involving production employees in the setting of goals and standards. Most of those who have tried it report that the employees tend to set higher goals than the management's and to achieve them with less difficulty. Human nature proves time and again that employees who have been a part of formulating a plan, setting a goal, or developing an idea work harder to bring about its success. After all, they are a part of it, and they belong to the group who said it could be done. They don't have to be sold. They sold themselves.

6. Plan the orientation of new employees

The new employee tends to be insecure when he faces a new job, a new boss, new working conditions, and new fellow employees. His need to feel that his work is important and that he belongs to the work group, to the department, and to the organization can be most effectively satisfied at the time he is the most impressionable—during his first hours and days under new supervision. Probably never again in his career in the department will he be more receptive to the supervisor's thinking, attitudes, and suggestions.

7. Train them well

Acquiring new skills and knowledge acts as a spur to better performance. The desire for excellent work grows with the employee's confidence in his ability to do the work. Good training and motivation go hand in hand—each contributing to the other. In the next chapter, we shall go into detail on the importance of proper training in motivating improved performance.

8. Communicate with them

In a recent survey conducted at the University of Wisconsin,* the supervisors who said they did not feel that they were a part of management cited lack of communication as the chief reason. The failure of management to communicate does more to tear down employees' morale and to frustrate their behavior than any other single shortcoming. Every incentive that the supervisor controls depends on communication as the vehicle for its implementation. Praise and credit must be communicated. The devices a supervisor uses to make an employee feel that he belongs or feel that he is important require communication. Employees want to know what's going on, where they stand with their supervisor, what changes are being contemplated, what their role in the successful operation of the department is, and what they can do to improve. Their feeling of being in on things is the result of how well the supervisor communicates with them.

A MATURE APPROACH TO MOTIVATION

Like communication, motivation is more an attitude and philosophy than a technique. Every suggested technique for motivating a work group is just so many words unless it is carried out with sincerity.

For several decades it was felt that the supervisor had very little to do with motivation, even though lip service was paid to his responsibilities in that area. The more we learn about motivation, the more we realize that the first-line supervisor is the real key to job satisfaction and high productivity. The importance of that responsibility should therefore motivate him to try to do his best to apply the philosophy discussed here. Since motivation theory is so intimately tied up with satisfying the needs and wants of others, a giving attitude seems to be the most desirable. In the last chapter we said that one of Dr. John Schindler's criteria for personal maturity was a giving

* From Bradford B. Boyd and Burt K. Scanlan, "Developing Tomorrow's Foreman," *Training Director's Journal,* May, 1965.

rather than a receiving attitude. Can we survey our departments, our jobs, and our people and ask ourselves, "What have I to give?" Carry that question to the specific suggestions contained in the preceding section on nonfinancial incentives, and we see that the opportunities for giving are numerous. Most of those with a genuine concern for giving will experience the satisfaction of witnessing higher morale, unsolicited cooperation, and greater productivity in their departments.

HIGHLIGHTS

1. The first-line supervisor is strategically situated to implement motivational practices which will have the greatest payoff in organizational effectiveness. No other level of management has more control of the incentives that stimulate greater effort on the job.

2. Dwight Eisenhower's definition of leadership—"the ability to get a person to do what you want him to do . . . *because he wants to do it,*" serves the management-minded supervisor as a working definition of motivation.

3. Striving for the things we want and need is what most psychologists mean by motivation. Satisfaction of needs represents the control supervisors have in motivating the improved behavior of employees. A man's needs or motivating drives are classified as:
   a. Physiological
   b. Security
   c. Social
   d. Psychological
   e. Self-esteem

4. Inability to find satisfaction for our drives results in frustration (negative behavior) that in work situations may take the form of excessive absenteeism, careless handling of equipment, frequent complaining, horseplay, slowdowns, argumentative behavior, or resistance to change. Before dismissing such behavior as unreasonable, we should try to understand what is causing it; for unless we understand and remove the cause, the frustrated behavior will continue.

5. People expect a great deal more than money from their jobs. Research has shown that such things as pay, fringe benefits, physi-

cal working conditions, seniority rights, and grievance procedures have greater capacity for dissatisfying employees than for stimulating improved performance. The factors which have the best potential for motivating high productivity include growth opportunities, achievement, freedom to act, participation, recognition, goal setting, and responsibility. It is in the latter area that supervisors have the greatest control.

6. Nonfinancial incentives that can be used to motivate employees in the supervisor's day-to-day contacts with them include:
   a. Treating employees as individuals
   b. Offering sincere praise and recognition
   c. Providing growth opportunities through delegation
   d. Reviewing their performances
   e. Providing for participation
   f. Planning the orientation of new employees
   g. Training them well
   h. Communicating with them
7. Opportunities to motivate improved employee performance seem to center on our own answers to the question, "What do I have to give my people?"

DISCUSSION QUESTIONS

1. In your own words, explain what is meant when we say that the supervisor has more control over the incentives that motivate improved performance than the members of any other level of management.
2. Why would employees in India or China differ from those in the United States in terms of what they want most from their jobs?
3. Describe the attitude of an employee whom you know who was not primarily motivated by money. What did he put ahead of money?
4. What are some specific things a supervisor can do to make an employee feel that he belongs in the work group and in the department?
5. We say employees need recognition. How many specific things can you list that a supervisor can do to recognize individual employees?

6. Cite an example—either on or off the job—when you thought another person's behavior was unreasonable. Can you now see the reasons behind his actions or attitude? Explain.
7. Explain the thinking behind the statement that praise insincerely given can have a negative effect.
8. Is it possible to praise too much? Why or why not?
9. Evaluate the philosophy of some managers that reflects the attitude expressed by the words, "You're doing all right as long as you don't hear from me."
10. Why would an employee try harder to improve his performance when he has had a voice in setting the standards that apply to his job?

SUGGESTIONS FOR FURTHER STUDY

Batten, J. D.
Tough-minded Management
Chapter 7, American Management Association, New York, 1963

Drucker, Peter F.
The Practice of Management
Chapter 23, Harper & Row, Publishers, Incorporated, New York, 1954

Ecker, Paul, John MacRae, Vernon Ouellette, and Charles Telford
Handbook for Supervisors
Chapter 4, Prentice-Hall, Inc., Englewood Cliffs, N.J., 1959

Kay, Brian R., and Stuart Palmer
The Challenge of Supervision
Chapter 4, McGraw-Hill Book Company, New York, 1961

CHAPTER
SEVEN

TRAINING
FOR
RESULTS

THE CASE OF THE UNTRAINED TRAINERS

Lack of time was the real reason Burt Hall delegated his training function. Besides, a good supervisor should delegate. It was one way of developing a sense of responsibility. No one had to tell Burt that training employees was his responsibility or that costs, quality, morale, and production are all affected by the kind of training employees receive. But you just can't be everywhere doing everything, and training takes time—a lot of it.

So Burt had delegated the training of employees in the department to three experienced men acknowledged by everyone to be good producers who knew their jobs backward and forward. Each of them had performed a number of different jobs, and among the three of them every job in the department was covered. None of them reacted negatively to the idea of breaking in new people as a part of their jobs, but their reactions were mixed.

Clarence "Squeaks" West, for example, radiated pleasure when Burt first discussed the assignment with him. Squeaks, who got his nickname because of a high-pitched, squeaky voice, was a smiling, gregarious employee, liked by everyone. Burt entertained a few doubts about using Squeaks as a trainer but decided his experience and popularity would overcome any handicap his voice might pose.

Sam Pitman, the youngest of the three, shrugged his shoulders, grinned, and said, "Yeah, I'll give it a try," when Burt approached him. Sam had come to work in the department right out of high school. He was twenty-seven years old but already was an old hand with ten years' experience. His competitive spirit made him an outstanding producer. It was only natural that Burt had developed a high regard for Sam.

Joe Meyer was the old-timer. At fifty, he had twenty-seven years with the company and fourteen years in Assembly Department B. He had dropped out of school in the ninth grade, knocked around doing odd jobs, and got a stock chaser's job as the company was working its way out of the depression in the late thirties. Joe was fond of calling himself a graduate of the "school of hard knocks" and took great pride in being a steady worker who appreciated the chance to do a job well— an outlook, he felt, that was "missing in the young people we hire these days." Joe wasn't keen about working with youngsters but said he would if Burt wanted him to.

As new people were brought into the department, Burt would greet them and spend about ten minutes in giving them a quick tour of the department. He felt it was essential for him to have this contact with new employees. With those who transferred in from other departments, he skipped the tour, assuming that they knew their way around. With the preliminaries out of the way, Burt turned the new employee over to the one of his training trio who had the most experience in the job to be learned.

"Full responsibility and authority for training these people will be yours," Burt told his trainers. "You know the jobs better than anyone, and therefore you're the best qualified men I have to do the training in our department," he told them as he wound up a brief meeting before putting his plan into operation.

It was only in recent weeks that Burt had come to the realization that almost all rejects and rework were being caused by people who had come into the department since he had taken over as supervisor. At first he had subconsciously written off the problem as one of new people learning the ropes. Recently, in analyzing the roadblocks to more efficient production, it dawned on him that it was those people trained specifically by Sam and Joe who were producing over 80 percent of the work rejected by inspection. Further analysis revealed that a couple of what he referred to as his attitude problems—the gripers— were in that same group.

Rather than blame Sam and Joe immediately for poor training practices, before he was even willing to admit that training was the problem, Burt decided on a course of observation and checking. First he planned to talk with the last person each of the trio had trained and then to observe each of his trainers in action with new people who would be hired in the coming weeks.

Sarah Weeks, obviously nervous when Burt called her in to discuss how things were going on her new job, felt certain that she was going to be called on the carpet for producing too much rejected material. She said that her job overall was all right and that she was sure she would get the hang of it. The first couple of days were pretty hectic, though, she told Burt.

Asked if she felt she had sufficient training on the job, Sarah said no without hesitation. She didn't want to criticize a whiz like Sam, she said, but she just couldn't keep up with him.

As she described her training, these patterns became evident. Sam had demonstrated the job several times, going so fast she couldn't see his hands move. He laughingly apologized for being so slow, saying that the other girls set a pretty stiff pace and that he was out of practice. She was sure Sam thought she was hopeless. She felt both relieved and tense when Sam left her alone. Yes, he had said she could ask questions, but she couldn't think of any before he left her on her own. The other girls helped her whenever she asked them.

Al Wagner welcomed the opportunity to talk to Burt, since he was thinking of quitting anyway. To himself, Burt thought he wouldn't mind his leaving at all, since Al was a griper. When they got around to discussing his training, Al revealed an immense dislike for Joe, though he grudgingly admitted that Joe was a good hard worker.

"But you get the feeling that if you don't copy everything he does, you're no good," Al told Burt. "Once he called me a young punk. He pretended he was kidding, but I knew that's what he was really thinking. He went so slowly when he showed me the job, he must have thought I just got out of kindergarten. When I had an idea for speeding up a part of the job, Joe said I should wait until I knew something about the job before I start telling old-timers how to do it."

Al said he understood everything Joe had told him, but he felt that Joe might be holding back a few tricks that would have been helpful. He felt this way because he had picked up a few watching the guys working next to him, and an old-timer like Joe sure could have passed them on if he wanted to. After a few words of encouragement from Burt, Al said he appreciated the opportunity to talk about his job. He promised to be a little more careful about his quality.

Alice Draper thought Squeaks was just about the nicest guy around. She described how he had made her feel right at home, took her down to final assembly to show her where her work fit into the finished product, and introduced her to the other girls around her before they sat down at her bench. She particularly remembered how he stressed going slowly at first so that she would only produce quality work. Squeaks had told her that there wouldn't be any difficulty working up to standard after she had been there a couple of weeks. She remembered being all thumbs at first and that she and Squeaks had several good laughs over her clumsiness.

"It's a wonder he didn't go crazy with all my silly questions, but he had the patience of a saint. The first day, I knew I was going to like working here, and I haven't been wrong."

Burt couldn't believe it when he saw identical situations develop as each of the trio tackled their next training assignment. It was, Burt thought, like seeing a movie a second time. Each of them apparently had developed a style he felt worked for him, but Sam and Joe certainly weren't helping build a strong department.

While watching Squeaks work with a new young man, Burt noticed him referring frequently to a sheet of paper in his hand and was puzzled about it. Squeaks seemed a little embarrassed when Burt asked him about it over a cup of coffee that afternoon. "I'm not good enough at these jobs to keep everything in my head," Squeaks explained. "Unless I sit down beforehand and make a checklist, I'm sure to forget something or get things all out of sequence. It's not very fancy. I just jot down each step of the job and anything special along the way that I have to remember. It may not be very professional, but it sure helps me get my thinking organized."

Grinning from ear to ear, Squeaks answered Burt's question about how he liked his instructing assignments. "I ought to be paying the company for that time instead of letting the company pay me. Seriously, Burt, I like it. These new employees are so eager to do a good job, they make me feel I should really learn something about instructing so I could do a better job for them."

As Burt began to evaluate his checking and observing of the three trainers, some things were so obvious that he was ashamed that he hadn't seen them before. Sam and Joe weren't contributing much to his goal of quality production. Squeaks, with a humble view of his own instructing ability, was getting results which anyone could be proud of. Burt wondered about several other things.

1. Should a supervisor delegate the training function to others in his department?
2. What made Squeaks so superior as an instructor to both Sam and Joe? Squeaks, after all, was the only one Burt had had any doubts about in selecting his trio of trainers.
3. What do employees really learn from their trainers? Isn't it a lot more than just how to do a job?
4. Just how important is training in the smooth functioning of a department?

THE TRAINING RESPONSIBILITY OF THE
MANAGEMENT–MINDED SUPERVISOR

What Burt Hall was learning the slow, painful way, many have come to appreciate very early in their careers. Unfortunately some supervisors never learn it. The responsibility for a well-trained work force is just about the most important responsibility a supervisor has. From the top executive to the foreman, every manager must accept the obligation to train and develop those who report to him. This principle is so vital to the progress of any organization that most large successful companies spell it out as a matter of policy.

The results supervisors achieve in production, costs, quality, safety, morale, and methods are proportionate to the quality of the training employees receive when they begin their jobs and while they are on the job. We all recognize, for example, what a mistake it would be to discount the effect employees' attitudes have on the major areas of supervisory responsibility. Nor can we fail to recognize that the most potent factor in shaping those attitudes is what happens when employees learn new jobs.

More supervisors than we like to admit have a negative attitude toward training because, they say, it takes so much of their time. Yet we see them taking time to correct mistakes, assign rework, and put out the fires that proper training would have prevented. We can always find time to correct those things that we didn't have time to do properly the first time—but sometimes this fact is slow to dawn on us.

Perhaps there is a deeper reason for disliking the job of training. Most of us like best the things we do well. Supervisors who have been deprived of the opportunity to learn how to train have in most cases been deprived also of the satisfaction that any good teacher experiences in working with his students. Squeaks West was one of the fortunate few to whom the skill came naturally. The trial-and-error approach to job training yields about the same results that it does in any other area. There will be a few who "luck out," but not many. The odds favor our falling victim to one or more of the common mistakes in training, which we'll analyze soon. When we do make any of these mistakes, dissatisfaction results and the dislike for training deepens.

We can all learn a lesson from a supervisor in a Minneapolis firm whom I'll call George Westphal. He was participating in a supervisory institute at the University of Wisconsin a few years ago when the discussion turned to the benefits of good training to the supervisor. George popped up his hand and said, "It's fun." Almost to a man everyone in the room did a double take and waited for George to explain that remark. Few of the men who were there that day will forget George's little speech.

"The thing I hate most about my job," he said, "is criticizing people. I don't like the look on their faces, and it just plain makes me feel lousy. When I don't train them right, I've got a lot more criticizing to do. That's one thing.

"I don't know how many of you stopped to think about it," he continued, "but a new employee is just about the most anxious-to-please person in the world. They want to do a good job. Sure, they're nervous, but it's mainly for fear that they won't be able to satisfy us. When you know that the impression they get in the first couple of hours is going to stick with them for a long long time, you know your work is cut out for you. That's when the fun starts. They're like putty in your hands. A lot of personal satisfaction comes in feeling that what you're doing is helping people learn the skills that will earn their living for them. You feel the responsibility, too. I guess I just enjoy being with people when they're so darned cooperative."

What a philosophy! Imagine what it must be like to come to work as new employee and meet George. Imagine, too, what kind of attitudes grow out of George's enthusiasm for teaching people how to do their jobs. This kind of attitude enables a supervisor to establish himself as a true leader and to experience the personal satisfaction we all seek from our jobs.

Empathy is a much-needed quality in discharging the training responsibility. A good teacher needs the ability to put himself in the shoes of his students—to see their needs and to understand their fears and tensions. The ability to empathize will help the supervisor recognize the anxiety experienced by the new employee as he stands for the first time in his work area facing a new boss, new surroundings, new fellow employees. Empathy will help the supervisor see the job from the learner's viewpoint rather than through the eyes of one with years of familiarity with the operation.

A little empathy helps the supervisor see the hopes and expectations the employee has as he begins a new job. To the extent that we can generalize about these hopes, the following desires would apply to most people on the day they face a new job, a new boss, a new department or company, and new fellow employees:

1. The hope that their job is important

We've all read and joked about the janitor who wants to be called a sanitary engineer or the trucker who prefers "materials handler" as a job title. Supervisors are proud of having attained a position of some standing in the company. Even the person coming in to do the most routine job wants to feel that he is doing something worthwhile. A management-minded supervisor capitalizes on this desire by assuring the employee that the service he will perform is needed. By so doing, he stimulates even further the desire of the employee to succeed.

2. The hope that they'll get along well with their supervisor

We frequently lose sight of the fact that most people want to enjoy friendly relations with the boss. It's good to be able to say, "My boss is a real good Joe." These hopes of new employees make the supervisor's job much more pleasant if he recognizes them.

3. The hope that they will do well in their jobs

As we've recognized before, we all need something to work for. We want to feel that we're accomplishing something. The management-minded supervisor who shows an employee how to measure his own performance builds in self-motivating incentives. The employee wants to see what progress he's making, against realistic standards. Through good performance he pleases his boss and satisfies his own need for a feeling of accomplishment. This natural need is especially high when an employee is beginning a new job; this need gives rise to the conclusion that new employees are anxious to make good.

4. The hope that their supervisor will set high standards
of performance

Every worker entertains the hope that the boss expects the best from him. While the supervisor's expectations from employees during the learning period must be moderate, they want to know that their supervisor has a sufficiently high regard for them to expect them ultimately to perform to high standards. Mistakenly, many managers play down standards to show their consideration, but in doing this they are removing incentives for top-notch performance. High but realistic standards are a compliment to an employee. Being a good guy by suggesting that they want people to take it easy may salve managers' egos, but it does very little for the employee eager to show them what he can do.

An employee's first few days on the job are full of high hopes and expectations. The supervisor who is able to empathize recognizes these hopes and takes advantage of them. In so doing, he finds his own role as an instructor infinitely more satisfying and more productive.

Delegating the Training Function

Common practice among a majority of supervisors is to delegate the function of job training to others—lead men, setup men, older employees, top-producing employees. Burt Hall's approach to training in his department is frequently followed. Unless special steps are taken, experiences like Burt's with Sam and Joe are the result. The problems and concerns discussed in this chapter must be faced by those who do the job training in the department. It doesn't make much sense for a supervisor to know the principles of job training and then not pass them on to the person who will actually train departmental employees.

We should recognize some factors concerning delegation in determining the desirability of delegating the responsibility for training. There are those who say that responsibility can't be delegated. It's a moot point. When a supervisor delegates, he creates a new responsibility—that which a subordinate has to him. He does not, however, delegate his own responsibility for a well-trained employee or department.

When a supervisor delegates, he gives others the right to perform in his name, to make his decisions for him. He shares with the subordinate the results of his performance. The subordinate's performance is the supervisor's performance. If there are mistakes, they are the supervisor's mistakes. He cannot view an employee's substandard performance, shrug his shoulders, and tell the boss that his assistant's poor training of the employee is responsible. He is just as much responsible as if he had personally handled every step in the training procedure.

It stands to reason, then, that the person to whom the supervisor delegates his training function must be adequately prepared to carry out the responsibility. He should understand the impact that good job training will have on the total results of the department. The trainer's training should include analysis of the learner as an individual, identification of the common mistakes made in training, finding out how people learn, learning techniques for preparing to instruct, and guided practice in teaching a job using a systematic approach.

Delegation is very effective in developing subordinates. Burt Hall, however, didn't appreciate that training requires special skills apart from knowing the job to be taught. Before a supervisor delegates training activities, he should understand thoroughly the principles and techniques of good job training. Then he must teach them to his trainers. If he cannot do this, he must at least arrange for the trainers' training and review carefully their performance as they begin to assume the supervisor's responsibility.

Tangible benefits accrue to the supervisor who properly delegates training in his department. He develops much-needed and extremely important skills in his subordinates. Having people specialize in training can result in a higher level of job performance in the department. Finally, the supervisor is freed to accomplish other important work in the department. The risks in delegating are obvious. But they can be minimized by an even greater emphasis on *training the trainer* than on training the new employee.

Common Errors in Teaching Employees Their Jobs

The assumption that anyone who can do a job can teach another how to do it has led to countless errors in the instruction process. Many of us have been the victim of one or more of these errors. Others have seen them committed. Perhaps a few of us have even been guilty of a couple ourselves. Some of the more common mistakes made by supervisors and trainers are listed here. Later we will discuss an approach to training that is designed to eliminate such errors.

Feeding too much at one time

Like the overeager parent who shovels food into an infant faster than he can swallow, a supervisor can heap a multitude of details on the learner so fast that they can't possibly be assimilated. This tendency is an easy trap to fall into, since the trainer knows the job so well. He assumes that pictures he carries in his head are easily and quickly received in the mind of the learner. He lacks sensitivity to the special problems of the learner in digesting new concepts, and proceeds on his merry way to compound the confusion.

Telling without demonstrating

Anyone who has ever seen the classroom exercise of having a supervisor tell a discussion leader how to put on a coat or open a pack of cigarettes will quickly testify to the fact that *telling alone is not enough.* Semantic problems for the trainee are often major barriers to learning. The learner must receive the words and visualize what is wanted. Being strange to his environment, he finds these visualizations extremely difficult. While his mind is trying to understand one concept, two or three more have gone in one ear and out the other. An example or two may dramatize the problems this error can create.

In a Midwestern pharmaceutical plant, a new employee was sent up a ladder to tighten down the cover of a pressure-cooking vat. The cover was clamped down by a stud and a palm-sized wing nut which swung up into a U-shaped projection on the rim of the cover. The supervisor told the employee, "Clamp it down good and tight." The shape of the nut, of course, indicated that he meant hand tight. But, being as eager as most new employees are, the employee got himself an 18-inch pipe wrench and proceeded to get the cover down "good and tight." In the process of following instructions, he snapped the stud off. The delay ruined chemicals with which the vat had been charged, production schedules fell behind, and customer relations suffered, all because the employee had tried to do "only what he had been told."

A Chicago manufacturer of small brass fittings provides another example. One of the foremen who had a new employee on his hands had to go to a production meeting. He needed something to keep the new man busy while he was gone. He called the man over, pointed to a large pile of fittings on the floor, and said, "Start cleaning up that pile of fittings, and I'll be back with you in a couple of hours." He intended the employee to clean the burrs off the fittings—a pure, out-and-out make-work assignment. After the boss left, the new man lost no time in securing a 55-gallon scrap drum, a shovel, a broom, and handtruck. Cleaning up the pile took little more than an hour as the employee hauled four loads of fittings to the company dump.

It took a crew of three men the better part of a day to sort out and recover about two-thirds of the fittings from the debris in the dump. Head in hands, the new man could only mutter, "I just did what he told me."

These examples may seem extreme. Yet, who among us can't find many examples, just as ridiculous, of what can happen when the trainer relies on telling without demonstrating.

Lack of patience

For many, learning is a slow process that demands frequent repetition and careful explanation. To the supervisor anxious to get on with running his department, the temptation to lose his patience is great. Burt Hall, we'll recall, was beginning to see that a learner learns more than the job being explained to him. He observes the attitude of the trainer and reacts to it. Impatience on the part of the trainer produces tension in the learner. Tension slows learning. Slow learning taxes the trainer's patience, and so it goes. Sam Pitman's approach was a fine example of this vicious cycle at work.

Lack of preparation

Good training doesn't happen by accident. Distractions caused by an instructor who has forgotten to have materials, supplies, tools, and prints ready before job instruction begins can only slow the learning process. Inhibition of learning is also caused by the trainer who doesn't present the job in its logical sequence. Confusion is the inevitable result of backtracking during instruction. An unorganized approach to training will create an image of an unorganized boss or department in the mind of the new man.

Failure to build in feedback

The instructor who fails to avail himself of feedback opportunities during instruction is asking for trouble. Imagine the trainer who tells the learner how the job is performed, shows him the operation, and then says, "Well, that's all there is to it. You know everything I know. Good luck."

Good luck! They're both going to need it. Who knows at that point what the trainee has learned, if anything? Job training requires effective two-way communication. An instructor who is not oriented to the needs of his student and is concerned only with his presentation does only half the job.

How does the trainer build in feedback? He can do it in a number of ways. During his explanation of the job, he's getting constant feedback through the facial expression and attitude of the learner. Any instructor who is sensitive to his student can read that "I don't have the faintest idea what you're talking about" expression on the learner's face. And he can feel the eagerness that communicates understanding and readiness to try out the job.

Another opportunity for feedback is created when the instructor invites his trainee to explain the job as he understands it. It helps to encourage the learner to ask questions about anything he doesn't understand. The dedicated trainer recognizes the vast difference between *encouraging* questions and simply saying at the end of an instruction, "Now, do you have any questions?" The latter approach makes questions almost impossible by creating the feeling in the trainee that he would demonstrate stupidity if he asked about anything —or, even worse, that he would be implying criticism of his instructor's explanation. One of the most effective and crucial feedback techniques, which should never be omitted, is to have the learner perform the job two or three times to demonstrate his understanding of it.

Failure to reduce tension

"Put him at ease" is a phrase we often come across in discussions of how to handle any face-to-face relationship with an employee. This concept is especially important in job training. Clear thinking is necessary during the learning process; but tension inhibits learning, and a new employee has plenty to be tense about. Usually he has just come from the personnel or employment department, where he has had explained to him his wage scale, deductions of many varieties, life and health insurance plans, vacations, hours of work, overtime pay, regulations concerning his joining a union, and countless other considerations which constitute conditions of employment. His head is filled with these facts as he faces his supervisor, the department, the job, and his new fellow employees.

Why should he be tense with such amiable fellow employees? The problem is that he doesn't know the other employees yet. Much will depend on how they reveal themselves to him in those first few hours. How valuable it would be if the members of the department could only see his mental picture of them during those first hours. A simple concern about what that image might be would undoubtedly cause a majority of them to make some positive adjustments in their approach.

Stimulating a Readiness To Learn

Everyone who had seen his children through the elementary grades has been made aware of the principle that children must be ready or interested in learning before real learning can take place. Teachers have cautioned parents not to panic if reading or math doesn't sink in immediately. Johnny has to be ready to learn, they counsel.

Because a job and a means of earning a living are at stake, it is easy to tend to take readiness to learn for granted when dealing with workers. True, new employees tend to be anxious to please, but supervisors cannot afford to overlook the importance of stimulating a readiness to learn. It's as important to job training as explaining the sequence of the job to the employee. Common sense tells us that once the learner is motivated to learn, the supervisor's job becomes easier and his training efforts are more effective. Motivation to a large extent depends on the employee's feeling that the job he will be doing is dignified and will contribute in a significant way to the overall work of the department and the organization. How often, for example, has a supervisor tried to reassure an employee that a job will be easy to learn but downgraded its importance instead? Instead of stimulating interest, this leaves the employee wondering, "If a ten-year-old can do it, why should I?"

Consider for a moment the approach of a foreman in a plant in Racine, Wisconsin, who made it a practice to greet every new employee with a smile, a firm handshake, and these words, "John, am I glad to see you. This job you're going to be doing really needs some attention."

In his very first words he tells the employee that the plant needs him and that his job is important. Sincerity, of course, is the keynote in his approach. But it's easy to be sincere when we recognize that people don't get paid for jobs that don't need doing. No matter how menial the tasks to be performed, that foreman in Racine could voice his greeting with the deepest conviction.

If the job to be taught is menial, routine, and easily learned, the supervisor has a golden opportunity to stress accuracy and quality. Even the sweeper makes an important contribution to good house-keeping, making a better place to work and indirectly contributing to the efficiency of production employees. When the supervisor can see every job in the department as a substantial contribution to the overall effort, he's on his way to transmitting this same outlook to individual employees. If people are our most valuable assets, why not communicate that fact to them? Empathy will help the supervisor see an individual's job as his whole work life. His standard of living and his feelings of personal worth are tied up in his job. A management-minded supervisor recognizes this and cultivates the employee's pride in the work he will be doing, and in the process he conditions the employee to learn with enthusiasm.

How to Facilitate Learning

Having recognized what a vital part of the supervisor's job training is, we might examine the skills that promote effective teaching. Most supervisors can't achieve the skills of the dedicated professional teacher, but they can borrow a few ideas to make the discharge of this key responsibility easier and more satisfying. Translating the principles of the educational psychologist into the commonsense language of the supervisor, we find a number of aids to good teaching. Let's consider what makes learning and the job of training easier.

1. Repetition

Difficult or complex operations may have to be explained several times and in several ways. A good instructor will find a variety of methods of presenting the job to an employee in order to maintain interest at a high level. For example, he might have the employee observe someone else performing the job as the first step. He might then explain the job in words in a logical sequence and follow this with a demonstration of the job in which he both tells and shows. Another variation, if further repetition is desirable, might be for the instructor to do the job as the employee gives directions. The last method is particularly useful in the operation of machinery when damage to equipment or injury to the employee might result from faulty handling. The degree of complexity will naturally determine how much repetition is needed. Without insulting the intelligence of the employee, the supervisor or instructor can capitalize on the knowledge that repetition does make learning easier simply by varying the method of presentation.

2. Arousing curiosity

A key technique in stimulating thinking or learning is arousing the learner's curiosity. Others will say the same thing this way, "You can't learn them nothing until you gets their attention." In effect, we're using this approach in this book. Burt Hall finds himself in situations that have confronted many beginning supervisors. He is faced with problems they have faced and ponders questions that they have asked. As we think about his problems, we open our minds to the suggestions of thousands of experienced supervisors who have shaped the text of each chapter.

Arousing the learner's curiosity is easily accomplished in the training situation by an occasional query—"Joe, do you have any idea why we do it this way?" "Why do we do it in this sequence?" "What does this part do?" Joe may or may not have an idea, but in either event he will want to know why—his curiosity has been aroused. If he has guessed incorrectly, he will listen carefully to the proper explanation, provided that we haven't belittled his effort. If he says he doesn't have the slightest idea, we can bet he's receptive to the answer. Selecting two or three key points in the operations to pique the curiosity will serve to reinforce learning where it is especially important.

3. Careful use of competition

Most people like to compete, especially if the competition is fair and there's a reasonable chance of succeeding. The competitive urge drives people to try a little harder—something everyone would like to see in new employees. Competition can enter into job training in a number of subtle ways. For example, if the trainer points out that it takes an average operator two weeks to achieve a certain level of production, he has indirectly set a goal the employee will try to reach. A caution, however, is in order. The goal set should be fairly easily attainable lest we produce a frustration that will have a negative effect on his effort. Remember Sam Pitman, Burt Hall's young trainer? Sam had needled Sarah Weeks about how his speed was no match for the other girls' performances and he had given Sarah a hopeless feeling that she could never come up to standard.

Employees can compete against time. If it takes five minutes to complete a unit of work the first time, how long will it take the second, the fifth, the tenth, etc.? Then how many units per hour will he average after a week, a month, and so on? Wherever it is possible for the employee to record or graph his production, he has an opportunity to compete with his own achievements.

4. Knowing the knacks

Many jobs revolve around certain key points, special timing, tricks, or knacks. A thorough knowledge of the job on the part of the instructor will include an appreciation of these knacks or principles. His teaching will be more effective if he can highlight these, convey an understanding of them, and show the balance of the job as revolving around these principles. For example, an instructor might tell a new assembler, "The trick to this whole job is matching these two surfaces." Or he might advise, "Once these two wires are properly soldered, the rest almost fall into place."

When the learner sees that a particular knack is a key to successful completion of that job, he'll be likely to focus extra effort there. If we have been judicious in identifying the knacks of the job, the employee's extra effort should pay handsome dividends.

5. Enthusiastic instruction

It's not very likely that someone will get excited about a job or quality production if no enthusiasm is shown by the trainer. Experience in many fields proves to us that enthusiasm is contagious, and this is especially true in teaching. Positive attitudes toward the job are best developed by men who can communicate those same positive attitudes. The quiet enthusiasm reflected in the attitudes toward instruction shown by Squeaks West and George Westphal is a valuable asset to anyone charged with the responsibility of training another. Common sense tells us that people are far more responsive to the instruction of an enthusiastic trainer.

6. Satisfaction in accomplishment

Perhaps the most potent stimulant to learning is the satisfaction the employee finds in making progress on the new job. As his fears and anxieties are replaced with confidence, his interest deepens and his effort increases. We can easily see this phenomenon at work in children. Even the mildest encouragement brings an immediate response. Tell little Johnny you're proud of the way he can sound out words, and he'll try to read everything in sight. Until, that is, he tackles a few words that are too tough—then he backs off to safer ground. Although adults are more sophisticated in their behavior and have learned to disguise their feelings, the inner positive response to praise and encouragement still exists in most of us.

The learner needs encouragement. It affects his behavior in a most positive way. It is easiest and most natural to encourage the learner when he has actually earned the praise. False flattery is quickly recognized by the employee. The real challenge to the instructor is to plan his training in such a way that the learner has the opportunity to recognize his progress during the learning process.

Helping the employee experience satisfaction in accomplishment is not difficult and well worth the effort. The technique is simply one of breaking the job down into sufficiently small elements to allow mastery of each one with relative ease. As he works with the learner, the instructor can sense how quickly or how slowly he may proceed and still allow the learner to feel that he is progressing. Interestingly enough, encouraging the learner is one of the most satisfying aspects of training for the instructor. As the learner feels satisfaction in his accomplishments, the teacher's own satisfaction in a job well done grows.

How to Inhibit Learning

Practical experience has taught many training people that they can unknowingly slow the learning process. Without proper preparation for training and without a sensitivity to the problems of the learner, seemingly insignificant factors can become a part of training patterns which have a definitely negative influence on learning. At the risk of repeating some of the points already raised in this chapter, we might profit by identifying what prevents learning efficiency. If learning efficiency is impeded, training effectiveness is reduced.

1. Fatigue

Learning is hard work. It requires effort. We tire very quickly in learning situations, and the mental processes slow down. To avoid undesirable consequences of fatigue, the instructor should schedule training, whenever possible, at a time when an employee is both physically and mentally fresh. Usually this time is early in the shift. Efficiency diminishes as the day wears on. There is little doubt that the poorest time to attempt any training is during the last hour before quitting time. Many supervisors have suggested breaking up the job and teaching it in segments. Training sessions which go on and on reach a point of diminishing returns.

2. Monotony

Teaching a neophyte how to do a job that doesn't challenge the trainer's abilities can easily be regarded as a chore, and this attitude will result in a monotonous presentation. A very detailed job which may appear to require a recitation of a great deal of factual information can likewise be monotonous to both instructor and learner. The most logical remedy for avoiding monotony in training seems to be an employee-oriented approach to teaching.

Even the most routine job is new to the employee—it's a puzzle and a challenge. Recognizing this fact helps many supervisors generate enthusiasm for teaching old jobs to new people. The situation is similar in many respects to that of a successful Broadway actor beginning the five hundredth performance of a play. The temptation to give less than his best, to walk through, to recite lines rather than live them, is ever present. The actor continually needs to remind himself, in the tradition of the theater, that no matter how many times he's performed the play, it's still the first performance for the audience.

To those who say, "yeah, but that's what he gets paid for," the supervisor can reply that effective training is his job. Fortunately the supervisor's pay comes not only in dollars but in the satisfaction of teaching and in the performance of well-developed employees.

3. Distractions

Anything that interrupts the employee's concentration during training slows the learning process. Some distractions cannot be avoided. Others can be anticipated and eliminated. When the training is done at the workplace, many distractions must be contended with. For example, the curious eyes of fellow employees at adjacent work stations or desks may distract the learner. This disturbing influence is reduced if the new employee is introduced to everyone in the department before actual job training begins.

Noise from machinery, typewriters, or people generally must be tolerated when training at the workplace. Where the noise level is especially distracting, as much of the job as possible should be discussed in an isolated area. Mockups or models have proved useful in many plants and offices to introduce the employee to job principles.

If the instructor is often interrupted to answer the phone or other employees' questions a real deterrent to learning can develop. If the trainer makes it known he is not to be disturbed during training, he will head off most of the distractions in this category. All too often, though, the distractions are of his own making. Any time the training sequence must be interrupted because the instructor has forgotten certain materials, supplies, forms, tools, or equipment, he creates the worst of all distractions. We noted before that the employee learns a good deal more during the job training than just how to do the job. If he must sit and wait while his instructor is off getting some tool or supplies, what does he think as he idles away his time? The obvious step to remove this barrier to learning is better planning—perhaps a checklist.

4. Anxiety

We needn't dwell on the obvious. Tension and anxiety are not conducive to thinking or learning. Research in one division of Texas Instruments, Inc., proved conclusively that the removal of anxiety shortened the time it took for operators to reach a satisfactory level of competency.* Special effort was made to minimize anxiety by stressing, for example, the extremely high percentage of people who succeed on the job. This helped new employees to anticipate some of the joking by experienced employees about the high rate of failure. Every assurance of help and consideration was given. In short, each possible cause of anxiety was identified and eliminated before the employee was given instruction on the job to be performed. The results proved, beyond question, that eliminating learners' anxiety will reduce greatly the time needed to reach standard performance.

Opportunities for Training

If we have created the impression, by frequent references to the "new employee," that training is necessary only with newly hired personnel, let's take a quick look at other opportunities that call for expert training. Any time a new method is introduced in the department, the opportunity arises to reestablish the importance of quality, costs, safety, and housekeeping. The installation of new equipment or machinery provides a similar opportunity. Changes in products, in the model produced, or the addition of new features open the door to renewed emphasis on job pride.

It goes without saying that excessive waste or scrap demands investigation and additional training. The same is true of serious accidents or increases in the rate of accident frequency. Poor attitudes; excessive gripes, complaints, and grievances; turnover; higher than usual tardiness; and absenteeism are all conditions which might be improved by training.

With the increased emphasis on automation and technological improvement, many employees will be moved from job to job and from department to department. Every transfer to a new job creates a new opportunity to train for improved employee performance.

A Systematic Approach to Training

Many will say, "All this talk about principles, theories, and suggestions is fine, but give me something specific to guide me." Is there a

* From Earl R. Gomersall and M. Scott Myers, "Experiment in On-the-Job Training," *Harvard Business Review,* July–August, 1966.

simple system to incorporate the principles of good training and avoid both the common mistakes made in training and the things which inhibit learning? Yes, but the system is a stepwise procedure and, like any four-, five-, or six-step approach, it must be followed with care if it is to be valuable. We often seek such a system, find it, and dismiss it as oversimplification or claim that it's fine for someone else but that our situation is different.

Here, then, is a six-step system for teaching a job—any job. Conscientious application of these six steps will almost guarantee improvement in training effectiveness. We must say *almost* because the final result depends on the care taken in preparation and on the individual skills of the instructor. It will be easy to see how the principles of good training are built in—the system simply organizes our thinking.

Step 1: Prepare the instructor

Many supervisors, trainers, and educators claim that adequate preparation is more than half the job of teaching and that even the most skilled communicator severely limits his effectiveness through inadequate preparation. Conversely, good preparation can compensate greatly for the lack of a flair for talking.

The instructor in his preparation should consider, for example, how much time he will need to do a good job and when and where he and the learner will be able to accomplish the most. He will see to it that all the supplies, materials, and equipment are available to ensure uninterrupted learning.

Perhaps most important is to have a training plan which breaks the job down step by step to tell the instructor *what* to present. The same plan will include points to stress to tell him the *how* of each step, or the knacks of the job. Figure 7 shows a blank training plan which will facilitate preparation. The same essentials can be covered with any breakdown form, even on the back of an old envelope. Remember that Squeaks used a homemade checklist to accomplish the same purpose.

Step 2: Orient the operator

The instructor should remove the new employee's anxiety and tension by putting the learner at ease. A smiling face works wonders. Helping

Job Training Plan

Job _____

Estimate of time required _____

Date and time of training _____

Location of training _____

Supplies needed _____

_____

Tools or equipment _____

_____

Job sequence (*What*)	Points to stress (*How*)
1.	1.
2.	2.
3.	3.
4.	4.
5.	5.
6.	6.
7.	7.
8.	8.

Figure **7.**

him see where he and his new job fit into the departmental and overall picture is important. The instructor can build his teaching on a sound foundation if he finds out what the employee's previous experience has been. The key in this step, of course, is to make the employee interested and eager to learn the job. He learns a great deal about his boss and the attitudes he will be expected to cultivate during this step.

Step 3: Explain the operation

Here's where the training plan is put to use. The trainer gives a step-by-step explanation of the job in its logical sequence and demonstrates each step as he goes along. It is essential that he doesn't proceed so quickly that he loses the learner. Facial feedback is the best clue to how well the learner is grasping our explanation. It may be necessary to repeat the operation several times to ensure his understanding. A final test of his comprehension is to have the learner explain the job to his trainer.

Step 4: Test performance

Once the instructor is confident that the employee completely understands each step in the operation—how and why it is performed—it is time for the employee to try the job. Consideration in correcting errors is important. While it is essential that the learner turn out accurate, high-quality work, the trainer can't lose sight of the fact that the learner needs encouragement in abundant doses. The trainer should remain with him until he has demonstrated that he can perform the job without 100-percent supervision.

Step 5: Release the operator

The new employee is now ready to strike out on his own. Before leaving, the trainer should check again to see whether he has any questions, stressing that he should never go ahead if he's in doubt about anything. A characteristic of most learners is that they're gamblers. It's nearly impossible for the instructor to cover every situation that is likely to occur on a job, so the new worker should know where to go for help if he needs it. If a fellow employee is designated as a source of help, it is essential that the employee be informed so he doesn't show annoyance at requests for help.

Step 6: Follow-up performance

This is the step that trainers so frequently overlook or where they tend to take shortcuts. Checking several times a day during the first week to offer encouragement, suggestions, and friendship helps the employee develop good work habits and helps him recognize the trainer's interest in him as an individual. As he demonstrates competence, he is checked less frequently until he is a full-fledged member of the work force.

These six steps can be applied to almost any operation—office, factory, or sales. In clerical work modified application of these steps may occur several times as the employee faces a variety of jobs that he will be expected to perform. Training is hard work, but it's work that saves work, and little else in supervision is as satisfying as seeing a novice develop into a reliable performer.

HIGHLIGHTS

1. Training is a prime responsibility of the management-minded supervisor, and it greatly influences the results he achieves in production, quality, costs, methods, safety, and morale.
2. Seeing the job from the employee's point of view, we recognize the hopes and desires he brings to it:
   a. The hope that his job is important
   b. The hope that he'll get along well with his supervisor
   c. The hope that he will do well in his job
   d. The hope that his supervisor will set high standards of performance
3. When a supervisor delegates the training function, he does not absolve himself of the responsibility for a well-trained work force. The supervisor should see that whoever does the training in the department knows the principles of good training and has the skill to apply them.
4. Unskilled trainers tend to make these common errors in teaching people their jobs:
   a. Feeding too much at one time
   b. Telling without demonstrating
   c. Showing a lack of patience
   d. Failure to prepare to instruct
   e. Failure to build in feedback
   f. Failure to reduce tension
5. A person doesn't learn until he's ready to learn. He must be mo-

tivated by seeing that the job he will be doing is important to the operation.

6. Some factors which tend to facilitate learning or make learning easier for the employee are:
   a. Repetition
   b. Arousing curiosity
   c. Careful use of competition
   d. Knowing the knacks of the job
   e. Enthusiastic instruction
   f. Satisfaction in accomplishment

7. Unknowingly, the supervisor can inhibit the learning process and make his own job tougher. Factors which slow down learning are:
   a. Fatigue
   b. Monotony
   c. Distractions
   d. Anxiety

8. A six-step system for training
   a. Prepare the instructor
   b. Orient the operator
   c. Explain the operation
   d. Test performance
   e. Release the operator
   f. Follow up with checks on performance

DISCUSSION QUESTIONS

1. Explain the effect that good training will have on production, costs, quality, safety, and morale.
2. What, specifically, can a supervisor do to get an employee interested in learning a job?
3. In your own words, explain why empathy is so important for anyone instructing a new employee on the job.
4. What are the advantages and disadvantages of a supervisor's delegating the training of new employees to others?
5. Many offices follow the practice of having the outgoing girl train her replacement. What are the limitations of this procedure?
6. Six common errors in teaching people their jobs were identified in this chapter. Can you identify at least four more?

7. Explain in your own words how the instructor's enthusiasm, or lack of it, is likely to affect the learner.
8. What can a supervisor do to put a learner at ease before beginning his instruction? Be specific.
9. Make a job training plan (like the one in Figure 7) for a simple job from your department.
10. Teach somebody a job using the six-step system presented in this chapter. Evaluate your experience using this system.

SUGGESTIONS FOR FURTHER STUDY

Bittel, Lester R.
What Every Supervisor Should Know, 2d ed.
Chapter 13, McGraw-Hill Book Company, New York, 1968

Ecker, Paul, John MacRea, Vernon Ouellette, and Charles Telford
Handbook for Supervisors
Chapters 7 and 8, Prentice-Hall, Inc., Englewood Cliffs, N.J., 1959

Famularo, Joseph J.
Supervisors in Action
Chapter 5, McGraw-Hill Book Company, New York, 1961

Gardiner, Glenn, and Associates
Managerial Skills for Supervisors
Chapter 11, Elliott Service Company, Mount Vernon, N.Y., 1960

Kay, Brian R., and Stuart Palmer
The Challenge of Supervision
Chapters 8 and 9, McGraw-Hill Book Company, 1961

CHAPTER
EIGHT

DISCIPLINE
AS A
WAY OF
THINKING

THE CASE OF THE DISAPPEARING CARPENTER

"I'm so mad I could chew nails. Have you got a couple of minutes, Ray?" Burt Hall was standing in the doorway to Ray Ford's office after the shift had left for the day.

Ray motioned Burt in, saying, "Come on in and grab a chair. Frank and I will have things wrapped up in about thirty seconds." Ray affixed his signature to a requisition, handed it to Frank Connors, toolroom supervisor, and turned to Burt, saying, "Now, what can I do you out of?"

Before Burt could answer, Frank started to go; but then he asked Burt, "Is this a private fight, or can anybody get in?" Without smiling, Burt said, "If you've got a few minutes, Frank, stick around. Maybe three heads are better than two, or should I say one. I think I've just lost mine."

"It sounds serious," Ray said. "What's up?"

"It's that Slim Carpenter we hired about a month ago. Rules just don't mean a thing to him. If I could have found him tonight, I'd probably have fired him or given him a week off to think things over," Burt started out. "For the third time in a month he's walked out of the department without checking—without permission. And these last two times he can't claim he didn't know about the rule because I explained it clearly the first time it happened. I don't know . . ."

"Wow," Frank interrupted. "You've really got him. Lower the boom. Teach him a lesson he won't forget so easily this time. You've got to show these new young punks who's boss, or they'll run all over you."

Burt nodded and went on to explain that he had been in the production office just before the end of the shift. He had been given a small but routine rush order that had to be ready for shipping late the next morning. On his way back to the department Burt decided that Slim could handle it if he got at it first thing in the morning. Slim should have finished that Apex order before quitting time. When Burt arrived at Slim's bench, Slim was nowhere in sight. His bench was cleaned up for the night. It was still five minutes before quitting time. Burt asked the man on the next bench where Slim had gone and was told by Slim's neighbor that he wasn't sure. He said that Slim had been talking about wanting to sign up for the softball team just before he left and that maybe he was going to take care of that. "Now how do you like that?" Burt asked Ray. "He just ups and walks out to sign up for softball after two warnings in less than a month about leaving the department. Maybe Frank is right. Clobber him."

"You bet," smiled Frank. "Get tough with him and get him in line."

"Now wait a minute," Ray cautioned. "Cool down. He's your man, Burt. Whatever you decide to do, I'll back you up. But let's be sure we're doing what's best for everyone concerned before we move. If I understand you correctly, we're not sure at this point why Slim was absent from the department tonight. Shouldn't we find out why before we decide to fire him or give him time off?"

Burt somewhat sheepishly said, "I suppose you're right. I only figured it's just like him to pull a stunt like that."

"Let's quit pussyfooting around," Frank snarled. "You'll get a beauty of an alibi. You can count on that. Give a guy like him an inch and he'll take a mile every time. No sir, I say you crack down hard before he gets to thinking he's got you hoodwinked."

"Burt," Ray asked. "What kind of a worker is Slim? Has he given you any other kind of trouble?"

"No, actually he's pretty good. He was a quick learner. I can always count on him to get a job done on time, and his quality is all that anyone could ask. But, Ray, I can't have a guy ignoring the rules in the department without giving everybody the idea that rules don't matter."

"You're right, Burt," Ray admitted. "Rules are made for everybody, and we can't be making exceptions. If we do, we're asking for trouble. Something will have to be done as soon as you find out why he was gone. What about the first two times? What happened then?"

Burt explained that maybe the first time shouldn't count, except that the rule was violated and he had taken the time to explain the rule to Slim. The first week that Slim was on the job he had gone over to the next department during the morning break to buy a candy bar. The machine in Assembly Department B was empty. Burt explained to

Slim that the rule about leaving the department included break periods. Not every department took its breaks at the same time, and it wasn't fair to be bothering other departments where people were working. He also explained to Slim that as supervisor it was his job to know where his people were at all times. Slim said that he could see the point. He told Burt that he understood and that it wouldn't happen again. Burt told Ray that Slim was so cooperative that he didn't think of it as a warning and hadn't even made a note of it.

The second incident happened about two weeks later. The personnel department sent a note asking Slim to sign some insurance forms that they were processing. Burt said that this time he'd been waiting for Slim when he got back and that he called him into the office immediately. Slim told Burt that he thought a note from Personnel took care of the rule and that he was only doing what he was told. He hadn't meant to create any trouble, he said.

Burt pointed out that absence from the department for any reason should first be cleared with the supervisor. Burt also told Slim that he accepted his explanation but that Slim could consider their conversation a warning. He told Slim that another violation would force him to take stronger action. Burt concluded by telling Slim that he had confidence that it wouldn't be necessary.

"And now," said Ray, "it seems we have another violation a little over a week later."

"Seems? Hell!" snapped Frank. "What more do you need to prove what I've been saying. If you're smart, you'll let him know what it's like not to have a paycheck coming in."

"We've got a fair investment in him, Burt," Ray said, ignoring Frank's last remark. "But we can't afford to let him disobey rules either. Find out what he has to say in the morning. You decide whether or not he's worth trying to save. Either way, I'll back you up. It's your department. Just as a final check on your decision, you might give some thought as to whether or not it will accomplish what you want it to."

By the time Burt got to work the next morning, he was thinking more clearly. Slim, he had decided, was too good a man to lose in a burst of temper. He actually hoped that Slim had a better excuse than signing up for softball for being absent from the department again. He wanted something that would take him off the hook. He had outlined four alternative courses he could take, depending on Slim's attitude and his reason for being gone. First, if Slim had a good reason, he could let him go with another warning. Second, Burt could send a written warning to become part of Slim's personnel file. That would be stronger. Third, there was the possibility of a three-day suspension without pay. That would give Slim something to think about. And, finally, if Slim's attitude was poor, Burt might recommend discharge. He didn't want to do it, but it was a possibility.

In the office, Burt started out by asking Slim what he had to say for himself. Slim turned red and said that he was sorry and that he had wanted to check with Burt first. Slim said that he had found out yesterday afternoon about the company softball team. Then he found out that the deadline for signing up had passed that noon. The personnel department had told Slim on the phone that Barney Stilwell had the list and was taking it down to the city recreation department on his way home from work. It was 3:00 P.M.; there was no way to phone Barney in the maintenance department, and Burt was gone.

"Gee, Burt, I didn't know what to do. I kept hoping you'd get back in time for me to ask you. I was sure you'd say OK," Slim said apologetically. "I play a pretty good game at first base, and I was sure I could make the team. You know it kind of makes a guy feel he belongs to be able to play on a company team. Well, I finished the Apex job, and it was too late to set up for the next one. Actually, I pushed pretty hard to finish so you could let me run over in time to catch Barney. But you didn't come, and you didn't come. Finally, I had to take the chance that you wouldn't get back before 3:30 and find out that I was gone. Burt, I'm sorry. I shouldn't have left, but it was only six or seven minutes, and I caught him just as he was walking out the door. What else could I do?"

Burt told Slim to go back to his bench until he had time to think. He gave Slim the rush job and told him to come back to the office at break time, when they would decide what should be done. Burt mentally eliminated his fourth alternative—discharge. Slim's attitude was all right. He knew what he had done and was sorry. "But where do I go from here?" Burt asked himself. "Ray and Slim both expect my decision. Why in blazes did it have to be the softball team?"

1. What did Ray have in mind when he cautioned Burt to determine whether or not the decision he makes will accomplish what he wanted it to?
2. What might be the results of implementing each of the three alternatives Burt has left?
3. How should we evaluate Burt's handling of Slim Carpenter up to this point?
4. How should we evaluate Frank Connors' advice to Burt?
5. What objectives should Burt be trying to reach in deciding how to handle Slim Carpenter?
6. What should Burt do under the circumstances?

THE MEANING OF DISCIPLINE

Applying the principles of sound discipline is a difficult job for many supervisors. Most supervisors don't think much about discipline until faced with rule violations. They accept without question the responsibility for enforcing the rules of the organization. And not until an incident occurs that calls for correction does the word *discipline* cross the supervisor's consciousness. At that point there's a strong temptation to react as Frank Connors did when he heard about Slim Carpenter. Crack down, straighten him out, show him who's boss, get tough, clobber him, lower the boom—these and many other thoughts direct the supervisor's thinking about discipline along the lines of punishment.

Rationally, we readily realize that disciplinary action and discipline represent two widely differing stages. It's important to understand that when we reach the point of getting tough, the probability is that discipline has already begun to fall apart. Disciplinary action is the action taken when discipline breaks down. Burt is at a point where he must decide whether disciplinary action must be taken with Slim.

For the purposes of our discussion in this chapter, we should take note of several definitions of *discipline,* keeping uppermost in our minds that the management-minded supervisor wants to stress its positive side as much as possible. The word *discipline* and the word *disciple,* which was originally used to describe the followers of the teachings of Jesus Christ, both have the same source. But the disciples were more than followers. They were also teachers and leaders after Christ's crucifixion. Those who choose to relate modern concepts to biblical origins will say that discipline means either following rules of conduct or leading people and training them. For our purposes both concepts are extremely useful.

The military recognizes the discipline of troops as essential—the unquestioning acceptance of authority and orders. The college professor speaks of his discipline as a field of study. The dictionary meaning defines discipline as the training that encourages self-development and self-control. It is also a system of rules governing behavior; and it is also punishment. Industrial training directors will generally agree that discipline involves controlling employees' performance.

Now let's see whether we can find a working definition that fits the job of the front-line manager. First we can agree that it would be better not to think of discipline as punishment. Since the supervisor is charged with maintaining control of his department, we might simply say that *discipline means control.* If that control includes the idea of people voluntarily following rules of conduct, we might add that *the ultimate goal of discipline is self-discipline,* or self-control. Probably one of the best tests of discipline in a department is to find out what happens when its supervisor is away from it. Does business go on as usual with everyone tending to his own job? *Discipline,* then, is *the training that makes punishment unnecessary.*

To summarize what many truly management-minded supervisors have said, we find that discipline is a positive concept involving building and teaching and is not a negative concept with the connotations of punishment and revenge. Good discipline encourages self-control. Discipline actually can be regarded as a morale builder instead of a threat to morale. Truly, discipline is a way of thinking. It requires sound leadership, the creation of a healthy climate, and expert teaching.

With this background, we can begin to see the end of the road that Frank Connors was trying to lead Burt down. Punishment was undoubtedly the focus of Frank's thinking about discipline. He followed the bull-of-the-woods approach, using fear and threats to keep his people in line. We don't have to be told that Burt probably would have lost Slim if he had taken Frank's advice, but more important, he would have sowed the seeds of disrespect among the other members of his department. An unhealthy desire for revenge might have been temporarily satisfied—but at what cost?

Ray Ford demonstrates qualities of a good boss. Without suggesting what decision Burt should make, Ray's first step was to calm Burt down. Anger or temper greatly inhibits the ability to reason. Ray helped Burt see both sides of the problem—Burt's and the company's long-range interest. Without humiliating him, Ray showed Burt the error of making a decision until he knew the facts surrounding Slim's disappearance. And finally, he assured Burt that whatever action Burt might want to take, it would have his full backing.

The implication was there that Ray's support would be forthcoming even though he might not agree with Burt. Clearly, Ray was demonstrating excellent leadership by showing confidence in Burt's ability to make a wise decision. By his example, he was suggesting that Burt should demonstrate the same strength in leading his department. From a management point of view, we can see the wisdom of Ray's suggestion that Burt decide what objectives he was trying to reach with his decision.

If we compare Ray's approach and that of Frank Connors with the definition of discipline we developed, we can see that Ray comes as close as one can to demonstrating that discipline is the training that make punishment unnecessary. The objectives of members of management are to train, develop, and mold a body of workers in their departments. Every rule violation or incident of misconduct should be regarded as an opportunity for training. Even when strong action to stop an undesirable practice is indicated, supervisors need to think about what kind of action to take in terms of how well it will teach, not how much it will punish.

Creating a Climate for Discipline

Creating a climate in which employees willingly and naturally abide by company rules is not simply a matter of devoting so much time per week to discipline. Everything discussed so far has a marked impact on how people respond to leadership. Communication, motivation, and training all contribute heavily to building a responsive, responsible work force. The cornerstone for sound discipline is respect for authority. How supervisors handle job assignments, respect the feelings of people, satisfy their needs, keep them informed, and teach them their jobs influences the way their employees conduct themselves.

It would be unrealistic to think that we could ever reach that state of perfection in which no one ever broke a rule. What supervisors do when violations do occur will also help create the climate in which they manage. The great majority of employees accept rules and directions as a condition of employment. They wouldn't think of breaking a rule. These same people, however, will observe and evaluate our conduct in handling those few who may get out of line. Everyone is concerned with getting fair treatment. It is not good for morale either to see someone else get away with violating rules we abide by or to witness unduly harsh disciplinary action. Supervisors should ask themselves whether their disciplinary methods contribute to good departmental control or threaten it.

Common sense and years of successful supervisory experience suggest some practical guidelines to follow in creating a healthy climate for constructive discipline.

1. Make sure employees understand the rules

This is so obvious and basic that many supervisors take it for granted. First, of course, the employees need a thorough knowledge of the rules themselves. Not only do they need to know what the rules are, but more important, they need an understanding of why the rules exist. Burt Hall's explanation to Slim Carpenter of the reason for the rule about not leaving the department even during a break was much more effective in building understanding than simply reading the rules out of the book. Burt also was willing to go easy on Slim because the possibility existed that Slim didn't understand or had forgotten the rule. He was much more concerned with the second violation. If we expect people to follow rules, they must know what the rules are.

2. Enforce rules consistently

Rules are made to be followed by everyone in the department. It's extremely difficult for an employee to understand on-again, off-again enforcement. The supervisor's position in relation to enforcing rules becomes quite untenable if the violator can come back with, "Yeah, but you didn't say anything when Joe did the same thing last week." Reprimands may not be necessary with every violation, but it is extremely important that every violation be acted upon. The circumstances surrounding the violation and the intent and attitude of the violator will influence such action. But the supervisor should not overlook the opportunity to demonstrate his concern and to teach the violator the error of his ways. For example, Burt was quick to explain to Slim that he shouldn't leave the department even during the break. His action couldn't be construed as a reprimand—he didn't even make a note of it—but he did act. Any time a supervisor turns his back on a violation and does nothing about it, he is, in fact, condoning the act. Such conduct can only make it difficult to correct future violations.

3. Make the disciplinary action fit the crime

It is a temptation to quote the Gilbert and Sullivan dictum "Make the punishment fit the crime." When disciplinary action must be taken, it soon becomes common knowledge in the department. A supervisor's actions will be judged by every member of his department. What would

Burt's employees have thought if Burt had followed Frank Connors' advice and discharged Slim Carpenter? Burt had to take some action, but few, if any, of us would recommend Slim's discharge. The test of training which would make punishment unnecessary is a good one to remember in considering what disciplinary action is most appropriate.

Most plants have certain rules which call for automatic discharge if violated. Examples of such rules include theft of company property, insubordination, fighting, sabotage, intoxication on the job, and smoking in hazardous areas. Even with discharge authorized on the first offense, a supervisor is inclined to weigh very carefully all the circumstances surrounding the incident before taking such drastic action.

Determining the appropriateness of disciplinary action should come only after serious consideration has been given to (1) the circumstances surrounding the violation, (2) the seriousness of the offense, (3) the past record of the offender, (4) the intent of the offender, and (5) disciplinary action taken in similar situations.

4. Make certain that actions correct, not punish

One plant of the Western Plywood Company, Limited, of Canada is so concerned with teaching their foremen the importance of eliminating punishment from their concepts of discipline that whenever disciplinary layoffs are necessary, the employee is paid for the time spent at home. They maintain that the purpose of the suspension is to give the employee time to think over the consequences of his behavior— to decide whether he wants to be a part of the team and abide by the rules. Loss of pay is punishment. Time to think without loss of pay tends to be more constructive. Expensive? According to an executive of the company, every time an employee was sent home without pay, a grievance resulted. Under the new program, grievances seldom grow out of suspension since there is no punishment involved. The expense of grievance meetings, he reported, was much greater than the cost of paying an employee for time off while he thought about his future with the company.

It's not likely that many companies will institute such an unusual procedure. It is important to understand the principle behind this method. Even in the case of disciplinary layoffs, the company was adhering to the principle of training and education rather than punishment.

Ray Ford was steering Burt's thinking along similar lines when he counseled Burt to consider what he was trying to accomplish. Constructive discipline requires the supervisor to show the offender how to make the necessary corrections, to explain the rewards for doing so, and to set forth the consequences of failing to conform to acceptable standards. Firm, fair, patient handling of rules violations is much more likely to produce the desired result than impulsive, insulting, humiliating treatment.

5. Remember to give credit

Most supervisors when pressed for an answer will admit that they criticize and correct far more often than they give credit. But they all know that giving credit is much more pleasant and satisfying than criticizing. Why should this be? Some say it's their job to criticize and correct. But isn't it just as much their job to give credit, particularly since creating a climate for sound discipline depends on gaining the respect of employees?

Others will say that they don't know how to give credit. Three considerations will perhaps encourage supervisors to credit good work. First, they should be alert to the opportunities for giving credit. These arise when a worker shows commendable initiative, sets a good example for other employees, performs better than was expected, shows evidence of good planning or good housekeeping, extends help or cooperation to fellow workers, makes a good suggestion, keeps his temper under stress, supports management's position to fellow employees. When these and countless other opportunities present themselves, why not give proper credit to the deserving person? Mark Twain once said, "When a man has credit due him, now is the time to give it to him, for he cannot read his tombstone when he's dead."

Second, supervisors should consider the advisability of crediting the work, not the worker. If the emphasis is put on skill, the giving of credit is a business matter rather than personal flattery, and there will be much less likelihood of creating any feeling of embarrassment.

Third, it is possible to give credit indirectly. By asking for suggestions, for example, a supervisor shows respect for the knowledge and ability of the employees under him. Checking on the progress of work is another method of recognizing the individual. Noticing improvement in a worker's performance, however small it may be, is still another.

Most supervisors who credit the performance of their employees find their employees praising them. And that's a nice climate to have!

How can we recognize a good climate for constructive discipline? If a department's employees abide by rules willingly and naturally, if suggestions for improvement replace gripes and complaints, if employees are enthusiastic about achieving the goals of the department, if employees are cooperative in helping one another, if employees accept assignments cheerfully, if employees will go out of their way to help the supervisor, if employees generally support management policies, and if employees show initiative in doing the best work possible, the chances are that the supervisor has done an outstanding job of creating the proper climate. Certainly we can see that if the above conditions exist, there's little likelihood of disciplinary problems, and disciplinary action will rarely be necessary.

Frequently new supervisors will ask for the do's and don't's of creating the proper climate for constructive criticism. At the risk of oversimplifying a complex aspect of our management job, let's consider what to avoid and what to do.

What to avoid	**What to do**
Sarcasm	Consider feelings of employees.
Loss of temper	Cool down, analyze each situation.
Humiliating an employee	Show confidence in the employee's ability to make necessary changes.
Profanity	Carefully explain the nature of the violation and the correction expected.
Public reprimands	*Always* reprimand in private.
Threats and bluffs	Outline specific consequences of future violations, and follow through.
Showing favoritism	Give every employee fair treatment.
Delay tactics	Give prompt attention to violations.
Unduly harsh penalties	Define the objective of disciplinary action.
Inconsistent enforcement	Deal promptly with all violations of rules.

Just reviewing such a checklist can be a reminder of the consequences of poor disciplinary methods. A breakdown in discipline is a great deal more difficult to repair than a breakdown of machinery or equipment. How much easier it is to build a healthy climate than to weather the storms of discontent and disobedience.

When a Reprimand Is Necessary

If we had reached that utopia where no one was ever guilty of a rule infraction and where cooperation and harmony were the only responses to supervision, then we could forget any consideration of the reprimand. We haven't, though, and rules will be broken—unintentionally or otherwise. Corrective measures must be taken, or else the idea that obeying rules isn't important may take hold.

Fortunately, few people ever need to be reprimanded. But good climate is encouraged by expert handling of those occasions when disciplinary action becomes necessary. The challenge is to correct mistakes without arousing resentment. We're thinking now particularly of those situations that require more than a simple suggestion or a casual corrective remark—those situations when an infraction is serious or when the negative behavior has become chronic. Slim Carpenter's three infractions amounted to what we might call a chronic tendency.

In analyzing how to reprimand, we should remind ourselves that corrective action and not punishment is the proper objective. The reprimand is a training situation. It requires careful consideration of the individual to achieve a positive response rather than resentment. As simple as this may seem, it's very difficult to remember and achieve. When a situation is serious enough to require a reprimand, the supervisor's control is being threatened, his leadership challenged, and his patience strained. The temptation to resort to impulsive, harsh treatment of the offending person is great. Yet, here in a calm, rational discussion of discipline we can easily see that it is the calm, thoughtful approach that keeps the supervisor in control of the situation and lets him move positively toward his goal.

Since it's generally easier to remember and understand an organized approach, let's think of reprimanding in terms of these six steps:

1. Control your temper

Little constructive disciplining is ever accomplished in anger. We tend to say things we're sorry for and make accusations that are difficult to retract. There's little need for concern about saving face if we control our temper. We don't think clearly when we're angry, and common sense tells us that we want to maintain every advantage we can. We'll recall that Ray Ford's first advice to Burt was, "Cool down." He was telling Burt, in effect, to stop reacting and start thinking.

2. Be sure of your facts

Gossip, rumors, and hearsay evidence all too often prove to be inaccurate. A supervisor wants to be certain that an employee is deserving of a reprimand before he issues it. Burt was ready to take drastic action before he even knew why Slim had left the department. What were the circumstances of the infraction?

What, specifically, did the offender do wrong? What are the consequences of the infraction? What could they have been? Has he been guilty of similar infractions in the past? How long ago? How frequently? The better equipped the supervisor is with the facts, the less likely he is to get caught off base. We have probably all known supervisors who have impulsively reprimanded an employee only to discover that the reprimand was not justified. A few such incidents can go a long way toward building a climate of disrespect.

3. Talk to the offender in private

The training objective of our reprimand demands that it be done in private, where the possibility that the offending employee will lose face in the eyes of his group is minimized. Safety violations which endanger other employees or company property will, of course, have to be stopped on the spot; but even in these cases the reprimanding interview can be conducted in private. Humiliation and embarrassment produce tension and make people less receptive to corrective suggestions.

A short postponement of a reprimand interview until it can be done in private gives both the supervisor and the employee some time to cool down. If one or the other, by chance, does allow his temper to flare up, how much better it is to have it occur in private. In fact, the supervisor who knows he has a short fuse should make doubly sure that reprimands are handled *only in private*.

4. Get the offender's side of the story

Empathy helps in trying to understand why a person might have committed an infraction. There is no substitute, however, for allowing an employee to explain his side of the situation. Even a criminal is entitled to his day in court and, we might add, is considered innocent until proved guilty. By listening attentively and courteously to the offender's full explanation, the supervisor demonstrates his concern for fair treatment of the employee. We might recap what Burt learned by listening to Slim's explanation: (1) Slim knew he was violating the rule. (2) He deliberately risked Burt's finding out. (3) He did want to clear with Burt and abide by the rule. (4) He wanted, through softball, to feel that he belonged. (5) He had put forth extra effort to finish his work to make time for his errand.

How strong a reprimand to give and what disciplinary action to take, if any, will be based on the attitude of the employee, his intent when he committed the infraction, his understanding of the rule he had broken, and his interest in mending his ways. It's almost impossible to get this kind of information without listening to the employee's explanation.

5. Be firm but fair

It is to be hoped that nothing in this chapter has conveyed the idea that a supervisor should be anything but firm in dealing with rules infractions. Being firm does not mean, however, getting tough or throwing your weight around. Consideration of the employee's feelings is what we mean by fairness. Being fair also includes explaining why the behavior is unacceptable, how it violates the rules of good conduct, and why the rule exists.

A fair reprimand requires the supervisor to outline for the employee what corrective action or behavior is acceptable. If disciplinary action is to be taken, he should explain what he wants that action to accomplish. Even in the extreme case of discharge, there is little justification for humiliating the employee. A highly respected training director has always maintained that the real test in discharging an employee is to do it in such a way that he says "thank you" at the end.

6. Express confidence in the offender's ability to improve

Since the objective in a reprimand is training, it is impossible to ignore the encouragement that should be given any trainee in learning his job. The sting of a reprimand can be removed by the supervisor's showing that he has confidence in the ability of the employee to modify his behavior. Showing confidence in the employee is a strong positive way to conclude the reprimand. We know that employees would rather please than displease. Doesn't the supervisor need to demonstrate the kind of supervisory behavior that makes pleasing him easy? A supervisor should expect an employee to change his behavior and should show his confidence in his ability to do so, for the more he asks of an employee, the more the employee is likely to give.

How can a supervisor be sure that, once the reprimand interview is concluded, he has successfully discharged his job? In the long run, if the employee makes the desired correction without resentment and causes no further difficulty, the supervisor has succeeded. Most supervisors would like a quicker evaluation, however, and answering these questions should help determine the effectiveness of a reprimand:

1. Did I maintain a positive corrective attitude throughout?
2. Did the employee understand and acknowledge what he had done wrong?
3. Did he realize the possible consequences to himself and others of his error?
4. Does he know what is expected of him now and in the future?
5. Does he feel that I have tried to help him?
6. Does he feel that I have been fair?
7. Is he free from any feelings of resentment?

Unless the supervisor has handled the reprimand in a way that will make the employee more interested and enthusiastic about his job, rather than hurt or resentful, his use of authority has been harmful to the best interests of the company he represents.

Stages of Disciplinary Action

Most labor contracts outline the steps to be taken in applying disciplinary action. Even in the nonunion organization, supervisory manuals will outline a variation of these same stages. They are designed to ensure fair treatment of employees—to protect them against impulsive, unduly harsh punishment for wrongdoing. In industry, as in society, the rights of the individual must be protected. These steps represent that protection:

1. First offense: oral warning

It is presumed that the employee did not understand the nature of his wrongdoing. The rule or standard of conduct is explained, and it is made clear that continued misconduct will not be condoned. The employee is warned that future violations will make stronger action necessary. A written record of the time, place, and circumstances of the warning is recommended by nearly all companies.

2. Second offense: written warning

The employee is informed in writing that his misconduct is in violation of rules or standards of good conduct and that another infraction will result in loss of pay or job. A copy of the warning is given to the employee, a copy is put in his personnel file, and a copy is given to the superior of the supervisor issuing the warning. If a union exists, the steward and/or the union also receives a copy. In effect, all parties concerned are informed of the action taken.

3. Third offense: disciplinary layoff

The employee is suspended from his job without pay for a period of time consistent with the seriousness of the offense. Most such suspensions range from one to five working days. Coupled with such action is the usual warning that another violation will call for discharge.

4. Fourth offense: discharge

It is presumed that by this time the employee has been given every opportunity to conform and that he has little concern for doing so. The best interests of both the company and the employee are assumed to be best served by complete separation.

Obviously, as we noted earlier, some infractions are so serious that discharge is permitted with the first violation. In other cases, the seriousness of the offense or the antagonistic attitude of an employee might dictate a shortcutting of these steps. On the other hand, many supervisors have added a fifth step. Before any of the above actions are taken, they will have a man-to-man talk with the employee at the first offense. An example of such action would be Burt's first talk with Slim, after Slim went out for a candy bar. For most employees this is all that is ever necessary.

It is most important to remember that even in disciplinary cases the training objectives of the action be recognized. Our goal is not to fire employees in whom we have a substantial investment, but to train them to be well-disciplined members of the work group. In determining what action should be taken after an infraction has occurred, many supervisors have been guided by asking themselves the following questions:

1. What is the past record of the employee?
2. Do I have all the facts that bear on this situation?
3. Has the employee had a reasonable chance to improve?
4. When was he given a fair warning of the seriousness of misconduct?
5. What actions have been taken in similar cases?
6. What effects will this action have on the rest of the department?
7. Should I consult anyone else before taking action?

The last question particularly is worth turning over in our minds. Discussing contemplated disciplinary action with the boss or with a staff specialist (personnel or labor relations) is not ducking responsibility. These are the people who will be having to support the supervisor's actions. Another person, one who is not emotionally involved and whose judgment the supervisor respects, might very well add another dimension to his thinking. Ray Ford played this role in "The Case of the Disappearing Carpenter."

DISCIPLINE: WHAT IT IS AND ISN'T

In concluding this discussion of discipline, we might benefit by reviewing what a positive, constructive approach to discipline means to the management-minded supervisor. For purposes of comparison we should also identify some commonly held ideas that should have no part in management-minded thinking about discipline.

First and most important, discipline is the training and development of a cooperative work force striving together for the realization of management goals and objectives. Disciplinary action has the purpose of teaching and molding. Planning and implementation of such action should never lose sight of that purpose. Punishment has no place in thinking about discipline.

Discipline is best achieved by creating a climate of respect through sound leadership. The supervisor who demonstrates respect for his work group finds that group respecting him. Many supervisors find it helpful to think of discipline as a program of preventative maintenance —heading off trouble before it starts. Discipline should not be ignored until trouble starts. It is not a policing action that begins only after infractions and misconduct have occurred and must be dealt with under conditions of stress.

Discipline in the work force is best demonstrated by self-discipline —people working in harmony, abiding by departmental rules and standards of good conduct. When discipline is good, cooperation with supervisors and fellow employees is at a high level. Discipline is not the use of fear, threats, and punishment to keep people in line.

Discipline is a means of maintaining and boosting morale. By providing for fair treatment to everyone, equal application of rules, and considerate correctional methods a supervisor establishes a climate of trust. Discipline is not rigid, unbending supervision that fosters resentment. It encourages rather than discourages, molds rather than destroys, rewards rather than penalizes, creates profits in human relations rather than deficits. It's a way of thinking.

HIGHLIGHTS

1. Discipline means control. Its goal is self-control. It is the training that makes punishment unnecessary.
2. Anger, temper, punishment, and revenge have no part in the management-minded supervisor's concept of discipline.
3. Discipline in the department is largely a matter of creating the proper climate. Practical guidelines to follow in creating a climate for constructive discipline include:
   a. Making sure that employees understand the rules

   b. Enforcing rules consistently
   c. Making disciplinary actions fit the offense
   d. Making certain that actions correct, not punish
   e. Remembering to give credit
4. Naturally, some offenses will occur. Corrective measures against these inevitable rules infractions require skill in reprimanding. To be constructive in reprimanding, the supervisor should:
   a. Control his temper
   b. Be sure of his facts
   c. Talk to the employee in private
   d. Get the offender's side of the problem
   e. Be firm but fair
   f. Express confidence in the employee's ability to improve
5. Four or five stages in taking disciplinary action are outlined in most labor contracts and supervisory manuals to guarantee the employee fair treatment. A five-stage procedure might include:
   a. First offense—man-to-man talk
   b. Second offense—oral warning
   c. Third offense—written warning
   d. Fourth offense—disciplinary layoff
   e. Fifth offense—discharge
6. Discipline should:
   a. Encourage rather than discourage
   b. Mold rather than destroy
   c. Reward rather than punish
   d. Create profits in human relations rather than deficits

DISCUSSION QUESTIONS

1. Expand on the statement that discipline can be regarded as a morale-builder rather than as a threat to morale.
2. List four reasons why it is important for a supervisor to keep his temper under control when handling disciplinary problems.
3. Evaluate the philosophy that many managers follow when they support a supervisor in his disciplinary actions even though they may not agree with his decisions.
4. What is your evaluation of the practice of paying employees for time they are away from work for disciplinary suspensions?

5. Would you support the policy of paying employees during disciplinary suspensions in your company? Why or why not?
6. Cite as many reasons as you can for a supervisor to give credit to his employees.
7. What, in your opinion, are the main reasons why supervisors don't praise more often?
8. Describe a situation in your experience in which the disciplining of an employee was poorly handled. What, in your opinion, should have been done to leave the employee with a positive feeling toward his job and supervisor?

SUGGESTIONS FOR FURTHER STUDY

Bittel, Lester R.
What Every Supervisor Should Know, 2d ed.
Chapter 18, McGraw-Hill Book Company, New York, 1968

Famularo, Joseph J.
Supervisors in Action
Chapter 8, McGraw-Hill Book Company, New York, 1961

Lateiner, Alfred R.
The Techniques of Supervision
Chapter 4, National Foremen's Institute, New London, Conn., 1954

Stessin, Lawrence
Employee Discipline
Bureau of National Affairs, Washington, D.C., 1960

Stessin, Lawrence
Practice of Personnel and Industrial Relations
Chapter 3, Pitman Publishing Corporation, New York, 1964

CHAPTER
NINE

HANDLING COMPLAINTS AND GRIEVANCES

THE CASE OF GRIEVING KAMINSKY

Burt wore a worried look as he joined two of his buddies for a beer before going home Friday afternoon. He had been eager to accept the invitation to have a beer because he wanted to talk. Seated in the booth as Burt dropped into his seat were Jack Holt, supervisor of final assembly, and Kevin "Mac" McNeil, supervisor of the molding department. Both men had over ten years of supervisory experience. Burt hoped they could shed some light on the uncharted territory he was entering.

"What's up, Burt? You look as if you're about to lose your last friend," Jack said.

Smiling weakly, Burt told them that he was about to be slapped with his first formal grievance. Burt's tone of voice, his facial expression, and his general attitude showed that he felt that his ability to manage was being challenged— that this was a black mark on his record. It was clear that he did not relish the situation.

When Mac asked Burt what had happened, here's the story he told. Boris Kaminsky had been a chronic absentee problem. He had been away from the job eighteen days in the past year, usually a day at a time. Most of his absences were excused for causes that both Burt and his predecessor Harry Gates felt were questionable. Their suspicions were deepened by the fact that twelve of the absences occurred on Fridays or Mondays. A headache or an upset stomach appeared to be a convenient way of extending the weekend to three days. Boris was usually careful to call in, as the rules required, when he was going to

179

be absent. Even so, it was a problem to find a replacement for him or to reshuffle work assignments on short notice.

After the first three absences, Burt began to talk to Boris about the problems his absences created and the obligation of employees to be on the job since they were counted on every day. Burt's lectures seemed to have little effect on Boris. He usually replied that he couldn't help it.

Three weeks ago Boris didn't show up on a Monday. As soon as he showed up on Tuesday, Burt called him in and handed him a written warning pointing out that he had been talked to repeatedly about the absences and that any future absences would be cause for considering more severe disciplinary action. Copies of the warning had been given to the union steward and to Ray Ford and placed in the personnel department files.

Boris was clearly angered by the warning. He said it was a dirty trick to give him a warning without finding out what his excuse was. He claimed that his wife and child were visiting her sister out of town and that he was home alone. He said he was too sick to get out of bed to phone in until late in the afternoon, and by then he didn't feel it made any difference. When Burt asked him how he felt, Boris simply said, "I'm here, ain't I?" The written warning was not contested, but Boris brooded for several days afterward.

After ordering a round of beers, Burt told Jack and Mac that he had had a phone call at home from Boris around 9:30 the night before. When Boris said that he wouldn't be in in the morning, Burt asked why.

"My reason is personal," was the answer. Burt explained that he couldn't accept personal business as an excuse and that he would have to know why Boris couldn't show up for work. Boris simply replied again that his reason was a personal one.

Burt admitted that he'd been annoyed. He told Kaminsky again that his not showing up would create a real hardship. "If you had an acceptable excuse, I'd play ball with you. But I'll be darned if I'll swallow 'personal reasons' so you can have another three-day weekend. Now, either you tell me what your personal reason is, or I'll assume it's not legitimate and act accordingly."

"You can't accuse me of goofing off," Boris retaliated. "I'm trying to cooperate by giving you plenty of advance warning. If I tell you it's personal, that's all you have to know. You have no right prying into my personal life. I'm not coming in, and that's all there is to it."

"Not quite," snapped Burt. "I'm giving you a five-day suspension starting Monday if you're not there ready for work tomorrow morning." Burt said that Kaminsky then hung up without saying any more.

"Boris wasn't there this morning, so I had to reshuffle the work of three people and ask them each to work an hour overtime tonight. That's why I was late getting over here. The guys seemed glad enough to help me out, but they weren't very happy to have to be covering for Kaminsky," Burt told his audience.

"What makes you think you've got a grievance on your hands?" Mac asked. "It seems to me you're within your rights. I'd probably have done pretty much the same thing if I'd been in your shoes."

"I'm glad to hear you say that," Burt told Mac. "About the middle of the afternoon Sam Bassett, the steward in my department, came in to say that they were filing a grievance. Kaminsky apparently had called him from home or wherever he was on his personal business. They're claiming that he gave me more than the required advance notice and that I have no right to discipline him. They also are going to claim that it's not our business to pry into his personal life and that a five-day suspension is excessive under any circumstances. I've always gotten along pretty well with Sam. We've leveled with one another. I figure he wouldn't go along with Kaminsky on this thing unless they thought they could win it. I've never had anything like this happen to me. I hate like the devil to run to Ray Ford again. It's going to look as though I can't control my people. What did I do wrong? Don't we usually get beat on these grievances?"

Mac thought that statement was strange, coming from a supervisor, and suggested that Burt sounded as if he was giving up before things really got started. He told Burt that every employee had a right to grieve and that the union had the obligation to represent him.

"Management has the right to manage—to run the plant efficiently and to make a profit," Mac explained. "Now, we're a part of management, and you were doing your job with Kaminsky. You probably won't get the grievance until Kaminsky gets back from suspension. Then you'll have to write an answer to it. This sounds like one the union might take all the way to arbitration if they don't get satisfaction before then. Keep Ray Ford posted, because he'll be in your corner all the way. This will be good experience for you, Burt. Take advantage of all the help you can get from Ray and Personnel."

"Hey, Burt, I've got an idea," Jack said. "Both Mac and I have had grievances go all the way to arbitration. We'll describe the situations. You put yourself in the arbitrator's shoes and see if you reach the same conclusion they did."

"I'm game. Go ahead," Burt mumbled.

"Well, you know me," Jack started. "I've got a fair temper when I get riled up. I had a guy by the name of Hank Boyle who had a temper like mine. The difference between us was that I'm a fairly nice guy when I'm not mad. Hank, though, was sullen. We used to say he was sore as a boil most of the time. He did his work but never more than just enough to get by. He seemed to resent orders, and you were never sure if he was going to follow them. We had several arguments. I don't mind saying that I didn't like him and that it was hard to be civil to him. One day we got into a hassel about a job I thought was taking longer than necessary, and he got smart. I lost my head and decided I wasn't going to take any more. I told him that he was lazy—that he had better shape up or ship out. It wasn't hard to see I was getting under his skin. Finally he blew up and called me a damned s.o.b—loud and clear for half the department to hear. You can guess what happened. I tied the can to him right then and there. We had a grievance before the day was over, and it went through all the steps to arbitration.

"We based our whole case on insubordination, claiming that a supervisor can't afford to have insubordination in his department if he's going to maintain control. The contract permits discharge on first offense. Boyle and the union claimed that I had provoked his outburst, that his record was good, that he had not had any previous warnings or disciplinary action against him, that a short suspension might have been in order—but not discharge. Now, Mr. Arbitrator, how would you rule on that one?"

"Well, from what you've said," Burt mused, "I'd side with the union. It's pretty rough to can a guy the first time. I would guess that the arbitrator made us take him back with the loss of some or all of his pay."

"Well, you're wrong," Jack smiled. "The discharge stuck. The arbitrator said that a plant couldn't operate if employees were allowed to curse or abuse their supervisors. He said that control was essential and couldn't be maintained if public abuse were permitted. Then he slapped my wrist for provoking Boyle and said that he probably would have ordered Boyle's reinstatement if the incident had occurred in private. It was what you might call a close call, and I learned a lesson. Boyle had more of a following than I thought. It took quite a while for things to get back to normal. OK, Mac, tell him about your trip to arbitration."

"Well, Burt, this happened several years ago," Mac said. "I was really out on a limb."

Burt was already deciding that Mac had won the case because he liked Mac. To Burt, Mac was the ideal supervisor—well-liked by his men, highly thought of by higher management, level-headed, firm but fair, and always in command of his operations. Mac ran a tight ship and was respected by his employees. Burt couldn't remember, either as a supervisor or employee, any disciplinary problems coming out of Mac's department.

"We had a young fellow, Les Harder, who was a wise guy. In some respect he was like your Mike Moran—a good worker, but he found plenty of time to bother other people without hurting his own production. Part of being a wise guy, I guess, was the way he liked to show off. He gave the impression that he knew more than anybody else. Every management policy or rule was a lot of kid stuff to him, and he let people know it. I don't think I ever told him to do anything without getting a lot of smart talk or sarcasm. A couple of times I called him in for a straightforward man-to-man talk about his attitude. I gave him every chance to get straightened out and become one of us. Nothing helped. He just seemed to enjoy making fun of me, of management, of the company, and of anything else that we took seriously. Finally, I recommended to Oscar Palmer, who had just become plant manager, that we fire Harder. Even though he was new to the job, Oscar backed me up.

"Well the fur began to fly. Harder filed a grievance with full union backing, saying that he never had a written warning of any kind. They claimed there was nothing in the contract requiring him to like his supervisor. His production was never the subject of any criticism, and if any discipline was called for, he should have been properly warned in accordance with mutually accepted disciplinary procedures.

"In our defense we claimed that we didn't have to put up with people who were consistently and openly hostile to management, that Harder's attitude was a disturbing influence on other employees, that he had been given plenty of chances to straighten out, that even though no single incident warranted a warning, his attitude in total constituted grounds for discharge. Remember, Burt, we had no precedent for taking such action. How would you rule on that one?"

"Just because it's you, Mac," Burt smiled, "I'll rule for the company. Seriously, I think an arbitrator would make you take him back. You can't fire a guy for having a poor attitude."

"That's where you're wrong again, Burt," Mac came back. "The discharge was upheld. The arbitrator said that Harder or any other employee has no right to ridicule management and its directives. He said that if Harder hadn't liked his supervisor, he could have asked for a transfer. Since there was no evidence that he had, the discharge was justified. But the thing you have to remember, Burt, is that the next arbitrator might rule differently. We were lucky. Well, let's knock it off. I've got to get home."

Driving home, Burt felt a little better, and he was sure it wasn't the two beers. Maybe a grievance wasn't the worst thing in the world that could happen to a guy. He was hoping that it could be settled without going to arbitration, but he didn't see how he could back down from the suspension he had given Kaminsky. It was good to know that all arbitration cases weren't decided in favor of the union. Looking ahead to the possibility of going all the way, he decided that every move he made would have a bearing on the case. He'd have to be careful.

1. How should we evaluate Burt's handling of Kaminsky in this last incident?
2. What did Jack Holt mean when he said he had learned a lesson from his arbitration case? What might he have learned?
3. How can we account for Burt's feeling that the union always seems to win out in arbitration matters?
4. What should Burt do now that he knows his handling of Kaminsky will result in a formal grievance? Outline some of the steps he should take.

THE MANAGEMENT–MINDED SUPERVISOR'S ROLE IN HANDLING GRIEVANCES

The supervisor who's doing the best job for his company in the area of grievance handling is probably the supervisor who spends less time handling grievances than any other supervisor. Does this seem like a contradiction? It doesn't if we accept the idea that the most valuable role a supervisor can play is in preventing grievances—notice we did not say squelching them or sitting on them. Certainly he has a primary responsibility to protect management's interest—management's right to manage. If he can do that with sound leadership, fair discipline, and wise administration and can resolve differences before they become grievances, is he not fulfilling his role? Management judges a supervisor's effectiveness in terms of how few grievances are generated in his department.

Misapplication of this criterion has led to mistakes, however. It does not follow that a supervisor with no grievances is necessarily doing a better job than one who has two or three grievances to his credit. We could, for example, hardly criticize Burt Hall for taking the disciplinary action against Boris Kaminsky which resulted in a grievance. He was simply protecting management's interest in the regular attendance of its employees. There will always be a few employees who stretch the rules to the breaking point and who become shop lawyers when they are called to account. The real test to be applied to grievances filed against a supervisor is whether or not proper handling of the situation might have prevented a formal grievance. From the evidence we have, we can conclude that Burt did a reasonably good job of trying to get Boris straightened out. If anything, he might be criticized for being too lenient, so that when the disciplinary action finally was taken, it came as a shock. Yet, how many would have let the matter go one more time in hopes of straightening it out?

Enforcement of rules, assigning work, running the department, administering the labor contract if there is one, and in general, representing management—these are considered to be the supervisor's responsibility. Implicit in that statement is his protection of management's right to operate an efficient, profitable enterprise. When misunderstandings (an early stage in the development of grievances) arise, he is the point of first contact. His willingness to listen and understand and to explain and perhaps sell a decision determine in most cases whether or not there will be a formal grievance. A supervisor has the power to eliminate most misunderstandings with employees. Misunderstandings cause grievances. The supervisor therefore plays a key role in preventing formal grievances and minimizing the time spent in hearing them, weighing them, and deciding them at higher levels. But, above all, it is his function to safeguard the interests of management.

As Burt Hall was driving home, he looked ahead to the possibility that his grievance would go all the way to arbitration, and he decided that every move he made from then on would have a bearing on the case. Just a moment's thought reveals the wisdom of his thinking. A supervisor's handling of every request, gripe, complaint, or grievance determines the strength of the case he may someday have to defend. He is the defendant in grievance matters. Before an arbitrator he has to be able to show that his actions were fair, considerate, and in good faith. He can expect the plaintiff—the grievant and the union—to take advantage of any and every mistake he makes to win their point. Day in and day out his interpretations of the labor contract or company policy help shape and define the real meaning of the contract. The contract or policy may say one thing, but if everyday administration and interpretation demonstrate a different way of operating, the grievant's case will be strengthened. Many cases have been lost before an arbitrator or have been conceded by higher management when the grievant has been able to say, "Yes, but that rule was never enforced until now."

In summary, the management-minded supervisor recognizes that management's rights in directing the work force are maintained by exercising those rights. He recognizes the right of the employee to grieve when a misunderstanding develops. His job, he knows, is to listen with respect, correct any errors, adjust where possible, or explain courteously the reasons for refusal. He acts with promptness and consideration, acknowledging that no matter how unrealistic a complaint might be, it is reasonable in the eyes of the person making it. The result of this approach in most cases is a minimum of formal grievances and a minimum of time spent arguing them.

THE ANATOMY OF A GRIEVANCE

A fundamental principle of sound employee relations is the provision of a means for employees to express their complaints and have them fairly considered. Through negotiation, unions have been able to guarantee this right for their members by having it written into the labor contract. Service to members is provided by the union through its willingness to represent the employee in his complaints against management. In the nonunion firm which prefers to remain nonunion, formal grievance procedures are a must because they provide this vital right of employees. Management has the right to manage; the employee has the right to grieve.

In its embryonic stage a grievance is a dissatisfaction with some condition of employment which is expressed either in the form of a request or a complaint. The justification for the complaint may be either real or imaginary, but it is vital to understand that from the employee's point of view it is real. Downgrading the importance of a complaint or ridiculing an individual only adds fuel to a fire that is just starting. It is at this stage in the development of a grievance that the supervisor recognizes his key role in preventing grievances. Anger and resentment are absent or minimal. Now is the best time to reach an amicable agreement. Ideally the complaint or request should go no further. The supervisor either grants the request, modifies it, or sells the employee on the reasons for his refusal. Some typical examples of causes of complaints include bids for higher-rated jobs, improvement of physical working conditions, clarification of rules or policy, claims of favoritism, requests for pay adjustments, claims of pay inequities, unfair distribution of overtime, and claims of unfair disciplinary actions. There are hundreds of others. These are typical.

Inability to reach an understanding at the first stage results in the formalizing of the grievance—which usually means putting it in writing. It's important to consider the words "inability to reach an understanding." The supervisor should recognize the role of his communication skill in creating understanding. Granting every request or bowing to every complaint is not a good way to handle grievances. Safeguarding the company's interests often requires the supervisor to say no. How successful he is in getting the employee to understand the reasons for his refusal is the real test of his ability. The times when he can say, "Yes, you're right. I'll take care of it right away," pose no problem. Getting the employee to say, "I understand why it can't be done," challenges his ability and helps determine his supervisory effectiveness.

It's usually with the initiation of this second stage that anger and resentment begin to cloud the logical reasoning of either side or both sides. When there is inability to reach understanding, attitudes become more rigid and opinions more fixed, and the opportunity for compromise or agreement goes out the window.

Again the supervisor's response to the grievance at this second stage (for now it is a grievance) will either strengthen or weaken his position in future stages. Anger, temper, ridicule, sarcasm, or profanity are luxuries he can ill afford. It is not at all uncommon for a steward or union official to goad the supervisor into a display of temper. Control of the emotions is essential if he is to represent management with dignity. The grievance at this stage is his to answer. The decision is his, but it should not be made without recognizing that higher-level management might be put in the position of defending it. Burt was reluctant to discuss his problem with Ray Ford—an attitude he should change. He has the obligation to analyze the situation, to justify his action, and to recommend a course of action. But to go it alone would be shortsighted. Once Kaminsky convinced the union that it should support his grievance, Burt should see the wisdom of consulting his superiors and the labor relations people who will be in his corner and whose support he expects. If the answer to a grievance is to be negative at this second stage, a supervisor will want to deal with the issues fairly, setting forth the reasons why a denial is justified. Nothing should be done to add fuel to the fire.

In the eyes of many managers, the next stage really sets the machinery of the grievance procedure in motion. Up to this point the matter is essentially between the employee and his immediate supervisor. It is true that the union steward assisted in writing and presenting the grievance. It is also true that the supervisor may have consulted his superiors or staff experts in responding. But the grievance was a complaint to the supervisor by the employee, to be answered by the supervisor—the common definition of the first step in the grievance procedure. The stages from this point on, however, invariably involve union and management officials at increasingly higher levels. Then it is really during the second step in the grievance procedure that the wheels get in motion and the machinery starts functioning. We'll discuss the steps in formal grievance procedures later in this chapter. With respect to the anatomy of a grievance, we should note that generally it goes through three stages of development while it remains in the supervisor's domain.

Stage one: A *request:* no anger, under supervisor's control
Stage two: A *complaint:* some resentment, under supervisor's control
Stage three: A *grievance:* considerable resentment; under supervisor's control, but generally with consultation

What Can Be Learned from Grievances

Handling grievances, as disagreeable and as distasteful as it may be, is a learning process. Jack Holt said he had learned from his experience of having a grievance go to arbitration. But what had he learned? More than likely, the "slap on the wrist" from the arbitrator shocked him back to an objective analysis of his role in the development of the grievance. Undoubtedly, his narrow escape caused him to see that his own temper had nearly lost him the case. He might also have come to the realization that it's possible to win an arbitration case and still lose. We'll recall his telling Burt that Boyle had more of a following than he'd realized and that it had taken a while for his relationship with his workers to get back to normal. Perhaps he learned that it had been a very costly victory.

In measuring the cost of handling a grievance all the way to arbitration, there are many factors to be considered. For example, hours and hours of productive time are lost by those who must argue the case. More time is lost by employees who spend time just talking about the problem. The effect on the morale of the department should be weighed. The cost of the arbitration hearing alone is considerable— fees, wages, salaries, and expenses of witnesses. The problem of settling down to normal operations after a hard-fought case can also be costly. Deciding whether or not it was worth it—whether the settlement justified the cost—is truly a learning experience. One such experience may teach us that the "ounce of prevention" adage has much to recommend it.

After every request, complaint, or grievance a supervisor handles, he should evaluate what he has done. Did he create understanding, or did he miss opportunities that would have helped create it? Was he fair, objective, considerate, respectful, and courteous in dealing with the individual? Or did he allow anger, ridicule, sarcasm, profanity, or abuse to creep into his treatment of the employee? In short, did he add fuel to the fire? If he made mistakes, does he know where he made them? If he was successful, does he really understand why he was? Did he keep his lines of communication open with the employee, the union, and management? Above all, what has he learned that will help him demonstrate to the employees in his department that all requests and complaints will get a fair and honest hearing? Every request, complaint, or grievance he handles, regardless of whether it is accepted or denied, should be a building block in the foundation of sound employee relations.

Understanding the Union Steward's Role

The chief function of a union steward in a department is to represent its employees in any complaints or grievances they might have against management. The steward is a specialist in processing grievances. He is in the department as the union's assurance to its members that they will suffer no injustices at the hands of management. Grievances are the reason for his job. While the supervisor concerns himself with costs, quality, production, methods, training, and a hundred other duties, the steward is concerned about one thing above all else—the grievance.

While there are exceptions, the steward is usually well trained to handle that phase of his job. When an employee has a legitimate gripe or complaint, the steward knows how to present it. If a grievance develops, he's an expert in preparation and presentation. Generally, he's intelligent enough to perceive when there's no chance of winning a grievance, and he can be an ally of management in convincing an employee not to press an issue.

It should come as no surprise that a steward's training in how to handle grievances runs closely parallel to the supervisor's. Where stewards tend to gain an edge is in their ability to concentrate or specialize on this one facet of their job while supervisors are inclined to set it aside as an unpleasant adjunct to the job. The steward would prefer to have grievances to handle—even to the point of looking for them—whereas the supervisor would prefer to avoid them if he could. The steward is trained to listen carefully to an employee's complaint and to be able to document the case. He is trained in interpreting labor contracts—from the union's viewpoint, of course. Pinpointing the clause in a contract that will help the union member win his grievance is the steward's job.

His training teaches him to investigate the facts, get evidence of unfair treatment, find previous decisions that would be precedent for his case, and secure witnesses to build a sound case. To top it off, he is trained in how to deal with or handle the supervisor. He knows the strengths and weaknesses of the supervisor just as the supervisor should know his. If the supervisor loses his temper easily, he can expect that characteristic to be known and exploited. The steward knows how and where to look for loopholes and how to use them to advantage. If the supervisor makes mistakes, he can expect those mistakes to be isolated and used with full force against him. Both stewards and supervisors are taught to win. In the strength of both sides it is to be hoped that justice and fair treatment for both employees and the company will prevail.

The union is a political organization. In it the steward holds a political office. He is judged by higher officers and his electorate by the quality of the service he renders its members. His effectiveness is measured in terms of how well he succeeds in gaining concessions on employees' complaints and grievances. Like a baseball pitcher, he's concerned about his won-and-lost record. This being so, the supervisor can generally count on his pursuing with vigor and skill any issue that becomes a formal grievance. He may be an irritant. He may create friction. He may even challenge the supervisor's leadership. But irritants, friction, and challenges have a way of stimulating, polishing, and motivating, and it may be that a good steward will spur the supervisor to more effective supervision.

In dealing with the steward, supervisors might find it helpful to remember a few brief don'ts:

1. Don't lose your temper with him
2. Don't stall or pass the buck.
3. Don't get sidetracked from the main issue.
4. Don't use profanity.
5. Don't ridicule or use sarcasm.
6. Don't guess—have the facts.
7. Don't bluff or make threats.
8. Don't be afraid to stick to your guns.

The Grievance Procedure

An effective grievance procedure, whether it be in a union or nonunion firm, makes it possible for an employee to express his complaints without fear. Management finds that when a grievance procedure is working properly, it is an effective means of locating and correcting legitimate causes for dissatisfaction among employees. The procedure makes it possible to handle disputes peacefully—minimizing heat and friction. A good grievance procedure provides a way of preventing minor complaints or problems from growing all out of proportion into major grievances. For these reasons, most companies have found it advantageous to spell out and guarantee the procedures whereby an employee can have his complaints or grievances heard fairly by the top authorities in the organization.

Essentially the principle on which an effective grievance procedure is built is the right of an employee to have his grievance heard at the next higher level if he is not satisfied with the decisions rendered.

Grievance procedures should be written and published so that employees understand their rights and supervisors know their responsibilities. In the unionized company the grievance procedure is well known—after all, it is the union's stock-in-trade. In the nonunion company, however, the procedure frequently does not get the same publicity. The supervisor can contribute to better employee relations by making certain that new employees are informed of the existence of a grievance procedure. The procedure assures the employee that he will get a sympathetic hearing and fair treatment. Nonunion companies that have successful procedures for enabling employees to adjust their difficulties continually emphasize the need for assuring employees that no reprisals will result from the use of the grievance procedure.

Grievance procedures, of necessity, vary in their structure. No one standard procedure could be devised to fit every business enterprise. Size, organization, type of operation, kind of personnel—all affect the problem of tailoring the grievance procedure. The purpose of all grievance procedures is to assure the employee that he can get a fair, sympathetic hearing without fear of reprisal and to spell out the steps by which an employee can carry his grievance to the next higher authority if he is not satisfied at the first level.

The number of steps in a grievance procedure will usually vary from three to five. For our purposes let's look at a four-step procedure. Our prime concern will be to consider the role supervisors play in each step and to understand that a supervisor loses some control over the problem with each successive step. We should understand management's genuine desire to have grievances settled at the first possible stage. This desire, coupled with the structure of the grievance procedure, puts the supervisor in a strategic position.

Step One: The employee, with or without representation,
confers with the supervisor

The grievance may be spoken or in writing. Many procedures call for a written statement before a complaint is considered a grievance. This is, whether written or spoken, the critical step. Supervisors have complete control to grant or deny a grievance—a responsibility not to be taken lightly. They are the first point of contact. The willingness to listen courteously with genuine interest, to investigate and weigh the facts conscientiously, and to respond with respect for the employee's feelings are the hallmarks of effective grievance handling. The scope of the supervisor's authority is sufficient to settle most grievances. The best practice is to settle employees' complaints quickly, before heat and friction are generated.

A large Midwestern manufacturing company, plagued by a backlog of hundreds of grievances every time it entered contract negotiations, decided finally to embark on a comprehensive program of settling all grievances at the first level. Higher-line management and staff specialists were put at the disposal of the foreman to help him reach a satisfactory settlement. Prompt, on-the-site, settlements became the rule rather than the deliberate delaying procedures previously used. The foreman was the key. He had, however, all the support he felt he needed to reach an equitable acceptable agreement. Concentration on early settlement with support from above worked. The backlog of grievances was eliminated, and negotiations from that time on were begun in a much healthier climate.

The complexity of the grievance will determine how much investigative work must be done before a supervisor can respond to a first-step grievance. He should gather all facts that might have a bearing on the case. He needs to have a thorough understanding of the rule or contract clause being contested. He will want to know of any previous actions, decisions, or rulings that might provide a precedent. He can be sure that the union will also be very thorough in making similar preparations.

In his handling of the first step the supervisor should remain objective and use an analytical approach. It's possible that he may be deliberately goaded into a display of anger in the hopes he might say something that can be used against him. He would do well to be wary of such tactics.

The supervisor's response to the grievance, after thorough investigation, should be firm, specific, courteous, and respectful. There should be no doubt as to what his decision is—nor should there be any room to doubt that a fair sympathetic hearing was given the employee's complaint. If the grievance does go beyond the first step, the handling of the initial phase will provide the basis for future discussions and arguments.

Step Two: The employee and his representative present the grievance in writing to next higher authority (usually general foreman or superintendent)

If the supervisor has done a good job of communicating, this step will come as no surprise to the boss. He will have some knowledge of the issues in dispute. It is assumed that since he is in a position of greater authority, he will be able to call upon broader experience which might lead to a satisfactory agreement. The supervisor's hope is that he will have the full support and backing of higher authority when his decision is challenged in this second step. His thoroughness and judicious handling of the first step will ensure this backing, but he must recognize now that the decision is out of his hands. He can influence that decision, but reversal or support is for the boss to decide.

Step Three: The employee's grievance, with the support of higher representation, is taken to top-line management

In an organized company the top grievance-handling arm of the union represents the employee. This might be the chief steward, the business agent, the president, or a grievance committee. On management's side the grievance is directed to the general manager, plant manager, branch manager, or president. The company's labor relations staff and the union's grievance specialists become involved in hearings and discussions. If only selfishly, the supervisor should note that his handling of the first step is under direct and close top management scrutiny. Perhaps this is what Burt had in mind when he decided he had better be careful about how he handled his first grievance. Everything possible will be done by the employee or his representatives to present his case in the best possible light. This means challenging everything the supervisor has done and said.

Management at the top level has just as great an interest in supporting the supervisor as his immediate boss. He is, after all, a member of management. If he has followed sound human relations practices and protected management's right to manage he can expect management's support. He needs to be realistic enough to understand, however, that at the top level the perspective is somewhat different.

The effect of granting or denying on the entire organization must be weighed. The risk of having the grievance go to arbitration has to be calculated. It is possible that the long-run interests of the company will best be served by a reversal of the supervisor's decision. Again the possibility of a reversal is minimized by his thoroughness in examining all facets of the problem before reaching his decision.

In a nonunion company, this is usually the final step. Provisions for hearing the grievance by an outside party are not usually made. The top manager makes the final determination, and the employee must accept the decision. Management must understand that the employee is relying entirely on its fairness and impartiality.

Step Four: The grievance is taken to arbitration or conciliation

If agreement on the disposition of the grievance cannot be reached, it is taken to a disinterested outside party for consideration. Arbitration is commonly specified by contract as the means for final settlement of the dispute. In arbitration both parties agree on an arbitrator to hear the grievance, and both parties agree in advance to abide by the decision of the arbitrator. Conciliation, on the other hand, is the attempt of a disinterested outsider to help the parties find a basis for settling the dispute. The conciliator does not make the decision. He simply facilitates and recommends avenues of agreement. The failure to reach agreement in conciliation leaves the courts or the National Labor Relations Board as the remaining recourse for the grievant.

An arbitrator will conduct a hearing similar in some respects to a court trial. The degree of formality will vary with the individual arbitrator, but he will require a specific statement of charges, hear witnesses, weigh evidence, and render a decision. Because of the interest both parties have in winning their points, they are usually represented by legal counsel in the arbitration hearing. Obviously, with so many people involved, the supervisor's control over the grievance's disposition is nil. He is now simply a witness. He can only hope that his judgment in the first step will be confirmed.

The grievance procedure, in summary, is designed to guarantee the employee a fair hearing in his complaints against management. Everything contractually possible is done to protect this right and ensure a fair hearing. We can see that the attitude of both parties and the spirit in which they deliberate contributes significantly to the effectiveness of the procedure. In this brief consideration of the formal procedure, we can see the wisdom of preventing grievances or settling them at the first level, where the supervisor's control is the greatest.

Tips on How to Handle Complaints and Grievances

Complaints in even the best-managed departments are to be expected. In fact, a complete absence of complaints, say many experts, is an indication that people are afraid to voice their feelings and concerns. Enough has been said of the key role the supervisor plays in preventing complaints from becoming grievances. We can clearly see the importance to any management of having those grievances that do arise settled at lowest possible level. Here are a few tips on handling complaints and grievances at the supervisory level gleaned from thousands of successful and management-minded supervisors.

1. Listen with interest

Listening is perhaps the best way in the world of sizing up another person in a disagreement. Listening is a way of showing respect. It helps the listener understand the depth of feeling the employee has about his gripe. It's the supervisor's first chance to start developing an understanding of what is really bothering the person.

2. Consider the complaint important

Many complaints and gripes are without foundation and are the result of an overactive imagination. Still, to the employee the complaint is real. It took considerable thought and courage on his part to express it to the supervisor at all. The least the supervisor can do is demonstrate to the employee that he considers his complaint important and that it will get full and sympathetic attention.

3. Keep calm

Effective handling of complaints and grievances requires clear thinking. Most complaints challenge methods of supervision. The temptation to become angry is great, but anger may add fuel to the fire. The supervisor's objective is to stay in control. When he loses his temper, he tends to lose not only control, but his dignity as a member of management.

4. Get all the facts

The pressure is on the supervisor to make a decision as quickly as possible. Yet he should not reach a decision without the benefit of factual information. There is always the possibility that a complaint might develop into a full-blown grievance. He must be certain that he has the complete story. He can ask the employee questions, check records, review rules or contracts, check previous decisions for precedents, and investigate anything that will help him give an intelligent decision.

5. Give or get a direct answer

Stalling and hedging are annoying. It's safe to assume that anyone coming to a supervisor with a complaint or a grievance would like a direct answer. If it's within the scope of his authority to give an answer, he should want to give it in clear, definite, understandable terms. A decision outside his authority should be sought and communicated to the employee as soon as possible. If the answer is slow in coming, he will want to keep the employee posted on his progress and the reasons for the delay. Since the complaint is serious to the employee, the longer he must wait for an answer, the deeper his concern and convictions become.

6. Sell the decision

It's no problem to tell an employee he's right and that his request will be granted. The test of the supervisor's skill is in telling him no and in getting him to accept the decision. He should be made to understand that his complaint was given very serious consideration. Reasons that are understandable from the employee's point of view should always be a part of rendering a negative decision. A hard, cold no does nothing to strengthen future relations. This, we know, is the critical point in preventing a complaint from becoming a grievance or a grievance from going to a higher level.

The handling of complaints and grievances demands the sharpest human relations skills from beginning to end. This skill can frequently make the difference between a satisfied, cooperative employee and an employee who is a constant source of irritation and trouble.

HIGHLIGHTS

1. Every employee has the right to grieve, complain, or question when a misunderstanding develops. Supervisors are the point of first contact for the grieving employee. Their job is to prevent complaints from becoming grievances while safeguarding management's interests.
2. A grievance usually develops in stages. It starts as a request, becomes a complaint, and, if unsatisfied, develops into a grievance. Resentment and anger, absent in the first stage, tend to increase throughout the process.
3. Grievances provide learning experiences. Every request, complaint, or grievance handled, whether it is accepted or denied, should promote sound human relations.
4. The union steward is a well-trained specialist in handling grievances. His training is similar to the supervisor's with regard to processing and winning grievances. His job is to demonstrate to the employee the value of the union in getting him a fair hearing.
5. Grievance procedures are clearly defined to guarantee the rights of an employee to be heard at the next higher level without reprisal if he is not satisfied. A typical four-step grievance procedure would permit the employee, with or without representation, to carry his grievance to higher levels:

   Step one: To his supervisor
   Step two: To a superintendent or middle management
   Step three: To top management
   Step four: To arbitration or conciliation

6. Here are a few tips on how to handle complaints and grievances properly gleaned from practical experience. A supervisor should:
   a. Listen with interest
   b. Consider the complaint important
   c. Keep calm
   d. Get all the facts

e. Give or get a direct answer

f. Sell the decision

DISCUSSION QUESTIONS

1. Explain why it is so important for a nonunion company to have a formal grievance procedure.
2. Discuss with a union steward his ideas of his grievance-handling responsibility. How does his thinking differ from yours as a supervisor?
3. Evaluate the statement that a complete absence of grievances in a department does not necessarily mean that a supervisor is doing a good job of managing his employee relations.
4. What is your opinion of the statement that the union is a political organization and that the steward holds a political office? How does this influence the approach of unions and stewards to grievances?
5. Do you agree that a good tough steward can make a supervisor do his job better? Why?
6. Why is it so important to avoid profanity, ridicule, sarcasm, and threats when handling grievances?
7. Why should a supervisor be careful to make written record of a spoken warning on a first offense?
8. Describe, from your own experience, a grievance that went to the second or third level. Would it have been possible for the supervisor to have settled it himself without compromising management's rights?

SUGGESTIONS FOR FURTHER STUDY

Bittel, Lester R.
What Every Supervisor Should Know, 2d ed.
Chapter 19, McGraw-Hill Book Company, New York, 1968

Black, James, and Guy Ford
Front-line Management
Section 4, McGraw-Hill Book Company, New York, 1963

Ecker, Paul, John MacRae, Vernon Ouellette, and Charles Telford
Handbook for Supervisors
Chapter 13, Prentice-Hall, Inc., Englewood Cliffs, N.J., 1959

Famularo, Joseph J.
Supervisors in Action
Chapter 13, McGraw-Hill Book Company, New York, 1961

Stessin, Lawrence
Practice of Personnel and Industrial Relations
Chapter 4, Pitman Publishing Corporation, New York, 1964

PART
THREE

JOB KNOWLEDGE

The knowledge we have acquired ought not to resemble a great shop without order and inventory; we ought to know what we possess, and be able to make it serve us in our need.

GOTTFRIED WILHELM
VON LEIBNITZ
(1646–1716)

CHAPTER
TEN

PLANNING
AND
ORGANIZING
WORK

THE CASE OF CARL'S CONFUSION

"Burt, I need some help. Have you got ten minutes you can spare me?" Carl Cramer, wearing a worried expression, was standing in the doorway to Burt Hall's office. It was 3.35 P.M. Burt was cleaning off his desk before leaving for home. The man with the worried expression was the supervisor of the production testing department.

"I've got things pretty well wrapped up for the day. Come on in, Carl, and take the load off your feet." If things had gone well, and today they had for Burt, this was the part of the day Burt liked most. He could sit back and reflect on a day of accomplishment. It was a good feeling, and Burt was in a good mood. "What's on your mind, Carl? You look as if you've just lost your last friend."

"To tell the truth, Burt, I don't know which end is up. I'm getting to the point where I'm wondering whether I should throw in the towel and give up this rat race. Ray Ford just chewed me out in his gentle way and suggested that I might get some help talking with you. Frankly, the suggestion didn't set too well with me at first, but I am going in ten different directions at the same time. Ray felt that you were usually pretty well organized and on top of things. I guess he was telling me that I'm not, and what hurts is that he's right. If you can help me get straightened out, Burt, I'd appreciate it. If not, then maybe supervision isn't my cup of tea. Life is too short to live with all this pressure."

Burt was wondering what he could possibly do to take the pressure off Carl as he said, "That's a pretty tall order, Carl. I sure don't know what Ray had in mind, but if I can help, I'll try. Why don't you tell me more about this pressure?"

"Well, I told you I seem to be heading in ten different directions at the same time. There aren't enough hours in a day. The harder I work, the less I seem to accomplish. Ray said that the job seems to be running me instead of me managing the job. I honestly don't know whether it's me or the whole doggonned system. What do you think, Burt?"

"It can get pretty hectic at times," Burt said. "And I don't have a magic wand or a formula to cure your problems, Carl. What happened that you and Ray got into this hassel?"

Carl began to explain that it wasn't what would be called a hassel. He knew that Ray was annoyed because some arrangements for a semiautomatic testing device coming in the next week had not been made. The equipment had been ordered three months before. Deciding where it was to be located and arranging the production schedule changes during the installation had been Carl's responsibility. He told Burt that the three months slipped by without his doing the necessary planning. He hadn't forgotten. Practically every day he meant to get at it, but one thing always led to another, and time got away from him. When Ray stopped in that morning, it was to tell Carl that the equipment was arriving in a few days and to find out what arrangements had been made for it.

"He just caught me with my pants down," Carl moaned. "I hadn't done a single thing. Yesterday I started to check out one area I had in mind—you know, measuring the area and seeing how much other stuff would have to be relocated. On the way I saw Jack Adams getting ready to set up a machine that I wanted some repair work done on. I got him going on something else and went back to my office to call maintenance. Before I could get away from the office, I had three more calls for information, and two guys came looking for help on their jobs. By the time I got the information and returned the calls, the afternoon was shot. I was determined that nothing was going to stop me this morning, but it was the same old story. Ray was there wanting to know my plans before I had a chance to step outside the door. When I told him I hadn't had time to get to it yet, you might know that he'd remind me that I'd had three months. It sounded weak even to me when I told him I had just been too busy. But doggone it, Burt, I've been running my tail off, and I get further behind every week. I don't know where the time goes. How in blazes do you keep up with it? Have you got some kind of a system? Ray seemed to think you have."

"I don't know if you could dignify it by calling it a system, but Harry Gates passed a couple of ideas on to me before he left. They've worked pretty well, too, except when somebody louses me up. Harry warned me that unless I took some time out each day for planning, I would be ready for the men in the white coats inside of six months. You seem to be getting ready to be a candidate, Carl."

"Time for planning," Carl groaned. "Where do you find it? Everything takes time, and I'm fresh out."

Burt tried to explain that it was time well invested and that it saved much more time in the long run. He said that he came in at 6:45 A.M. every day and spent fifteen minutes listing the things that had to be done that day. As the day went along, he crossed off the things that had been finished. What didn't get done was carried over to the next day. He also told Carl that he stayed half an hour late on Friday to block out the following week in rough form. The morning sessions refined the weekly plan.

"One of the things that the list does," Burt pointed out, "is show you where to delegate some of your work. It took me quite a while to catch on to that part of it because I had to know what I was doing before I could parcel out any of my work."

"Delegate! That's a laugh." Carl grunted. "You've got to have someone to delegate to. The way things are, I've got to do everything myself if it's going to be done right. Everybody in my department is so darned busy that I couldn't pile my work on them if I tried. Besides, Burt, it's easier to do it myself than to take all the time to show somebody else how to do it."

"You're right about that, the first time through," Burt countered. "But how about all the times after that? The payoff comes when you have somebody who can do the job every time it occurs. Believe me, Carl, it's worth taking some extra time to help a man do the job right for you the first time through."

"Yeah, but I never seem to find the time to do it that first time. All my jobs are rush jobs, and I don't have time to play nursemaid when I can do them in half the time myself. What I can't see, Burt, is how making a list of jobs every day is going to help much. I don't know when that blasted phone is going to ring or when one of my men is going to have trouble on a job that I'll have to straighten out. It seems that that's where most of my day goes. I never get around to the important things I want to do. I go from one crisis to another, and I just can't see how you can plan for a problem that hasn't happened yet."

"When you put it that way, I don't know either, Carl." Burt scratched his head. "I'll have to admit that I get upset when somebody fouls me up. Maybe that's the big disadvantage to planning. Once you determine what you want to accomplish, you want to do it. I find myself cursing anything that gets in my way. In the long run, though, the system does a pretty good job for me—especially if I don't try to cram too much into a day. Maybe that's the answer—keep it loose."

"Frankly, Burt, I had hoped for something more," Carl said. "There's so much confusion in my department that it's going to take more than a daily checklist to straighten things out. My guys are getting as jumpy as I am. Every time I catch hell for missing a deadline, I pass it on, and I know that's wrong. It's not helping morale any. Every breakdown, shortage of material, or rush order turns out to be my fault. Our costs have been going up. I haven't heard from topside on that one, but I will. Ray didn't actually say it, but I thought you had a real system for streamlining your whole operation that I could use in my department."

"For your sake, Carl, I wish I did," Burt replied. "My morning planning just seems to keep us all on track. We have a pretty good idea of where we're going and when we're going to get there. It's like starting out on a trip. You have a hundred miles to go, and you know it will take you about two hours if you don't stop. Gassing up, coffee or lunch breaks, or side trips add time to that two hours. It's the same here. We've got just so much time, so many people, and so much equipment to get the work done. If there's too much work, something has to give —adjustments are made—push back the deadline, work overtime, farm out some of the work, or add more people. With the daily and the weekly plans I can usually see the need for an adjustment before it's down around our ears—a crisis. Those morning planning sessions give me a feeling that I'm making things happen instead of having them happen to me. Do you know what I mean?"

Carl halfheartedly said that he did and asked Burt why he did his planning in the morning instead of during the day. Burt said that he thought deciding on the best time was an individual matter. The important thing was to find a time when there were no interruptions. Burt told Carl that Harry Gates always did his planning at the end of the day, but Burt felt that he did a better job in the morning when he was fresh. For some reason, he explained to Carl, he still liked Friday afternoon to look at the whole week. One thing was certain, no one hung around to bother a man on Friday afternoon.

"You mean the way I'm doing now," Carl said. "Seriously, Burt, I'm almost as confused about how your system could work for me as I am in trying to keep up with my job. But a drowning man will grab at anything. I'll give it a try."

"That's the only way you'll find out if it will help, Carl. After you try it a couple of days, maybe we can compare notes. Don't expect miracles. It will probably take a while to adjust to planning—that is, if you can call it planning."

    1. How much of Carl's confusion could be attributed to a lack of planning?

2. Burt seemed to have doubts as to whether or not his system could really be considered planning. Was it?
3. How should we evaluate Carl's reasons for not wanting to delegate?
4. Is there a relationship between supervisory planning and employees' morale?
5. Burt said that a disadvantage to planning was getting upset when he couldn't always achieve his objective. Is he right?
6. What did Burt mean when he said that his morning sessions made him feel that he was making things happen rather than having them happen to him?

PLANNING AND THE MANAGEMENT–MINDED SUPERVISOR

For decades we have been stressing job knowledge as one of the most important assets of a supervisor. To most of us, job knowledge means a mastery of the procedures, techniques of production, man or machine capabilities, and properties of materials. Job knowledge, as we commonly think of it, is acquired either through technical education or long experience with a variety of operations performed in the department. Great emphasis has been placed on this concept of job knowledge in selecting supervisors for many years. A man's knowledge of his job can be fairly safely evaluated, but it has limited value for predicting success in supervision.

Many have been handicapped by such shortsighted selection procedures. Supervision is management! Job knowledge for a supervisor should mean a knowledge of how to manage—not simply how to produce. As a new supervisor in the production testing department, Carl Cramer was technically qualified beyond a shadow of a doubt. But his conversation with Burt Hall reveals him to be woefully weak in knowing his job as a manager. Management is the achieving of results through people, and Carl was completely lacking in this skill. Every supervisor, if he is to experience the satisfaction of successful supervising, will have to learn the job knowledge of management—planning, organizing, motivating (directing), and controlling.

In Chapter 1 we identified the seven major responsibilities of the management-minded supervisor as (1) production, (2) quality, (3) costs, (4) methods, (5) training, (6) safety, and (7) morale. Application of the management process to people and work produces the proper results in those seven areas. It should not be difficult to see how excellence in any of these seven major areas of responsibility is dependent on good planning. For example, programs for the improvement of quality, costs, safety, or methods must be carefully planned if improvements are to be realized. It doesn't happen by chance.

Carl Cramer was typical of so many supervisors who remain producers instead of becoming managers. Most, if not all, of his time was occupied in doing routine work and jumping from one crisis to another. His thinking was centered on things and details rather than on planning and directing. His technical knowledge provided a security that wouldn't permit him to trust his people. Work makes people feel productive. A mental barrier limits many supervisors who have never learned the techniques of planning, directing, and controlling the work of others. For most, it takes some time to let go of the producing activities and find satisfaction in the management functions. Management-mindedness in supervision is reflected in a supervisor's ability to plan the activities in his department.

What is planning? Some have said that planning is merely deciding. in advance what is to be done. Burt Hall said almost the same thing when he told Carl that his morning planning sessions gave him the feeling that he was making things happen instead of having them happen to him. Others have said that planning is the substitution of thinking for worry. If Carl Cramer survives as a supervisor, he will, in time, come to appreciate that definition, for good planning surely does minimize the need to worry. Our purposes will best be served by defining planning as the determination of what needs to be done, who will do it, and when it has to be done in order to carry out major responsibilities.

In "The Case of Carl's Confusion" we found evidence to support the idea that good planning on the part of a supervisor tends to build respect for him as a manager. Employees, like supervisors, want to be a part of an organization that is accomplishing things—that knows where it's going. Burt Hall's men knew that Burt was running things and respected him as a manager. Carl, on the other hand, let the job run him, became what is known as a "crisis manager," and earned a sizable disrespect from the employees under him. Many executives have gone so far as to say, "If you can't plan, you can't manage." Ability to plan is therefore one of the first distinguishing characteristics separating a producer from a manager—a characteristic that employees are quick to sense in their supervisor. There seems little doubt that a lack of planning skills has been sufficient reason why many supervisors are not promoted, for each move up the management ladder requires a higher degree of planning skill. If that skill is lacking at the first level, a supervisor is not likely to be advanced to a more responsible position.

Management-mindedness demands more of the supervisor than a personal ability to plan. It challenges the supervisor to demonstrate an enthusiastic willingness to participate in the plans of others with whom he coordinates. Much of a supervisor's planning must fit into plans that are developed at higher levels. His responsibility is to implement those plans as efficiently as possible. For example, a manufacturing manager calls a meeting to announce a plantwide cost-reduction program. He sets forth general guidelines for the program, suggests areas that should be attacked, and sets up time limits for achieving a certain percentage of reduction. His supervisors have been given the job of implementing the plan. They must now develop their own plans—setting their own goals, determining who will do the work and when it will be done. Obviously, the more thorough the planning is at the supervisory level, the more likely it is that the plant will reach its goals.

Frequently a supervisor will be asked by the boss or by staff departments to participate in planning special projects or programs—more demands on his time. Yet a mark of management-mindedness is the degree to which he is cooperative in participating in the planning of others. His responsibility is for his department, but he also has an obligation to contribute his efforts to the benefit of the overall operation by making sound suggestions when plans are being formulated and by carrying out any personal assignments that might develop within the designated time limits.

MANAGING PERSONAL TIME

Carl Cramer is an example of a supervisor who has no concept of the critical need to manage time like any other resource. Those who make the familiar complaint, "If I only had more time," fail to recognize that they have all the time there is. They'll never get any more or have any less—twenty-four hours a day. What a man accomplishes in the approximately eight hours a day allocated to the job is dependent on how well he manages. It's a simple matter to recognize that if a man takes ten hours to do eight hours' work, he must take those extra two hours from his family, rest, or recreation. There's no way to recover a wasted hour or day, yet tomorrow is ready to be managed or used in any way we choose.

How often, like Carl Cramer, have people said to themselves, "I don't know where the time goes"? The first step in effectively managing time is to find the answer to that question. Just how am I spending my time? Am I chasing around putting out fires? Is half of my time consumed in answering the phone and chasing down information? Am I losing precious hours by arriving late, leaving early, extending breaks, and engaging in nonproductive bull sessions? How much of that forty-hour workweek is consumed in attending meetings, in routine clerical work, or in locating tools and materials? Many supervisors would be surprised at the ratio of their producing time to their managing time. Until they make an effort to find out how they spend their time, there's little likelihood that they will disturb themselves sufficiently to take corrective action. As in the solving of any other problem, they need the facts.

Burt Hall told Carl that it was necessary to spend time to save time, and so it is with respect to managing personal time. It will take some time for a supervisor to determine how he's spending his time, but that job can be made easier by using a chart like the Personal Time Analysis Chart shown in Figure 8. A precise time study isn't necessary. By using a check mark for each ten minutes, a supervisor can get a fairly accurate picture of how most of his time is spent. For example, if he attended a production meeting from 9:00 to 10:00 A.M., in each of the 9:00 and 9:30 blocks under "Meetings" he would put three check marks. If the first half hour was spent on scheduling and instructing an employee on a job, he might put two marks under "Scheduling" and one under "Instructing." It takes only about a minute to mark the sheet for the previous hour or two. Estimates of how much time he spends on the phone or talking to employees will have to be made, of course. He simply wants an approximate idea of how his time is being spent. No one else will ever see the analysis unless he chooses to show it. The same sheet can be used for the entire week, or individual sheets might be used each day. Generally, one sheet for the full week carries a greater impact at week's end. The total check marks for the week in each column multiplied by ten provides a good idea of how many minutes are spent in a week on each activity.

Personal Time Analysis

Time	Meetings	Personal contacts	Scheduling and assigning work	Inspecting	Instructing	Planning	Paperwork	Personal; breaks	Miscel- laneous	Comments
7:00										
7:30										
8:00										
8:30										
9:00										
9:30										
10:00										
10:30										
11:00										
11:30										
12:00										
12:30										
1:00										
1:30										
2:00										
2:30										
3:00										
3:30										
4:00										

Figure **8.**

The column headings in Figure 8 are for purposes of illustration only. Each supervisor will have to determine those which best cover his own activities. After a day or two he might want to modify the headings. For example, if his job involved large amounts of time spent in personnel contacts, he might want to break that down into types of contacts—safety contacts, grievances, personal problems, etc.

By the end of two weeks he should have better than a fair idea of where his time is going. To say the least, his analysis should be revealing. He can ask himself, "Am I wasting an hour or more a day in idle conversation and on breaks?" "How much of that time could be saved?" "Am I doing so much paper work that I might more appropriately be called a clerk than a supervisor?" "Am I a slave to the telephone and to my role as an expediter?" Many supervisors, for example, find in making such an analysis that they spend literally no time in planning. Carl Cramer would certainly be one of them.

After a supervisor has found patterns in his use of time, he should then start to determine how he should spend his time most profitably. Somewhere in that workday he will want to set aside a period for planning and creative work—the function of a manager. But how, and where?

Burt Hall set aside fifteen minutes at the beginning of each day to make a list of things that he wanted to do that day. He hesitated to dignify what he was doing by calling it planning, but that's exactly what it was. Determining what was to be done, who was to do it, and when it was to be done fits our definition of planning perfectly. Burt was managing his day rather than have things just happen. He found, too, that if he tried to cram in too much detail, he couldn't fulfill his plan. There must be some flexibility for emergencies, breakdowns, or demands from the boss or from other departments. No one is free from demands on time imposed by the boss or others in the organization.

Each Friday afternoon, Burt found the quiet after everyone had left an ideal time to look at the next week. Figures 9 and 10 are examples of forms he might have used to project some of the jobs that he wanted to accomplish—jobs which many supervisors put off until they get more time.

In a chart like the one shown in Figure 9, a supervisor would simply list in the "Work activity" column the jobs that he wanted to accomplish the next week, for example, review John Jones's performance, revise filing system, call departmental meeting on eye and foot protec-

Personal Planning Sheet

Week ending _____

Work Activity	Monday		Tuesday		Wednesday		Thursday		Friday		Saturday		Comments
	A.M.	P.M.	A.M.	P.M.	A.M.	P.M.	A.M.	P.M.	A.M.	P.M.	A.M.	P.M.	

Figure 9.

tion, and study method of reporting waste materials. To this, of course, should be added any regular known demands on his time, such as weekly production meetings, preparation of periodic reports, conferences with the boss, periodic inspections, and training meetings. As he lists each activity, he will put an X in the appropriate column— Monday, A.M., Wednesday, P.M., etc. Rather than trying to do everything tomorrow, he should force himself to evaluate activities, set priorities, and schedule each activity when it won't be crowded by a dozen others.

During the week as each job is completed, he will put a circle around the X. If he didn't get to it, he can use the "Comments" column to explain why he didn't and reschedule the job. The advantage of this kind of planning is that the explanations or alibis for not accomplishing the job are made only to himself. When a supervisor gets tired of explaining, he should discipline himself to get the job done by setting less important things aside.

Figure 10 combines a daily and weekly plan by identifying each hour of the day for a week at a time. The principle, however, is the same. Some will find one more convenient. Others will find perhaps even another method more convenient such as the monthly pocket calendars which are so popular. Simplicity and flexibility are important. Tying

Personal Time Plan

Week of _____

Hour	Monday	Tuesday	Wednesday	Thursday	Friday
7:00– 8:00					
8:00– 9:00					
9:00–10:00					
10:00–11:00					
11:00–12:00					
12:00– 1:00					
1:00– 2:00					
2:00– 3:00					
3:00– 4:00					
4:00– 5:00					

Figure **10.**

himself down with too much detail puts the supervisor in the position of spending more time revising the schedule than the system is worth. His objective is to save time and use it more effectively, not to spend it as a slave to a system.

To those who might ask, "Is this really planning or managing?" let's review it in terms of our definition. By this method the supervisor can determine *what* has to be done by analyzing how he spends his time and can decide how to make better use of it. *Who* will do the job is determined when he puts it down on paper—either he will do it personally, or he will assign it to a subordinate. *When* the job is to be done is designated by the time at which he schedules it in his daily or weekly plan. Having established that this is planning, we can ask, "Is this managing?" First of all, let's recognize that the first function of management is *planning* and *organizing*. *Directing* is accomplished when the supervisor says to himself, "This is what I will do and when I will do it." *Controlling* enters the picture, when at the end of the day or the week, the supervisor looks to see whether he has accomplished what he had planned. If corrective measures are needed, he plans them, and so he goes through the cycle again.

Many supervisors, like Carl Cramer, acknowledge that managing personal time sounds good in theory, but they back away when they look at the countless activities in which they engage every day. Feeling that it's hopeless, they never start. They put personal-time planning far down on the mental list of things they will do as soon as they get more time. Several supervisors have reported at university seminars that they were able to bridge this initial hurdle by making their first plans for weekends at home. It works the same way and with much less pressure. How many odd jobs are there waiting around the house for us to get more time—screens to be painted, garage to be cleaned, tools to be sharpened, appliances to be repaired, a room to be painted, shrubs to be trimmed? Scheduling a few of these jobs for particular weekends until the list is whittled down has proved to be an excellent exercise in personal time planning. Oddly enough, the exercise has also contributed positively to domestic relations when tried.

Consequences of Poor Planning

Where planning is poor or lacking in a department, it can be said that the department is operating without management. Certainly the supervisor who can't plan can't manage. Carl Cramer's department provides an excellent (or should we say miserable) example of what happens in the absence of good planning. A supervisor hopelessly bogged down in a never-ending deluge of details, Carl was ready to give up. Life, he said, was too short to endure the pressure of the job. Let's take a look at some of the specific consequences of poor planning and organizing.

Lower production

It stands to reason that lack of coordinating, overlapping activities, shortages of materials and equipment, and poor scheduling can't help but result in lower productivity. With production as one of the supervisor's major responsibilities, failure to plan is to cheat himself and to short-change the company.

Dissatisfaction among employees

Employees want to feel a satisfaction in accomplishment. If poor leadership creates chaos and denies them this opportunity, the natural result is discontent. A supervisor who gives sound direction to his work force will build respect. The ability to give that direction is dependent on sound planning. Carl Cramer and Burt Hall are examples of the effect of supervisory planning on the morale of their work force.

High costs

When productivity is lowered, morale is poor, rework is high, and costs inevitably rise. Another of the supervisor's major responsibilities is sacrificed to poor planning when he sees his unit costs increase and profits diminish.

Misunderstanding and confusion

Not knowing what is expected of him is disconcerting to the employee. Employees want direction, not a lot of if's and maybe's. Standing around because materials aren't available or equipment is missing adds to the confusion. Cramer was confused. His confusion, as hard as it was on him, was no greater than the confusion his employees experienced.

Pressure from above

Here poor planning really hurts the supervisor. He was put in his job by management to get results and results are expected—not alibis. Few supervisors haven't had the experience at one time or another of having these words stick in their throats, "Boss, I just haven't had time to get at it." When poor planning yields poor results, the pressure from above mounts, and well it should.

Poor-quality work

Quality, say some manufacturers, is built into their products; but quality, too, must suffer when confusion reigns in a department. Complaints from customers are inevitable when quality drops off, and what a way that is to draw attention to the supervisor in whose department quality has suffered because of poor planning. Quality improvement must be planned for just like any other improvement.

Accidents

Confusion and dissatisfaction in the work force tend to take people's minds off what they are doing, thus creating conditions ripe for accidents. Lack of planning often results in hurrying, poor housekeeping, substituting improper tools, using makeshift equipment, and taking chances—all known contributors to accidents.

Lessened chance for promotion

All functions in the management process are geared to the planning function. Directing and controlling are effective only when planning is thorough. The supervisor who can't plan can't manage. Common sense tells us that the supervisor who can't manage won't be promoted and will be penalized when salary increases for merit are considered.

Benefits of Good Planning

Other than avoiding the consequences of poor planning, what benefits to the supervisor and to the organization accrue as a result of good planning? Let's enumerate just a few.

Better coordination

Most departments relate to other departments and functions. Close coordination of activities is required. The planning which enables the supervisor to live up to deadlines, maintain standards, honor commitments, and render outstanding service marks the supervisor as a good team man.

More effective control of operations

As we shall see when we discuss how to plan, the early stages call for establishing the goals or defining the desired results. Goals, results, objectives, or standards are the basis for the controlling function of management. Until, through planning, the supervisor sets his objectives, he has little against which he can measure his effectiveness. If he seeks in his planning to increase productivity 6 percent, he has established a basis for control.

Easier delegation

Planning leads to organizing similar activities, setting priorities, and analyzing the manpower available. Good planning will point to the potential opportunities for delegation. When a supervisor sees what jobs can be delegated and who might be capable of doing them, some of the initial barriers to delegation have been hurdled.

More economical use of resources

By pinpointing duplication of effort, uneconomical use of materials, and overlapping functions, planning contributes to more efficient use of the resources under the supervisor's control. Defining skills required to perform specific operations enables him many times to utilize lower-level skills on some jobs.

Increased personal effectiveness

When we compare a supervisor who can plan with one who can't, the accomplishments of the planner stand head and shoulders above those of the nonplanner. Carl Cramer and Burt Hall are cases in point. As simple as his planning was, Burt overshadowed Carl by far in what he was able to achieve in a day or a week. Burt was managing his department; he gave it direction; he controlled it. Carl was batted back and forth by circumstances. Neither Carl nor any of his people approached their full potential.

Tendency toward improvement

There's a tendency on the part of a good planner to want to do a better job next time. As he implements his plan, he finds out what works and what doesn't. He retains what is successful and seeks to improve what is lacking. If he achieved one hundred units of production this month, he tends to shoot for an increase next month, and the month after that. When improvements are a part of the supervisory pattern, the supervisor's worth to organization rises to new levels.

Types of Supervisory Planning

There are those who claim that a first-line supervisor really does no planning and is not expected to. Their reasoning is that production standards are set at higher levels and are simply given to the supervisor to carry out. Further, they point out, staff specialists have taken over the planning responsibilities and the authority of the supervisor in the areas of quality, safety, personnel, methods, and labor relations, leaving him little more than an expediting function. Of course, it is these same so-called "experts" who claim that today's supervisor is not a manager. Those who have been a part of supervisory development hold quite opposite views. The supervisor is management, and if he is a manager, he plans. What does he plan? Let's look at some of the activities that call for planning on his part.

Participation in setting goals

Higher-level management is dependent on front-line supervision for the accurate determination of realistic goals. The supervisor is frequently asked to participate in planning production schedules and requirements. The man in the best position to know the capabilities of present production facilities is the supervisor. His role in the critical area of goal setting is significant.

Improvement programs

We're all familiar with quality-improvement drives, cost-reduction programs, housekeeping campaigns, accident-prevention programs, and methods-improvement programs. Whether a supervisor produces any concrete results in these improvement programs is determined by the effectiveness of his planning of departmental efforts. For example, in a cost-reduction program he may set a goal of so many thousand dollars or a general 3 percent reduction as part of an overall attack on costs. From that point he must plan how the goal will be reached and who will do what. He also determines how he'll measure his improvement against the results anticipated. The supervisor who, like Carl Cramer, doesn't have to plan these programs and hopes that something will improve is more likely to find the situation deteriorating instead of improving. These improvement programs, which are constantly recurring, provide an excellent opportunity for a supervisor to exercise and sharpen his planning skills.

Personnel management

The organizing of activities so they are performed most efficiently by qualified people requires expert planning. Determining how many people are needed so that there is sufficient help to get the job done with no extra people standing around calls for a high degree of planning. Disciplining an individual, reviewing his performance with him, handling a grievance, and discussing a change in job assignments should all be carefully planned to avoid misunderstandings.

Production

Production planning in a supervisor's department may call for a variety of planning activities. Scheduling and routing of production are planning functions. Having the necessary materials, equipment, facilities, and manpower available calls for detailed planning in many operations. Movement of materials in and out of the department requires planning. The degree of production planning required by the supervisor will vary with the nature of work performed in the department. For example, a job shop will call for substantially different plans from those required in a production line operation.

Organization of work

The problem at the supervisory level is not to develop detailed organization charts, but rather to answer the question, "How should the work of my department be divided and grouped?" While a supervisor may have inherited the basic organization of his department and may have had other changes dictated to him, he is still responsible for productivity and must set up a well-organized department. He is in the best position to know when a shift in job assignments will accomplish the work of the department most efficiently. The company may very well have organization specialists. At the first level, though, it's academic to try to separate the planning and organizing function. The basic purpose of organizing is to group the work to be performed to utilize manpower most effectively. This is done at the same time as the planning function.

Maintenance

Only the most reckless, foolhardy supervision operates expensive equipment until it breaks down or falls apart. Proper maintenance planning ensures a longer service life of equipment and provides uninterrupted production cycles. Determining when a machine needs service, the best time to do it, and the extent of the maintenance (for example, lubrication or complete overhaul)—all demand careful planning to ensure the least possible interference with production.

Paper work and reports

So many supervisors complain that an unreasonable amount of their time is consumed by paper work and reports. Generally they have no choice but to generate the information needed by other departments through this paper work. Good planning, however, can contribute significantly to a reduction of the time spent on paper work. Consideration can be given to delegating the paper work as a means of developing subordinates. Reports which are planned to present the information required in the most concise, usable form help both the recipient and the reporter.

Changes

Increasingly supervisors are faced with initiating changes in their departments. Resistance to those changes can be minimized by the proper planning of their initiation. Chapter 4 deals in some detail with the need for planning changes.

Communications

Effective department management depends on good communication. Important communications should be carefully planned. Chapter 3 discusses the need for careful planning in communication.

Personal time

Because the key to having sufficient time for performing his job is the planning and organizing of the supervisor's own personal activities, a major portion of this chapter has already been devoted to the subject. A supervisor cannot overlook the fact that he must be personally well organized to have a smoothly operating department.

In summary, almost every function the supervisor performs calls for planning to some degree. Short- and long-range plans are participated in daily. He is involved in carrying out standing plans and in formulating single-use plans. Planning gives purposeful direction to the management of a department.

Key Steps in Formulating Plans

A dynamic organization depends on planning, and it cannot ignore the basic fundamentals. Any plan must ultimately include the answers to some basic questions. We have seen them grouped so often that they seem deceptively simple: *what, when, where, who,* and *how.* Let's consider the role these questions play in planning.

What

Is the supervisor's goal clearly in mind? How will he know whether he has achieved his objective unless he has spelled out his objective? Answering the question *what* is the beginning of the planning process and is at the heart of the "management by results" concept. Goals are vital in planning. They give direction to the supervisor's efforts. Examples of goals he might set include: producing so many units of production; reducing the amount of time to complete a project; having a trained replacement available at all times for key jobs; reducing the percentage of scrap in a month or a quarter; reducing overhead labor costs to a certain level; reducing the percentage of turnover, tardiness, or absenteeism; eliminating defects; reducing by minutes, hours, days, weeks, or months the time usually required to do a job. Setting goals in terms of the desired results gives the supervisor a beginning and ending point to his plan. Administrative control of his operations depends for its effectiveness on having specific objectives against which to measure his progress.

When

Plans are designed to accomplish objectives in a given amount of time—on schedule. How long will it take to do the job and each part of the job? When is the best time to move from one phase to another? When is the best time to start? What is the completion date?

Where

The supervisor should determine the most effective place to accomplish the objective of his plan. Should a potential method of improvement, for example, be tested in the department or in some controlled environment like the experimental laboratory? Should a meeting be a tailgate session, held in his office or taken to the conference room to achieve maximum results? Should special clerical work be performed in the office or outside the company?

Who

A key determination in the formulation of any successful plan is who will carry it out. Who will give the best results? Who is best qualified? Who can benefit most by the experience the project offers? How many times does the supervisor fail to give consideration to these questions and by default wind up doing the job himself, adding to an already heavy burden of work? The opportunity for delegation and time saving becomes most apparent when careful consideration is given to the *who* in his plans.

How

The method the supervisor chooses to implement his plan will have very real impact on the results he achieves. Should it be done by traditional methods and procedures? Is there room for creative or novel approaches? The less he specifies specific methods when he delegates, the more he creates opportunity for growth. Can staff specialists assist him in finding a better method for reaching his goal? Their help may be well worth considering. That's why they are there.

As an exercise in formulating his plans, it would be well to determine whether or not he has answered all these questions. The chances are, that if he has, it is a reasonably well conceived plan. Another check on his planning skill would be to analyze a project gone wrong to determine which of these questions were ignored or improperly answered in formulating his plans. In the final analysis these questions are the key to sound planning no matter how elementary they might seem.

Difficulties in Planning

Supervisors ought to recognize that they face some genuine difficulties or limitations in their attempts to plan the work in their departments. The pressure of many jobs and responsibilities limits the time they have for planning. Supervisors lack control over some factors in their plans, such as goals which may be set for them. The frustrations of many supervisors are reflected in the following difficulties in planning:

1. Lack of know-how

Many supervisors shrug off their planning responsibility with the comment, "I haven't the faintest idea of how to go about it." For the great majority there's no reason for having to go it alone. This chapter contains some suggestions on how to handle basic planning; supervisors can also always find help from the boss, other good planners, or staff specialists. That Carl Cramer went to see Burt Hall is a good example of a way of getting started.

2. The time required

Planning inevitably requires time. Invariably it will save the supervisor much more time than it takes. Unfortunately planning time must be spent before the activity begins. It's too late to go back to plan after things go wrong. Planning is deciding in advance what is to be done.

3. Pressure of other work

Planning is a mental activity. Current work demands the supervisor's attention. When faced with day-to-day decisions, he tends to give planning secondary priority. Planning is difficult at best when he is interrupted by having to make on-the-spot decisions. That's why Burt did his daily planning before the shift began and his weekly planning on Friday afternoon, when things had quieted down.

4. Absence of similar problems

The expenditure of time and effort sometimes doesn't seem worth it when the problem or project isn't likely to recur. Why develop a plan that will never be used again?

5. Tendency toward inflexibility

Many supervisors report that plans limit their freedom of action, and well they might if supervisors don't retain their flexibility. Burt Hall became annoyed when things interfered with his projected plans. Once his plans were set, he was determined to accomplish his goals, perhaps even sacrificing time that might be required by more important developments. Sometimes supervisors have a tendency to rely forever on a good working plan. They think that if it worked for them last year, it's good this year and should be next year. This type of thinking naturally stifles creativity, but it's more a deficiency in the individual than it is in the concept of sound planning.

In summary, it is important to recognize that planning is frequently the difference between the haphazard, chaotic operation and the smoothly functioning department. Planning separates the manager from the door. If he can't plan, he can't supervise!

HIGHLIGHTS

1. Job knowledge for today's supervisor is only in part a knowledge of the technical aspects of the work done in the department. More important is his knowledge and skill in implementing the management process—planning, organizing, directing, and controlling. Management is planning.
2. Planning is determining what needs to be done, who will do it, and when it has to be done.

3. One of the keys to a supervisor's effectiveness is his ability to manage his own time. Personal time management starts with an analysis of how he is currently spending his time. Additional suggestions include finding some time each day for uninterrupted planning, laying out the work he wants to accomplish, setting priorities, and delegating.

4. Some of the consequences of poor planning are:
   a. Lower production
   b. Dissatisfaction among employees
   c. Higher costs
   d. Misunderstanding and confusion
   e. Pressure from above
   f. Poor-quality work
   g. Accidents
   h. Lessened chance for promotion and advancement

5. Benefits of good planning include the elimination of the undesirable consequences of poor planning and in addition these positive results:
   a. Better coordination
   b. More effective control of operations
   c. Easier delegation
   d. More economical use of resources
   e. Increased personal effectiveness
   f. Tendency toward improvement

6. Examples of the types of planning a supervisor gets involved in are:
   a. Participation in setting goals
   b. Improvement programs
   c. Personnel management in the department
   d. Production planning
   e. Organization of work In the department
   f. Maintenance
   g. Paper work and reports
   h. Changes
   i. Communications
   j. Personal time

7. Planning is fundamentally a matter of answering the key planning questions:
   a. *What* is to be done (goals, results, objectives)?

   b. *When* will it be done?
   c. *Where* will it be done?
   d. *Who* will do it?
   e. *How* will it be done?
8. Some of the very real difficulties faced in doing a better job of planning in a department are:
   a. Lack of know-how
   b. The time required
   c. Pressure of other work
   d. Absence of similar problems
   e. Tendency toward inflexibility

DISCUSSION QUESTIONS

1. What is your opinion of the attitude often expressed that if a man has leadership ability, he doesn't need job knowledge and can supervise in any department?

2. Do you agree or disagree with the statement that a supervisor who can't plan can't manage? Why?

3. Make a list of as many activities and duties as you can that occupy a supervisor's time during the day. What suggestions could you make to find more time for planning?

4. Are there any disadvantages to planning carefully all the department's activities?

5. Why should a supervisor's inability to plan have any effect on dissatisfaction among employees in his department?

6. What reasons might there be for the statement that there's a tendency on the part of a good planner to want to do a better job next time?

7. If you were planning a departmental house-cleaning campaign, what are some of the considerations you would take into account in your initial planning?

8. Suppose you were planning a new program to get everyone to cooperate in wearing eye protection. Outline how you would answer the planning questions *who, what, where, when* and *how*. Make whatever assumptions you like.

SUGGESTIONS FOR FURTHER STUDY

Batten, J. D.
Tough-minded Management
Chapters 5 and 6, American Management Association, New York, 1963

Bittel, Lester R.
What Every Supervisor Should Know, 2d ed.
Chapter 26, McGraw-Hill Book Company, New York, 1968

Black, James, and Guy Ford
Front-line Management
Chapters 24 and 25, McGraw-Hill Book Company, New York, 1963

Gardiner, Glenn, and Associates
Managerial Skills for Supervisors
Chapters 1 and 2, Elliott Service Company, Mount Vernon, N.Y., 1960

Heyel, Carl
Management for Modern Supervisors
Chapter 10, American Management Association, New York, 1962

CHAPTER
ELEVEN

GIVING
DIRECTIONS
AND
ORDERS

THE CASE OF SAM PITMAN

It had been four days since Burt Hall had delegated the supervision of a thirty-day housekeeping campaign to Sam Pitman. With over ten years' experience under his belt, Sam was an old-timer at the age of twenty-seven. Burt liked Sam, even though Sam rubbed a lot of people the wrong way. Sam was eager and enthusiastic. A topnotch producer, he had developed into a reasonably good trainer after some sad early experiences. Sam jumped at this new assignment as an opportunity to show what he could do. Perhaps he had been perceptive enough to see that Burt was trying him out on a job requiring supervisory responsibility.

Before Burt had even finished explaining that the campaign was to be plantwide, Sam was popping with ideas of what could be done in Assembly Department B. He would divide the department into three sections and have one man in charge of each section. Of course, he personally would supervise the overall campaign, but it would help to have someone closer to the work carrying out his assignments. Burt gave Sam full authority—within reason, he said—to make their department the sharpest in the company.

That same afternoon Sam came back to Burt with the organization of his campaign all set. He would put Phil Knudson in charge of the north section. Arnie Ross could handle the central section, and Gus Schulz could take charge of the south section, where Sam worked.

Burt asked Sam if he had cleared the assignments with the three "deputies." He hadn't. "Don't worry about that, though," Sam assured

230

Burt. "Getting their cooperation is my responsibility. You don't have to fret, Burt. They'll do what I want them to do."

It was clear to Burt that Sam relished this assignment. What was it he had been told about delegation? You have to give subordinates freedom of action and decision if they are to develop. Well, if Sam says not to worry about it, then maybe a hands-off policy is best, Burt thought. But, doggone it, it sure requires some confidence in your subordinates.

Burt didn't see much of Sam after that, but he knew Sam was busy. It almost seemed that Sam was avoiding him to prove that he was capable of running the campaign without help. Burt's pleasure at seeing Sam take charge outweighed his uneasiness in letting go of the reins in a project where Burt wanted to make a really good showing. As each day passed, Burt showed less concern about the campaign, confident that Sam would come for help if he needed it. Also there was evidence that cleanup activity was under way. His choice of Sam, he was now convinced, had been a good one.

Arnie Ross gave Burt the first clue that things might not be going as well as he had hoped. Four boxes of subassemblies that Burt had set aside for future use and that could now be utilized had been thrown out. They were perfectly good, but they had not met the government specifications for which they had originally been produced. Burt, rather than scrapping them, had saved them because they could be used on nongovernment orders. The production order calling for their use had reached Arnie, and he came in to tell Burt that the four boxes had been junked.

Burt asked why, and Arnie said it was orders from Sam. He asked Arnie if he hadn't told Sam that the parts were being saved for an order that was sure to come. "How could I?" Arnie countered. "You just said to store them over in the corner. You didn't say why."

A little impatient, Burt said, "For heaven's sake, Arnie, if I told you to store them, you should have known it was to use them. At least you might have checked with me before you junked them."

"Now wait a minute," Arnie said. "I don't like getting caught in the middle. I just do what I'm told. You said to store them in the corner. OK, I stored. Sam comes along and says to get rid of them. Sure, I started to question it. But Sam says they go out, and he's running the cleanup. So what am I supposed to do? Besides, I don't like the way Sam is bossing me around. He says you put him in charge, but a little bit of authority sure went to his head. He gives orders like my old drill sergeant. It burns me up being told to do things like a little kid. You've never been that way, Burt. Why does he have to be? Honestly, I thought of checking with you, but then I figured that Sam probably had already checked and that he'd get sore at me for second-guessing him. So I just do what I'm told—no trouble that way. If you've got a beef, see Sam—not me. I was just following orders, and that's what I'll keep on doing the best I know how."

Burt apologized to Arnie. He said that Arnie was right and that they would just have to write the whole thing off to experience. He complimented Arnie on the improved appearance of the central section, asked him to pass the good word on to the others, but asked him not to say anything about the problem of the scrapped subassemblies. The order would just have to be held up until they could be replaced.

It was Arnie's comments about Sam's way of giving orders that concerned Burt most. It was inconvenient not to have those subassemblies. The delay would be more costly than the dollar value of the parts. But if Sam's order-giving pattern was being repeated in the other sections, more trouble could be expected. Checking up on a guy behind his back is a sneaky thing to do, Burt thought. But it might be wiser than sticking your head in the sand and hoping nothing would happen. Heading north out of his office, Burt decided on a little talk with Phil Knudson and a brief informal inspection of the area.

Improvement in the appearance of the area was obvious as Burt glanced around, and he was smiling as he walked over to Phil's bench. Phil really was one of the old-timers, and as steady as they come. Any time you needed cooperation, Phil could always be counted on. Before Harry Gates retired Burt had thought that Phil would be the new supervisor. It was only the difference in their ages that had tipped the scales in Burt's favor; Phil had just turned sixty.

After a couple of friendly exchanges about the improvement in the appearance of the area, Burt decided to come directly to the point of his visit. "Sam is really going after things," Burt commented. "How are you two making out? He's not moving too fast, is he, Phil?"

Phil looked at Burt several seconds, weighing his answer. Then he smiled and said, "Maybe you're going to have some trouble because of him, Burt, but it won't be from me. He's an eager beaver, but he does have a head on his shoulders. What he lacks in tact he makes up in enthusiasm. You can get along with Sam if you know how to take him. He gets carried away with a program like this and kind of shoves his ideas down your throat—do this, do that. You know what I mean. Most of his ideas are pretty darned good, so I just overlook his manners, and we get along fine. We've gone him a couple better than he expected, and everybody feels good. Both the fellows and the girls want to show him they can do a better job than he ever thought of. He's quick to give them a pat on the back, and he fakes a big surprised look when he comes around and sees what they've done. They like him now, and the important thing is that things are looking better than they have for quite a while.

"Burt, I don't like to carry stories out of school," Phil continued. "But you may have a problem developing down at the other end. Gus was up here yesterday afternoon, and he was just plain mad. He claimed he was going to knock Sam's block off. You know what Gus can be like when he gets his dander up."

"Say no more, Phil," Burt replied, "I know you don't want to be telling tales. I'll look into it right away; and, Phil, I do appreciate the cooperation you've given us up here. Things really do look good." Deciding not to waste any time getting to Gus, Burt started walking down to the other end of the department. As he passed his office, Arnie, who answered the phone in his office, flagged him down. "Hey, Burt, Oscar Palmer was just on the phone asking where that stuff for the Allied job is. Everything is ready in final assembly except for our stuff."

"That should have gone down an hour ago," Burt said as he walked by. "I'm on my way down there now. I'll check on it." Burt wondered whether the truckers had fouled things up. The job had been pretty well along when he had checked it last night and promised Oscar that things wouldn't be held up on their account. Sam and Gus were engaged in heated debate when Burt approached. At a glance around the area, Burt could see that the Allied job hadn't progressed from the previous evening. Another hour, possibly two, would be needed to finish it up. Several employees were engaged in cleaning activities and were apparently enjoying the argument between Sam and Gus.

As Burt walked up, Gus was saying, "Don't hand me any of that 'That's what I mean' jazz. We're doing exactly what you told us, and you made it pretty damned clear that you didn't want it any other way. Now get off my back so I can get my cleaning done."

"I'm ordering you to get back on that Allied job and get it finished before Burt gets down here," Sam shouted.

"You're too late," Gus sneered. "Here he comes now. And who in hell do you think you are, ordering us to do production work? Are you the foreman now that you took over the cleaning detail?"

Burt had heard enough to know that a number of the employees were putting a priority on cleaning over production in order to spite Sam. Quietly he suggested to both Gus and Sam that they get hustling on the Allied job. Stopping at the workplace of each person who was involved in Allied work, Burt asked them each to drop what they were doing and rush the Allied subassemblies as much as they could. He explained to them that it was an extremely hot job and that all the other components were in final assembly waiting for them to finish. Each one seemed to be eager to cooperate and relieved to see the tension subside.

With everybody working on the rush job, Burt walked over to Sam and quietly asked him what had been going on. Sam said that every time he had tried to get any cooperation from Gus, he met with resistance. He got so fed up with the lack of cooperation from the whole gang that he ordered Gus and the rest of them to get the cleanup started no matter what—"I meant that I didn't want any more alibis and excuses." Sam told Burt that he was sure that Gus got them to set aside the Allied job just to make a fool of him.

Burt asked Sam if he could bring his lunch down to the office at noon and eat with him. The appointment confirmed, Burt stopped next at Gus's bench to get his side of the story. "For two cents I'd bust that smart aleck in the teeth," Gus blurted out, nodding his head in Sam's direction. "I hate to say it, Burt, but you really pulled a boner giving that punk any authority. He's another Hitler. He's been pushing us around ever since you gave him that cleanup job. There's not a one of us here that doesn't figure we could show those guys up at the other end, but we can't take Sam's bossing us like grade-schoolers.

"This morning before the shift ever started, he blew his stack. He said he didn't give a damn what we were doing, that we better get this place cleaned up or there'd be hell to pay. He acted as if he meant it, so I got the guys going. I think he just remembered the Allied job when you came up, because then he said we'd better get going on that. I told him we hadn't finished cleaning, and he blew his stack again."

Burt again asked Gus to put all his effort on rushing the Allied job along and simply said that they would get things straightened out as quickly as possible. Gus was industriously working, with a smile on his face, before Burt could finish his statement. Hurrying back to the office, Burt decided what he would say to Oscar Palmer when he called him. Then his thoughts turned to delegation. "It sure is a tricky business," he thought. "This is the second time I've gotten burned—and both times Sam Pitman has been involved. I've got to admit that I was to blame the first time for not teaching him something about training. This time it wasn't my fault—or was it?"

He was still talking to himself as he walked into his office, shut the door, and picked up the phone to call Mr. Palmer.

1. How should we evaluate Burt's selection of Sam Pitman to take charge of the housekeeping campaign?

2. What are some of the strengths and weaknesses in Burt's delegating techniques?
3. How can we account for the varied responses Sam got to his orders from Phil, Arnie, and Gus?
4. What principles of order-giving can we identify from Burt's and Sam's instructions to the employees in Assembly Department B?
5. What should Burt say to Sam at lunchtime?

MANAGEMENT IS DIRECTING

Once a supervisor has planned and organized the work of the department, the next step—the vital step—in the management process is to put his plans in motion. Giving directions unleashes his plans and begins their implementation. At this stage of the management process, everyone acknowledges the key role of the supervisor. Even those who play down the supervisor's role as a manager admit that he initiates the action in his department with orders he gives.

So much of what we have discussed thus far in this book culminates in the order-giving process. A supervisor's skills in motivation are reflected in how he gives directions. Good orders are a matter of communication and the creation of understanding between the one who gives the order and the one who receives it. It would be difficult to differentiate between giving directions and instructing. The principles are the same for training as they are for giving directions. Maintaining a positive climate for giving orders depends in part upon a supervisor's knowledge of individual differences and the philosophy of discipline. The process of giving orders and directions involves not only issuing an order but that part of the management process which gives direction to the entire department. Direction is the reason for a supervisor's being a part of management.

Giving orders is so basic to supervision we tend to take it for granted. Every supervisor gives orders. It's his job. How often does a supervisor evaluate the effect of his orders on personnel? Burt Hall took Sam's order-giving skills for granted, and the results were nearly disastrous. If anyone had asked Sam if he knew how to give orders, Sam would have been insulted. Of course he knew how to give orders. He'd told Burt not to worry, hadn't he? We can all communicate— give orders, give directions—so we forget that this can be done more or less effectively. This chapter reviews the critical elements of giving good orders.

THE ORDER–GIVING CLIMATE

Everyone who holds a supervisory position has been placed in a role of authority. He has been given the authority to make decisions and give orders to those under him. He is in charge or in command of his department by decree from higher management. Most supervisors start their supervision only with the authority of rank. People do what the supervisor tells them because they know he is the boss. Unfortunately, many supervisors never graduate from that level of authority. Sam Pitman was starting off down this road—order, demand, command. "Do it because I say so." "I am in authority." Unless Burt lets Sam see the consequences of such tactics, the chances that Sam will be able to mature in supervision will be slim. Using rank or authority only is the mark of immature management, and the resulting climate in the department is clouded by tension and hostility.

In contrast to Sam's first supervisory directing, Burt demonstrated that he had earned for himself an authority based on respect rather than rank. Burt had authority because he was Burt, not because he was boss. The authority of respect grows as employees develop confidence in their leader. It grows out of fair treatment and firm direction. The existence of respected authority in a department results in a climate of cooperation—voluntary effort to achieve more than is asked or expected.

As an exercise in analyzing climate, a supervisor might first look at how he feels toward the orders, directions, and instructions he gets from above. Is the feeling he has toward the boss the same one he would want the employees under him to have toward him? Answers, of course, will vary. What kind of climate exists now in his department, as a result of the orders he gives? Can he empathize—put himself on the receiving end of his directions? How would he feel and react toward the orders he gives? This exercise alone has caused many to modify the language or the approach they use in their instructions.

Generally we recognize three levels of climate, according to how a work force is directed. Let's identify each level and relate it to the case of Sam Pitman.

Climate of cooperation

When people accept a direction willingly and follow it enthusiastically by giving more than is asked or expected, we can assume that a climate of cooperation exists. We found evidence of the climate of cooperation under Phil Knudson's direction. Phil's was an informal authority born of respect. Here we saw employees giving more than they were asked. Most supervisors would naturally like to have this kind of response to their orders.

Climate of compliance

At this level people do what is expected of them—what they are told to do. They seldom do more or less than is ordered. Compliance is automatic, without any questioning of authority. There is no enthusiasm in this climate. Unintentional mistakes are frequently made because people do exactly what they are told. Arnie Ross responded in this manner to his direction from Sam. He said, "I was just following orders, and that's what I'll keep on doing the best I know how." He might have added, because he was thinking it, "Don't expect me to do anything on my own without being told." In a climate of compliance initiative on the part of workers and the creativity that results in ideas and suggestions for improvement are lacking. Compliance is compliance—no more, no less.

Climate of hostile compliance

Stormy weather! This response to orders is one of compliance with harmful intent. The one who receives orders complies because he must bow to the authority of rank. He waits for an opportunity, however, to do exactly what he is told and embarrass his supervisor in the process. Gus Schulz's attitude is a good example of hostile compliance. He had bucked Sam's orders until Sam told him to clean up no matter what. Gus's thinking probably would have sounded something like, "Ah-ha, did you hear what he said? 'Clean up no matter what.' Now we'll get this son of a gun. Let the Allied job sit. He said no matter what. OK, wise guy, we'll clean; and you can explain to Burt, or Ray, or Old Man Palmer why the Allied job didn't get finished. We're only doing what you told us, Sammy boy." There are very few who could give every order in such a way that it couldn't be followed in a hostile manner. Supervisors have to trust that their supervision will never create such an unhealthy climate.

UNDERSTANDING DELEGATION

Among the concepts of management that are frequently misunderstood and misapplied, delegation probably ranks first. Delegation can be the answer to many supervisors' problems, such as gaining time for managing, extending their effectiveness and influence, and developing subordinates. Misconceptions of what delegation means have produced results that can lead supervisors away from it rather than make them explore its full potential. For example, the supervisor who regards delegation as a means of dumping any unpleasant task soon finds his subordinates resisting rather than seeking it. This is also true of the supervisor who puts so many conditions on his assignments that he really isn't delegating at all because he permits no freedom of action.

Characteristics of Delegation

What is delegation? Basically, it's the entrusting of an activity to another person. It may be for an extended period of time or, as in the case of Sam Pitman, for the completion of a project. When we come right down to it, delegation means giving others the right to make our decisions for us. It's within the context of this last statement that we see the elements of risk that cause many managers to shy away from delegation. Let's look at four characteristics of delegation which define the risk more clearly.

1. Freedom of action

Delegation does not mean sending someone off on an errand or getting him to perform some routine menial task. It means giving another the right to act, to decide, and to direct in our place. One characteristic of delegation is that the individual has freedom of action—that the employee makes the supervisor's decisions for him. Most executives point to their responsibility for having to make decisions as a key factor in their growth. By encouraging a subordinate to make decisions, a supervisor puts him in a climate where he will grow. Growth is one of the prime objectives in delegation, but growth can't be realized unless freedom of action is allowed. A supervisor delegates the results he wants, leaving the method of reaching the goal in the hands of the subordinate. Sure, it's risky! Burt found that out when he turned the housekeeping campaign over to Sam Pitman.

2. Shared decisions

The subordinate's decision becomes the supervisor's decision. If he makes mistakes, they are the supervisor's mistakes. If he does well, it is a reflection on the supervisor. Many managers want it one way— share the credit, but pass on the blame. Still other managers see it another way—good decisions show them up, and poor decisions demonstrate how indispensable they are. They are the fearful ones to whom the risks of delegation are too great. One of the truly satisfying experiences in supervision occurs when a subordinate makes an excellent accounting of himself. An example of the shared decision can be found in Arnie Ross's junking the subassemblies on Sam's orders. Sam made a decision, and Burt shared in that decision as if it were his own.

3. Shared responsibility

We often hear the statement that responsibility can't be delegated. If a supervisor means to absolve himself of responsibility by delegating it, then responsibility cannot be delegated. He cannot rid himself of his responsibilities by giving them to others. He does, however, create new responsibilities when he delegates. His subordinates become responsible to him while he retains his responsibility to higher management. In this sense the supervisor does delegate responsibility. Burt was responsible for the success of the housekeeping campaign whether he delegated its execution or directed it himself. Sam was responsible to Burt, and Burt was responsible to the plant manager. Both have responsibility for the success of the campaign.

4. Granting of authority

Responsibility can't be created without bestowing commensurate authority. No one ever wants to be held responsible for an activity over which he has no control. Many supervisors today are deeply concerned about being responsible for the quantity and quality of production when they have no authority to make decisions that affect production. Whenever a supervisor delegates an activity to a subordinate, some of his first considerations should be whether or not he is giving him the authority he needs to perform.

Defining delegation in terms of these four characteristics demonstrates the potential risks and rewards inherent in the process. Enhancement of promotional potential is certainly not the least of the potential rewards. Many successful supervisors regard the opportunity to increase their personal contribution to the organization as reward enough for proper delegation. Why then, do so many resist delegation? Let's look at just a few of the reasons:

1. Fear of costly mistakes by subordinates
2. Fear that subordinates might perform too well and show up the supervisor
3. Fear of losing control of an activity
4. Fear of loss of prestige or status
5. Reluctance to give up activities that a supervisor performs well
6. Having no one to delegate to

Not having a subordinate to delegate to is commonly given as the real reason for not delegating. If it's an opinion shared by many supervisors, perhaps we should consider the problem of finding people to delegate to. It is not necessary for a supervisor to have a person designated officially as his assistant before he has a candidate for delegation. There may be several people who can perform an activity in an enlargement of their jobs. Figure 11 suggests a technique for finding potential employees to delegate to. It's a simple inventory of the activities a supervisor performs, why he performs them, who is able to perform them now, and who can be trained to perform them.

Burt Hall might have used such a technique to help him find assistance on his job. In Chapter 7 he picked out three men to perform the second activity listed in Figure 11. When the time-consuming housekeeping campaign was announced, Burt selected Sam in order to test his potential for supervisory work. If a supervisor can think in terms of the ability of several employees to perform a variety of activities instead of in terms of one assistant, he may be in a better position to ease into the practice of delegation.

What to Delegate

Activity	Why is it performed?	Who can do it now?	Who can be trained?
1. Plan job assignments	Utilize manpower; give everyone a chance to do his best	Smith	Jones
2. Train new employees	Increase productivity; improve job satisfaction; improve work quality		Smith Brown
3. Make out production reports	Inform management of department's progress; provide basis for corrective action and decisions	Smith	Olson

Figure 11. B 87 · is a fool.

Delegation Techniques

Here are some suggestions on how to delegate that have been gleaned from a large number of supervisors who have experienced the pleasure of watching their subordinates develop through the process of delegation.

1. Assign as many tasks as you safely can

There's a double advantage to this that should be obvious. First, it frees a supervisor for more real management activity and creative work. Second, the more people he has carrying out delegated activity, the more the growth in his department.

2. Expect and accept some mistakes

If mistakes can be looked upon as an opportunity for further training, delegation becomes a challenge rather than a threat.

3. Give sufficient authority to complete the task

If a supervisor can empathize and put himself in the shoes of his subordinates, he will very quickly see the need for that authority. He can't do his job without it—he shouldn't expect his subordinates to.

4. Delegate according to the results desired, not according to the method people should use

Here is the heart of successful delegation. For subordinates, the chance to demonstrate what they can do depends on the freedom of action they are allowed. Little real growth is likely when activity is narrowly and rigidly restricted.

5. Let others know to whom the task has been delegated.

To give his subordinates every possible chance to succeed, a supervisor will want to let anyone concerned know who is authorized to act in his place. Although Sam Pitman took advantage of his delegated authority and perhaps overstepped the bounds of good judgment in giving orders, there was evidence that Burt had let people know that Sam was in charge of the campaign. A supervisor can do much to pave a path of cooperation by letting others know that he wants his subordinates to receive the same help that he gets.

6. Call for progress reports, and schedule reviews

In other words, the supervisor shouldn't delegate and forget it. Mistakes can be minimized by inviting frequent progress reports until both the supervisor and the subordinate have confidence in the progress being made. Even though the supervisor has given a subordinate the right to make his decisions, the subordinate is accountable to his superior. The progress and review discussions provide the opportunity to coach the subordinate—to give him guidance.

The art of delegation is a delicate one. Trying to find the line between too much delegation and too little is difficult. How much freedom to allow has to be balanced against giving sufficient direction to guide subordinates. Too much direction tends to cause subordinates to lean on their supervisor. So he must give enough, but not too much.

Effective delegation requires a knowledge of the individual to whom a supervisor delegates and a clear idea of what he hopes to accomplish when he delegates. Successfull delegation allows the supervisor to fulfill his role as a manager who has a prime responsibility for the development of his subordinates. By relieving himself of the burden of routine, the supervisor will be in a much better position to spend his time on the management functions of planning, directing, and controlling. Management-minded supervisors delegate. In the process they increase their management-mindedness.

Order-giving Techniques

Sam Pitman said, "Get going on this cleanup right now—no matter what." And a little later, "I'm ordering you to get back on that Allied job and get it finished before Burt gets down here." Burt, on the other hand, asked each of the group to set aside the cleanup activities and get things going on the Allied job. Then he asked Sam to have lunch with him. Within the span of a minute or two they demonstrated the two most common techniques used in giving orders—the demand and the request.

To be sure, many variations often make the distinction between the two more difficult. A request may be stated with such an emphasis and tone of voice that it is received as a demand with no questions asked. Experience indicates that the milder, more tactful request is a much more pleasant form to use. By and large it gives better results, and with good reason. The request, even though it is an order, gives the receiver a sense of participation in an activity. It dignifies his position by allowing him to decide whether or not he will comply. For example, "Joe, will you see that those three boxes get down to shipping before three o'clock so they can go out today?" Joe responds in the affirmative; the boxes get to shipping; and the order goes on its way.

If there is some reason why Joe might have trouble carrying out the order, it is much easier to modify a request than a demand. Some supervisors feel that they weaken their position by framing their orders as requests, that no room for debate should be allowed the receiver, and that action is quicker when commands are given. But those who use the request find that it works well. It gets the work done and establishes a pleasant relationship between them and their subordinates without any relinquishing of control of the department. As a supervisor's relationship with his people matures and his confidence in his management ability develops, he will use the request form of order-giving almost exclusively.

Is there a place for the demand or the command? Of course there is. Emergency situations requiring quick reactions call for commands. An employee who has consistently resisted orders may very well justify the demand. For example, an employee who refuses to follow safety rules may be ordered to do so. The lazy, the careless, the indifferent, the chronic griper, the gossip—all may need more rigid direction. But by and large a supervisor will want to use the request as a means of getting better results in a climate more enjoyable for him and his subordinates.

Characteristics of a Good Order

The enthusiastic response and hostile compliance are the extremes in the reactions of employees to the orders they receive. The case of Sam Pitman illustrates both extremes. Everyone wants cooperation and enthusiasm to result from his orders, but what criteria determine whether an order has been good or not? The following five character- istics of most good orders offer an evaluation checklist. A supervisor might ask, "How do my orders measure up, and where might I improve them?"

1. Orders should be clear

An order is a comunication. The purpose of all communication is understanding. The supervisor's idea of what he wants when he gives an order is very clear. It's a challenge to see that the one who receives the order gets the same idea. Remember the blacksmith who told his new apprentice, "I'll hold the shoe on the anvil. When I nod my head, you hit it with the hammer." The result was a broken skull.

Making an order clear to the receiver is almost always helped by explaining why the order is given. Wanting to do well, employees can cooperate better and use their initiative more if they know why they're doing a job. For example, Burt told Arnie to store the boxes in a corner without telling him why. If Burt had told Arnie what he had in mind, there's no doubt that Arnie would have checked with Burt before scrapping the parts.

A supervisor's language should be as simple as possible, and his orders issued in words the receiver will understand.

2. Orders should be concise

Too much detail can be just as harmful as not enough. Why waste time by giving more detail than is necessary to accomplish the desired results? Employees tend to respect a supervisor who can say what he wants clearly and concisely.

3. Orders should be complete

As we noted in our discussion of delegation, giving orders requires a balanced approach. We have just said that supervisors should not burden an order with too much detail—that they should be concise. Yet the importance of giving all the information that is necessary remains. How much is too much? When the order has been issued, an employee ought to know what is to be done (that is, the results expected) and when it is to be done. He should understand what standards of performance will apply in judging his performance. In a previous example, Joe was asked to take some boxes down to Shipping. He knew his performance would be judged satisfactory if Shipping had the boxes by 3:00 P.M. That way they could be shipped that day.

4. Orders should be considerate

It would be more accurate to say that someone giving an order should be considerate. Courtesy and consideration make the one who gets an order more kindly disposed toward his assignment. If he feels he has a part to play in determining the successful execution of an order, cooperation (the highest level of response) is most likely.

5. Orders should be reasonable

Surely this goes without saying. A moment's reflection, however, might reveal that an order that is entirely reasonable to the giver may not at all be reasonable to the receiver. Are the time, materials, and equipment available to do the job? Is the job within the scope of his ability to perform? Has he had experience? Has he been taught? Have the standards of performance the supervisor has set taken into consideration the employee's abilities, experience, and training? Many supervisors have found that the effect on employees' morale of issuing unreasonable orders can be disastrous. This is particularly true when the practice is repeated frequently. Empathy can provide valuable measures of the reasonableness of orders.

The Order-giving Process

Early in this chapter we took note of the similarities between giving orders and instructing. They are both forms of communication. They both seek to create understanding and to achieve results through others. Therefore in analyzing the steps in the order-giving process, we can expect to find similarities to instructing. Following these commonsense steps in giving orders should improve effectiveness: (1) plan, (2) explain, (3) check, (4) release, and (5) follow up. To the experienced manager accustomed to giving orders and direction, these steps are done automatically without much conscious thought. More complex orders require more attention to each phase. Failures in giving orders can generally be traced to the neglect of one or more of these steps. Let's look at them in a little more detail.

1. Plan

The planning questions are considered almost instantaneously on a short, uncomplicated order, but they are considered. Let's take an example. "Joe, hand me that wrench, will you?" The supervisor has determined *what* he wants—the wrench near Joe. In a split second he decides *who* is to do the job—Joe, because he's nearest to it. His tone of voice and inflection revealed that now is *when* he wants action. Deciding that he wants the wrench in his hands right here answers the *where* question. *How* was determined, and he asked Joe to hand it to him, not to throw it. In getting ready to give any order or direction, we decide what action we want, who we want to act, and what kind of order we should use, such as a spoken request or a written directive.

2. Explain

The receiver of the order must know what is expected of him. What the supervisor has planned is now communicated to the receiver, who wants to know what he's to do, how to do it, and when and where to do it. He's likely to be more cooperative and use his initiative if the supervisor has explained why he wants it done. The supervisor ensures quality when he explains what standards the performance will be judged on. For example, "There shouldn't be any streaks or smudges on the windows when you've finished." If the order is complex, the supervisor's plans may very well call for the same type of step-by-step explanation discussed in Chapter 7 under instructing.

3. Check

The feedback principle again! The supervisor should be certain that the order has been understood the way he intended it. Asking and encouraging questions helps him check on understanding. Getting employees to repeat orders gives him a good check on their understanding and provides an excellent chance to correct any misunderstanding. The supervisor takes unnecessary risks when he gives an order and fails to check the receiver's concept of what he wants before releasing him.

4. Release

In most cases the release is accomplished with a few simple words, but only after it is certain that the order has been received and understood. Action is initiated with such simple statements as: "OK, let's go." "Get it started right away, will you?" "Check with me if you're not sure." "Good luck." "I'll see you when you've finished." Sometimes encouragement is needed, sometimes a challenge. But in this step the supervisor demonstrates his confidence that the employee will be able to carry out the directive.

5. Follow up

The final test of whether or not a supervisor's orders and directions have been successful is the degree to which his goals have been achieved. There are other considerations, however, which will guide his future orders. How did the receiver perform during his execution of the order? Did he have difficulties that can be remedied the next time around? What adjustments are needed, if any? Evaluating the effectiveness of instruction will lead to the improvement of techniques in giving orders.

To these steps which describe the process of giving an order, we might add the advice of several hundred supervisors who have debated the problem at University of Wisconsin Supervisory Institutes in recent years.

1. Be sure to identify the results wanted

The supervisor should give the employee something to zero in on. He'll be able to come to his superior and say, "I've done it!"

2. Condition the person receiving the order

The supervisor should get him interested in carrying out the order. Motivation is the key to the enthusiasm with which assignments are handled. There's no more critical time to practice motivational skills than in the order-giving process.

3. Explain the "why" of directions

Man is a reasoning animal. A supervisor helps his subordinate help him when he explains why he wants the action he is ordering.

4. Build in feedback

Why take chances? Feedback assures a supervisor that his objectives will be accomplished, and it's so much easier to get a quick reading on understanding than it is to require the work to be done over.

5. Identify controls and procedures for reporting back

The supervisor should let the employee know what he should do when he has completed the assignment. Is he to report back, bring a receipt, write a memo, call the supervisor over, call an inspector? If his performance is to be evaluated, then he ought to know the standards by which his performance will be measured. He'll be more likely to excel if he can measure his own progress as he goes along.

6. Maintain an attitude of helpfulness

How easy it is for a supervisor to take the attitude that employees exist to do his bidding and for him to give orders without concern for their feelings. He should remember that the employees under him want to make him look good. Maintaining an attitude of helpfulness in giving orders is bound to benefit the supervisor in the long run.

In the management process, the directing phase starts the wheels in motion. Directing or giving orders is the dynamic phase—the action phase. The best plans can be upset by faulty orders. Fulfilling management responsibilities requires expert direction, and no matter how often or how long a supervisor has been giving orders, a frequent reevaluation of his skills will pay off. Complacency has no place in developing management-mindedness.

HIGHLIGHTS

1. Direction in the management process is the step that puts plans in motion—initiates the action.
2. Giving orders is so basic and fundamental in supervision that there is a tendency to take it for granted.
3. How orders are carried out depends on climate. All supervisors start on their supervisory jobs with the authority of rank. As they develop confidence and gain the trust of their subordinates, they acquire a different kind of authority—the authority of respect.
4. There are three levels of response to orders:
   a. Cooperation
   b. Compliance
   c. Hostile compliance
5. Delegation means giving others the right to make our decisions for us, and it is characterized by:
   a. Freedom of action

b. Sharing decisions

c. Sharing responsibility

d. Bestowing authority

6. Common reasons why supervisors avoid delegation include:

a. Fear of subordinates' mistakes

b. Fear that subordinates will show the supervisor up

c. Fear of loss of control over an activity

d. Fear of loss of status or prestige

7. Order-giving techniques generally fall into one of two classifications—a request or a demand. The former usually yields better results and is a more pleasant approach to use.

8. Good orders or directions are:

a. Clear

b. Concise

c. Complete

d. Considerate

e. Reasonable

9. Giving orders is a five-step process. These steps are usually carried out with little conscious effort. The steps are:

a. Plan

b. Explain

c. Check

d. Release

e. Follow up

DISCUSSION QUESTIONS

1. Explain this statement in your own words: "Giving orders is so basic that we tend to take it for granted."

2. Describe a supervisor you know who through his way of giving orders creates a climate of cooperation. What are some of his typical attitudes?

3. Describe a supervisor you know or have known who has come close to creating a climate of "hostile compliance" in his department. What attitudes and actions on his part produced that climate?

4. What possible risks does a supervisor face when he delegates a part of his job to his subordinates?

5. Which is a better practice, in your opinion—giving orders by

asking or demanding? What are the advantages and disadvantages of each approach?

6. Why is it important that the reasons for an order be explained to the employee?

7. Five characteristics of good orders and directions were identified in this chapter. Can you cite any more?

8. Write a memo giving directions on cleaning up a work area to a second-shift employee. Make any assumptions you wish. When you have finished, check it against the criteria of a good order.

SUGGESTIONS FOR FURTHER STUDY

Bittel, Lester R.
What Every Supervisor Should Know, 2d ed.
Chapter 16, McGraw-Hill Book Company, New York, 1968

Black, James, and Guy Ford
Front-line Management
Chapter 26, McGraw-Hill Book Company, New York, 1963

Famularo, Joseph J.
Supervisors in Action
Chapter 7, McGraw-Hill Book Company, New York, 1961

Gardiner, Glenn, and Associates
Managerial Skills for Supervisors
Chapter 10, Elliott Service Company, Mount Vernon, N.Y., 1960

CHAPTER
TWELVE

CONTROLLING EMPLOYEE PERFORMANCE

THE CASE OF THE INEPT INTERVIEWS

Burt Hall sat looking at the pile of completed performance-appraisal forms on his desk. In ten minutes Norm Wiley would be in to discuss his performance of the past six months. Wiley had been scheduled first because Burt had wanted to get things off to a good start. After Wiley, the number two man would be Dave Bangs in the afternoon. That's the way it would go—one in the morning, one in the afternoon until he got through the whole department. By the evening of the first day, with two of his better employees reviewed, Burt felt that he could analyze his results and improve as he went along.

This would be Burt's second round of performance appraisals since becoming supervisor of Assembly Department B. The first time around could hardly count, and Burt was determined that this time he was going to do a better job. His predecessor, Harry Gates, didn't have much patience with the whole idea of performance evaluation and review. He filled out the appraisal forms for Burt as his last official act and left the review interview for Burt to do. His advice was to just tell each employee what his rating was and give him a chance to object if he wanted to. Harry felt that the quicker you got it over, the quicker you could get back to concentrating on production. He kept the ratings on the high side, he told Burt, because then there wouldn't be any difficulty with the employees and because it made the department look good by comparison with others.

That entire first review had gone without incident. Everyone liked Burt. They felt that the ratings were Harry's, and signed the forms acknowledging the interview without much comment. When he had finished, Burt was relieved. But he was concerned that nothing much seemed to have been accomplished.

Determined this time to show his employees that he knew what he was doing, Burt had spent a considerable amount of time preparing the forms. He worked on them three evenings at home in addition to the time spent in his office. Generally the individual evaluations were quite high, but they were deserved. The production results were right there to back them up, and quality in the department was excellent. Naturally there had been a few problems and problem children over the past six months, but on the whole Burt felt good about the evaluation of his department's performance represented by the completed forms on his desk. Burt regarded this job as a chance to get really close to his employees. That was why he scheduled Norm Wiley and Dave Bangs first. They were easy to talk to; they were cooperative; but most of all they had won high ratings from Burt, and it would be a pleasure to tell them so individually.

The procedure outlined by the personnel department called for the supervisor to make his evaluation of each employee, bring the employee in and discuss the evaluation with him, and get the evaluation form signed by the employee to show that the discussion had taken place. The signing of the form did not mean that the employee agreed with the rating but simply that it had been discussed with him. He had the opportunity to register any disagreement with the evaluation either on the form or by contacting the personnel department. There hadn't been a single such objection on Burt's first round six months ago.

The form was a simple two-page booklet calling for an evaluation of the employee's quantity or volume of work, quality or accuracy, reliability, cooperativeness, versatility, loyalty, strengths, weaknesses, and promotability. Training necessary to make the person a more valuable employee was to be covered in the last section.

Burt hadn't been satisfied with Harry Gates's off-the-cuff rating on all factors the last time—especially on quantity and quality of work. Since production records were available on almost all his employees, Burt pulled out the achievements of each and based his quality and quantity ratings on "the facts," as he called them. His evaluation of reliability was based on tardiness and attendance records even though he felt that a less objective rating was wanted. The rest of the form required him "to play God," as he said. Being human, he was never sure that his ratings were free of his personal bias. Whenever he could, Burt found specific examples to back up his ratings on cooperativeness, versatility, loyalty, strengths, and weaknesses. Many times he wondered, though, how much his choice of examples might be reinforcing his bias. He had done his best, however, and now he was ready to begin. Burt was so anxious to get started on the right foot with Norm that he trembled just a little bit when Norm poked his head in the office door and asked if the time had come.

Shaking hands with Norm at the end of the interview felt awkward to Burt, but it seemed to be the only way to signal the finish. Doggone it, the whole interview was awkward. It hadn't gone at all as he had wanted it to. From the time Norm walked in, he wasn't himself. He seemed to freeze up. His manner was pleasant enough. There was no disagreement with Burt's evaluation. Burt began to feel that they were like a boss with a rookie employee rather than two friends discussing a subject of mutual interest. Burt had wanted informality, but the result was formal and consequently uncomfortable for Burt.

Burt had avoided looking at the evaluations from the last period. He wanted to be certain that he was not influenced by them in any way. He was surprised to find Norm disappointed with the new ratings. It turned out that in most cases they were lower, even though Norm's performance had improved. His quantity of production, which had definitely improved, now had a lower rating. Burt's explanation that nobody rated any higher, and that he was using a new system based on factual information, had a hollow ring. Norm accepted the rating, but Burt had the feeling that he might go to the personnel department to explain that he hadn't really slipped.

For some reason, the whole tenor of the interview was more negative than positive. Burt had intended it to be very positive. He had wanted to tell Norm how pleased he was with his progress, but he wound up several times trying to justify the lower ratings. Burt explained to Norm that his philosophy was to rate a little low to stimulate improvement and that he actually thought more of Norm's work than the evaluation showed. Thinking about that after the interview, Burt felt that it was a stupid thing to say.

Burt rated Norm about midpoint on promotability. The definition on the form at that point said, "shows promise; could be promoted." There were two places above and below to make checks, so that Norm felt that Burt's rating really said nothing. His disappointment was obvious when he told Burt that he did hope to get ahead in the company. Burt wondered, as Norm talked, how many more would feel the same way. He had been very careful to avoid letting a high rating on promotability trap him into making a commitment. His thoughts so occupied him that he wasn't really listening when Norm said something to the effect that another department might possibly offer him a better chance for promotion. The affirmative nod of Burt's head brought another disappointed look to Norm's face, and the subject was dropped.

After that there were some offhand remarks from both intended to terminate the interview, but neither felt that he wanted to accept the responsibility for bringing it to an official conclusion—perhaps because no conclusions had been reached. The awkward pauses at last caused Burt to extend his hand to Norm and thank him for coming in.

A meeting, five phone calls, and a minor breakdown kept Burt from any mental analysis of the interview until it was time for Dave Bangs to arrive for his. In the back of Burt's mind he knew that he himself had been responsible for the unsatisfactory interview in the morning. He knew he had missed an opportunity to motivate Norm and to build his interest in the job.

The interview with Dave was almost a replay of the morning. Sure, the questions were different; the words were different; it was a different man across the desk. But the coolness was still there where warmth had been wanted. Disappointment masked Dave's face the same as it had Norm's. Tension got a firmer grip on Burt's feelings and strained his reasoning powers even more. The same awkward handshake terminated the interview and left Burt wondering how he would ever get through the rest of them.

"Why, oh, why," he thought, "didn't I compare these ratings with those from the last period? Just because I wanted these to be my own, I risked antagonizing two of my best men."

Dave had shown the same disappointment at the lower rating that Norm had. After getting Burt's explanation of what he was trying to do in quantifying the evaluation, Dave said, "Sure that's fine, but how do they know that in Personnel or in Palmer's office or wherever they decide on our raises? They look at this form and the last one and see my rating down. What chance have I got to get a raise?"

Burt explained that these evaluations weren't used to determine raises, but the words were hardly out of his mouth before the realization struck him that he really didn't know whether they were or not. Dave promptly asked what they were for if not raises, and Burt said he thought it was to be sure everybody got a chance to find out where he stood. Again, he wasn't certain that what he was saying was true. Dave mumbled something about not standing very well right now and Burt hastened to assure him that he was one of the best men in the department.

That last statement caused a wry smile to cross Dave's face, and he said, "Then a couple of other men are in for a rude awakening, because they figure they've been doing a lot better the last few months. They thought they got better than they deserved last time, so they've been looking forward to this time and getting what they deserve. Ha!"

Burt wasn't sure that he had said enough or too much, but when Dave was willing to sign the form, it seemed to be a good place to cut it off. Again there hadn't been any arguments. The real disappointment was that he hadn't achieved so much of what he had hoped for in these first two interviews. What had he hoped to accomplish? Well, he really couldn't put his finger on anything specific. He just wanted the relationship between him and his employees to be a lot better, and instead they seemed to be getting more strained.

Why, he wondered, when he was so pleased with his employees' performance, was he creating the impression that he was dissatisfied? Why, he asked himself, should good positive relationships suddenly become so strained at appraisal time? How could anything designed to be helpful and constructive have just the opposite effect? Burt put Dave and Norm's evaluation forms in an envelope along with those of Phil Knudson and Arnie Ross, whom he was going to talk to tomorrow. He would study them at home. Somehow he was going to have to find a way to improve his techniques. As things stood now, he was better off just going through the motions the way he had done the first time.

1. What strengths do we find in Burt's approach to appraising and reviewing his employees' performance?
2. How can we explain the results Burt had with his first two reviews in the light of his high hopes?
3. What objectives did Burt have for each review? What objectives should he have had?
4. How can he get better results from the reviews with the rest of his people?

MANAGEMENT IS CONTROLLING

We have defined the management process as planning, organizing, directing, and controlling. In the first chapters of this section on the supervisor's job knowledge, we discussed the planning, organizing, and directing phases of the cycle. Now we turn our attention to the final phase—control. The purpose of the control phase is to assure that what the supervisor has planned and directed is accomplished. Effective control is dependent on skillful execution of the planning phase of the management process, for plans provide the standards against which performance is measured in the control phase.

Management-minded supervision recognizes the controlling function as one of the most critical. Through the years with all the changes in the concepts of what supervision is, it has always been acknowledged that a supervisor controls his department, his people, his processes. He wants to know what the quality and quantity of his production is. If he is not meeting his standards, he takes corrective action to bring production back in line. The process of setting standards, measuring performance against those standards, and making the necessary corrections is what we mean by control. Even when the standards are set by higher-level management, the supervisor still functions as a controller in the measuring and adjusting activities.

The supervisor's control extends to a wide variety of departmental activities. First and foremost, production is his concern. In addition he wants to be sure that his use of equipment, tools, materials, supplies, and services yields the desired results. Control activities keep him abreast of his costs. One of the main items under his control is the performance of his subordinates. Individual improvement programs, such as cost-reduction and methods-improvement programs, also require control. To illustrate how often supervisors are engaged in control activities, here are but a few types of controls most of them use frequently: production schedules, production reports and records, time-and-motion studies, a wide variety of inspections for quality, blueprints and specifications, procedure manuals, standard costs, budgets, special cost reports, work measurement, audits and inventories, and employee performance appraisals. Most of the reports to members of higher management become the controls they use to measure progress on company plans.

It would be impossible to discuss specific controls in view of the wide variety of control activities supervisors engage in daily. For example, quality controls range all the way from proofreading a stencil in the office to 100-percent inspection of parts, to highly refined statistical quality-control programs. Our purposes will be adequately served, it seems, if we identify the key steps in the control function, relate control to other management functions, and finally analyze one major control system which is troublesome for many supervisors—employee performance appraisals or merit ratings.

Planning activities involve setting goals and objectives. These goals and objectives become the basis for control systems. For example, in planning a cost-reduction program, a supervisor may have set an overall goal of reducing his costs by $10,000 in a six-month period. He has a target! At the end of six months he will know whether he has exceeded his goal or fallen short of it. But why wait for six months to pass? Controls should give a means of determining progress throughout the cost drive rather than indicating failure after it's too late to do anything about it. The supervisor might decide to shoot for a $2,500 savings in each of the first three months, $1,000 the next two months, and $500 the last month. Now by comparing total achievement to date against his goals, he will know how successful his efforts are at any time during the cost-reduction drive. Thus he has performed the first two steps in the control function: (1) setting goals and standards at key points in a process, and (2) measuring performance against those standards.

The third step in the control function is taking corrective action or making adjustments. For an example, let's go back to our cost-reduction program and assume that midway through the six-month period total savings came to $4,500. At this point, the supervisor had expected to achieve $7,500. With only three months to realize the remaining $5,500, he is going to have to increase his efforts, change his strategy, or call for help.

The control function is a questioning activity that keeps the supervisor returning to the planning function in the management process. Planning and controlling are so integrated that it is difficult to set them apart. Planning sets goals; these goals become the basis for controls. If in the evaluation of progress the supervisor finds it necessary to revise his goals or standards, he is both controlling and planning. His plans are based on what his controls have told him in past experience is reasonable and possible, and his controls are set up on the basis of what he has planned. The two are so completely interwoven that it is difficult to discuss them separately.

Management-minded supervision and effective controlling are the same thing. The comment, "He's a supervisor who really knows what's going on in his department," is high praise. It is also an indication of effective control. Every supervisor wants to be regarded as a manager who is really in charge of things. Being in charge, being a manager, and being an effective controller are synonymous.

PERFORMANCE APPRAISALS: WHY?

Burt Hall, like many supervisors, has begun to wonder how performance appraisal, intended as a management control or tool, can have such devastating results. Intended to be constructive and helpful, it can blast morale to bits. The performance appraisal *is* a management tool, but like any tool, it must be properly used. Burt was using this tool with a deep-seated desire to use it well. It wasn't because of lack of effort that he experienced failure. His inability to achieve the desired results was caused by something revealed in his conversation with Dave Bangs. Burt couldn't explain to Dave why they were reviewing his performance. From his own standpoint, Burt hoped to build morale through free and open discussion of performance. Admirable, yes—but he failed to realize the full impact of performance reviews on the individual. He also failed to take into account the assumptions employees make concerning management's use of performance appraisals.

Burt began using a tool before he knew what he wanted to do with it or what the capabilities of the tool were. No one would pick up a power saw and start cutting lumber without knowing how the saw worked or what dimensions of lumber were wanted. In effect, that's what Burt was doing, and it didn't matter that he really wanted to cut lumber. He had no direction—no purpose to his activities.

The performance appraisal is a management control designed to provide a report of how well individuals are performing to standards. It provides the supervisor with a basis for corrective action. How the evaluation of an individual's performance is used above his level should be thoroughly understood by him and by the employee. This is the only way he can be fair to his employees. For example, if Burt knew that his evaluations would be used for determining merit increases by comparing them with those of other employees, his approach might have been entirely different. On the other hand, if both Norm and Dave could be certain that the only purpose for the review was for performance improvement and that no comparison would be made either in or out of the department, their concern over Burt's lower ratings would not have been as great. As it was, no one was sure just why he was doing what he was doing.

Does the performance appraisal fit the definition of control that we established? If properly conceived, the performance appraisal defines the standards of performance for each job, and the goal-setting phase of controlling is covered. Measuring performance against predetermined standards is a function of performance appraisal and a management control. The third step in controlling is taking corrective action, and this is accomplished in performance reviews in a number of ways —suggesting areas for improvement, planning for self-development, encouraging good working habits, and granting or withholding wage increases. So we can see that the performance appraisal meets the criteria of a control.

What are some of the uses to which the supervisor puts the performance appraisal? We'll identify a few, but only with the caution that the list cannot be all-inclusive and that we do not suggest that any given performance-appraisal system should have as its purpose every item listed. Obviously some contradict each other. A single program cannot be all things to all people any more than the same micrometer can be used to measure close tolerances and to crack hickory nuts. Here, then, are some of the purposes for using performance appraisal:

Improvement of performance

A periodic evaluation and review of performance points up areas for improvement in an employee's work. The evaluation is valuable in detecting performance slippage before it becomes a matter for disciplinary action. Supervisor and employee have an opportunity to agree on corrective action that both can take to improve performance. Planning for improvement is done in a positive climate. Because a definite time has been set aside for the review, the supervisor is more likely to feel an obligation to formulate specific improvement plans. The great majority of performance-appraisal programs set forth improvement of performance as their prime objective.

Basis for personnel action

Promotion, demotion, transfer, and salary increases are frequently tied to performance appraisals. The appraisal, it is felt, provides a much better basis for taking such actions than off-the-cuff judgments. Whether or not this is true depends, of course, on how accurate, honest, and objective the evaluations have been. Some theories hold that basing personnel actions such as wage adjustments on formalized appraisals is the most effective way of controlling employee performance. We can see the conflicts that are possible in the mind of a supervisor who tries to use the same program for wage adjustments and performance-improvement purposes. For example, Burt was apparently conservative in rating some of his best workers because he wanted to leave room for improvement. If he had been using those same ratings to try to justify wage increases for Norm and Dave, he would have been at a marked disadvantage in competing with a supervisor who had rated his people very liberally.

Determining training needs

Training directors and supervisors alike have found the performance appraisal helpful in spotting areas that require training for groups of employees. Widespread difficulties in performing one phase of a job call for training to be done as quickly as possible. Wherever patterns of similar problems suggest training, the supervisor will want to get help and advice from any staff specialists available to him. He may ask them to do the training as a corrective action, or he may simply get advice on how to do it himself.

Improving supervisor-employee communication

Properly handled, the performance review can contribute greatly to better communication between supervisor and employee. It sets a definite time for sitting down to talk about the employee's progress. This is something he wants to know and has a right to know. Undoubtedly, Burt Hall saw his performance reviews primarily in this light—a chance to tell his people how much he appreciated their cooperation and effort. He didn't consider the emotional pressures experienced by his employees, and their reserve threw him. He worked hard on the appraisal but didn't plan the interview. The interview can improve communications, but it must produce real understanding of what the supervisor is trying to accomplish. Half-truths and unanswered questions about the purpose of the appraisal can't possibly contribute positively to his relations with his people.

Feedback on standards and supervision

If two-way communication is encouraged in the performance review and the employee is confident that he can speak his mind without recrimination, the supervisor can learn a great deal in the appraisal interview about how his style of supervision is accepted by his subordinates. The employee should be given an opportunity to explain how fair the standards against which his performance is measured seem to him. Participation by the employee in setting goals is increasingly being heralded as a motivational technique second to none. Certainly an employee who has participated in setting a performance standard on his own job is going to try to exceed that standard.

To come anywhere near being an effective tool, the purpose of the performance appraisal must be clearly fixed. Knowing the purpose gives direction to appraisal efforts. It increases the likelihood that those efforts will result in an effective management control.

Objections to Performance Appraisals

Performance appraisals do take time, and the payoff for the time required is often difficult to see. Because of the time and the questionable results, supervisors raise many other objections. "There are too many problems." "It's too tough to get consistent ratings." "We don't like to sit in judgment." "People work better if they're not shaken up by ratings." "It just opens the door to unnecessary questions." And so on. To deny that there are problems in appraising and reviewing employees' performance would be dishonest. There are problems— real ones! In striving for a management-minded approach to performance appraisal, the supervisor should look at the problems in terms of how to overcome them. Let's examine a few of the more common problems.

Difficulty in setting standards

How can standards of performance be set on jobs where the output either is a service or can't be measured quantitatively? It's difficult in many areas, but it's even more surprising how a little ingenuity on the part of the supervisor and the employee will produce standards that both can accept. The standards need not have the preciseness of predetermined time standards, but they can be an adequate basis for agreement on how well the job is being performed. For example, a stock chaser's performance might be measured in terms of total orders filled—recognizing that over a period of time the one-item orders and the ten-item orders will average out. His performance might be measured in terms of the number of orders he holds more than twenty-four hours without filling. An exercise is to pick a job and try to find something that can be used as a standard. A supervisor can ask himself, "How about my own job? How many measurements are there of how I'm performing on my own job?"

Inconsistency of rating by different supervisors

How should a supervisor rate his people? Some supervisors tend toward high ratings on the theory that since it makes people feel better, there are fewer problems from employees and that high ratings make them seem to be better supervisors. Other supervisors lean toward low ratings because they feel that a high rating removes the incentive to improve, and high ratings leave them open to demands for more money and more privileges. All too often both of these schools of thought have lost sight of the fact that the supervisor is evaluating actual performance and is not using the form simply to nudge, needle, or bludgeon an employee.

The answer to this problem of inconsistency seems in part to be in the training of supervisors as raters. Certainly it would be to the supervisor's benefit to get some guidance from qualified people. A more practical answer to getting some consistency is for him to base as much of the appraisal as possible on objective standards and goals. There is little ground for disagreement when we can see that John Jones reached 95 percent of his goal or exceeded it by 5 percent.

Failure of forms to cover the job

If the forms don't fit the job, a supervisor can perhaps take some initiative to correct them. Forms, such as Burt Hall was using, which consider only quantity and quality of production and a few personal characteristics might very well miss the most important aspect of the job in the mind of the employee. Even if a supervisor is required to use a specific form in his company, he can suggest changes to the personnel department and add comments on his own to the evaluation form. A supervisor in a Wisconsin company who had to work with an appraisal form similar to that used by Burt Hall took the initiative by adding a supplement to the usual appraisal with six of his key men. He asked each of the six to make their own preparations for the interview. He told them that there were three things he wanted:

1. A listing of what each man considered to be the most important part of his job—production, quality, customer service, new ideas, etc.
2. A list of the problems each man felt were keeping him from doing as good a job as he would like to do
3. Any ideas each might have on what could be done to solve the problems

He discussed both the company's form and the answers they had prepared to his three questions with each man. The result was a far more meaningful interview with the men. Also, the company revised its appraisal form to make it more useful.

Dislike of the formality involved

Many supervisors experience the feeling that Burt did in talking with Dave and Norm. A warm, friendly relationship often seems to chill in the formality of the appraisal interview. Evaluation and review of performance is a touchy situation and is for many supervisors one of the most difficult aspects of their job. There is nothing wrong with the formality of the appraisal interview. It is a time for serious thought and discussion. Let's look at the situation for what it is—a boss discussing his evalaution of performance with a subordinate. It's an analysis of how the man performs his life's work—an analysis that may influence his advancement, his pay, his personal feelings of satisfaction, and his future training. Serious and formal? Of course it is! It's not a time for joking, certainly. The mere fact that we regard it seriously is likely to cause the employee to enter into the discussion constructively.

A brief summary here should take note of the fact that the problems aren't entirely the fault of the program or the control but in how supervisors as individuals administer the controls. A knowledge of what they want to accomplish and how they are going to accomplish it and a desire to make it work can bring positive results even from a poorly conceived appraisal system.

The "results" Approach Versus the "traits" Approach

So many recent problems have been attributed to the fact that appraisal systems have required managers to make subjective judgments about the personality traits of their subordinates. By defining the ideal employee in terms of personality traits and judging him on those traits, it was felt that supervisors could show him how he missed fitting the perfect mold and show him what modifications he would have to make. Think of the difficulties built into that approach.

What traits are really important? How should a trait be evaluated? How can bias and emotion be removed from the rating? How should supervisors tell an employee that they think he's lazy or that they think his judgment is poor? How do supervisors keep their values straight and true after rating twenty employees on twenty or thirty traits? How can they prevent one unpleasant incident from coloring their judgment about an employee? By the same token, can a supervisor be sure that those employees who have been cooperative are more deserving of high ratings than those who have created a problem or two for him? Of course not—but it always seems to come out that way.

These and hundreds of other problems have given managers no end of trouble in trying to carry out employee-evaluation programs. There has been change of terminology in these last two paragraphs. We started out by discussing performance appraisal and have now switched to employee evaluation. The difference between employee evaluation and performance appraisal has caused many companies to renew their efforts to make this control constructive. A supervisor should not try to evaluate people by using undefinable traits as a criteria but should instead strive to evaluate their performance by using quantitative measures wherever possible. He should have much less concern for what kind of personalities the employees working for him have than for how well they perform their jobs. The object of this control is to improve behavior, not to reshape personalities.

One of the reasons that performance is so much more difficult to control is the lack of sound acceptable quantitative standards. If a supervisor is asked how he is coming on the budget, his answer can be precise: He is running 3 percent over on his overhead costs, or his direct labor costs are right on the button. But let someone ask him how John Jones is doing, and he's likely to say that he seems to be doing all right and that, given a little time, he should be paying his own way. Why the hedging? He simply doesn't know himself just how well John Jones is doing, and he hopes that Jones might blossom forth in time to save the supervisor the embarrassment of having to make a decision about him.

Today, wherever and whenever possible, many are trying to find objective means of evaluating performance. This is part of the philosophy advocated by Edward Schleh and Peter Drucker—the idea of management by results or by objectives. Supervisors find themselves on much stronger ground when they can discuss performance with an employee in terms of whether or not he is meeting a standard. What are some of the measures that are used to evaluate employee performance? Let's look at a few:

Volume of production How many units, pounds, tons did an employee turn out per day or week on the average? What amount is acceptable? What goal should he shoot for in the next period?

Quality of production How is quality measured—in percentage of rejects or rework, pounds or tons of scrap, number of complaints by customers? What goals is the worker striving for now and next period?

Attendance How many times is an employee tardy or absent as against what is normally allowed?

Safety Has he had any accidents or been the cause of any? Has he contributed any ideas for improvement of safety?

Cost Is his cost record available? Has he contributed any cost-saving ideas? Are there examples of his practicing cost-consciousness?

Once goals have been set for an individual employee and he has accepted them, performance reviews can be conducted in a much less emotional climate. If production falls short of a goal, the supervisor's concern is with how he can bring it up next time; but there is no basis for argument with employees when the results are there for review. They may have a problem to solve together, but no emotion-laden charges need fly back and forth.

Another positive result of appraising performance quantitatively has been a self-generated tendency toward improvement. If an individual produced fifty-five units a day on the average, and if that exceeded his standard, he is more likely to set a higher goal for himself on the next round. Many supervisors attending institutes at the University of Wisconsin have reported experiencing this self-motivation to seek improvement. Some have even expressed concern about how to shut it off because, they say, some of the employees under them have exceeded all reasonable standards and yet keep going to a point where supervisors feel concern for their health.

When company appraisal forms require evaluation of traits, supervisors can still improve the effectiveness of their ratings by backing them up with specific incidents. For example, if the form calls for a rating on cooperativeness, it will help a supervisor make a fair judgment to have several examples of an employee's going out of his way to be helpful. Conversely, if he finds that he must rate an employee low, it will be easier to convince him that the rating is justified if incidents of his uncooperativeness can be cited. The same approach will help in rating other traits, such as dependability, initiative, and creativity.

As a management control, performance appraisal will work much more constructively if appraisals can be based on specific results achieved. The further a supervisor can get away from subjective judgments of personality traits, the better off he will be. The problem is that many of those traits do make a valuable employee. But until some way to quantify and measure cooperativeness is established, supervisors had better stick to evaluating quantity and quality of production.

THE APPRAISAL INTERVIEW

Even a poorly conceived performance-appraisal system can be an effective control if skillful appraisal interviewing is practiced. The make-or-break point in any appraisal program is the review interview with the employee. Essentially the supervisor is seeking two things in the appraisal interview. The first is to move the employee to improve his job performance or engage in self-development activities, or both. The second is to create a deeper understanding between the supervisor and the employee. It was the second objective that Burt was seeking, but he had only a fuzzy idea of what he wanted and no plan for accomplishing it in the interview. Simply holding the interview and wanting to do a good job is no guarantee of positive results.

Skillful interviewing takes practice, but unfortunately the adage "Practice makes perfect" doesn't work here. Practice doesn't make perfect unless a supervisor practices proven techniques. It should be worth his while, then, to consider some suggestions from personnel specialists. Backing up these guidelines is the experience of hundreds of first-line supervisors who have said, "These guides have helped me."

1. Prepare for the interview

Preparations for the interview should cover two factors. The first is the appraisal. Is it based as much as possible on specific results? The supervisor will be on stronger ground and represent management much more effectively if he can stick to objective measures of performance. Where company systems call for trait evaluation, his preparation will be more effective if he can back up his evaluation with illustrative incidents or examples. If he does this, he and the employee will be more likely to agree on the meaning of words like *dependability, initiative, loyalty,* and *creativity*. Double-checking the appraisal just before the interview is helpful.

The second factor in preparation is the interview itself. Here's where Burt Hall fell down. He did an excellent job of making his appraisals and supporting them with specific results, but he gave no thought to the interview other than hoping it would go well. The interview needs careful planning. There is little chance of a successful interview if a supervisor doesn't begin his preparations by defining his objectives. We have noted that as a control the appraisal seeks to correct or adjust. If performance improvement is his objective, he should recognize it. More important, he should know how much improvement he wants and what approach he will use to gain the employee's acceptance of those same goals.

The supervisor's preparation cannot ignore the personality of the individual whose performance he is reviewing. In view of the appraisal he has made, how is the employee likely to react? Empathy can be extremely helpful. The supervisor should ask himself, "How would I react if I were in his shoes? How can I put the appraisal so he will react positively?" If there's little chance of a positive response, can he at least make the employee understand without a display of emotion? Of course, a person who is on the defensive can't see any viewpoint other than his own, and this applies to employees and supervisors equally.

2. Encourage preparation by employees

If the supervisor's objective of creating a better understanding between him and his subordinates is to be realized, the employees should also be thinking about the appraisal. We have already mentioned the example of the Wisconsin supervisor who asked some of his key employees to prepare answers to three questions before the interview. Those who don't feel that preparations by employees should go that far will find value in speaking to an employee two or three days before an interview with him. The comment might go like this: "Harry, on Wednesday we'll have a chance to review your performance and mine for the past six months. I'd appreciate it if you would give some thought to your job and what we might do to make it more satisfying to you. If you have any problems in doing as good a job as you would like to do, let's discuss those too."

Now the supervisor has told Harry (1) that he will review his performance, (2) that Harry, too, has an opportunity to talk, (3) that the supervisor wants to create an even better working relationship, and (4) that Harry is free to comment on the supervisor's supervision. The chances are that Harry has a better idea of how well he has performed than the supervisor has, and he should come prepared to share his ideas.

3. Arrange for uninterrupted privacy

Since performance review is a touchy situation, the supervisor will naturally want to do everything he can to remove distractions and to protect the feelings of the employee.

4. Level with the employee

Stressing the need for seeking positive results from the interview sometimes leads to the mistaken idea that it's best to gloss over any deficiencies in performance. The supervisor is of no help to anyone unless he lets an employee know exactly where he stands. This can still be done with tact and consideration for his feelings.

5. Encourage the employee to talk

As he talks, the employee is participating and the supervisor is learning. Many times the employee will bring up deficiencies himself and make them easier to discuss. His participation is essential if he is to be motivated to improve his performance. The supervisors cannot assume, however, that he will talk without encouragement. No matter how free and open a climate the supervisor tries to create, he can't overlook the fact that the boss-subordinate relationship is strongly felt by the employee. That feeling may cause even the most talkative employee to become quiet. This is one time, say many experienced supervisors, that supervisors should be prepared to get the employee to open up. They can't accomplish the objective of the appraisal interview unless they do.

6. Try to set goals

Where appraisals have been based on specific results, the job of setting goals is much easier. The self-motivating feature of employee-centered appraisals isn't realized until the employee has participated in the setting of goals for the next period. The setting of goals puts the emphasis of the appraisal interview on tomorrow's performance instead of on yesterday's. Managers seeking to control their departments are much more concerned with what is going to happen than with what has happened. The primary function of controls is to adjust and guide future operations.

7. Appraise the interview

To his credit, Burt Hall was preparing to find out what whent wrong with his first two interviews. He hadn't done as well as he had hoped he would, and he wanted to take corrective action. Most supervisors will benefit from the same action. A supervisor should ask himself, "Did I reach the objective of the interview? If not, why not? What did I learn that will help me in future interviews?" Each interview should be a learning experience, but the supervisor should take the time to evaluate what he's learned.

8. Follow up

In the course of the interview, a supervisor may very well have made suggestions or offered help that should not be forgotten. The effectiveness of the entire performance appraisal system can be threatened by a failure to follow up on promises made during the interview. Such failure makes the appraisal appear to be a mere formality to be forgotten as soon as the interview is concluded. If the interview resulted in planning for improved performance or in trying to correct a performance deficiency, the supervisor will certainly want to check progress with the employee periodically rather than wait until the next appraisal interview. It's in his follow-up actions that the supervisor demonstrates his sincerity in trying to make the appraisal an effective control.

Skillfully handled, the appraisal interview is of great benefit to the employee, the supervisor, and the company. The employee gains a sense of direction and participation in the development of his career. He finds that he has a voice in managing his own job. To the supervisor comes the knowledge that he is controlling his department by correcting, adjusting, and upgrading.

HIGHLIGHTS

1. The purpose of the control phase of the management process is to assure the supervisor that what he has planned and directed is accomplished. Through control he takes charge of the department.
2. The three essential steps in controlling are:
   a. Setting goals and standards at key points in a process
   b. Measuring performance or progress against standards
   c. Taking corrective action or making adjustments
3. Performance appraisals are management controls which set standards of performance, measure or evaluate performance against accepted standards, and seek to improve employees' performances.

4. Some of the uses of performance appraisal are:
   a. To improve performance
   b. To provide a basis for personnel actions
   c. To determine training needs
   d. To improve supervisor-employee communication
   e. To gain feedback on performance standards and supervision
5. Appraising employees' performances is avoided by many supervisors. The problems that they cite are:
   a. Difficulty in setting standards
   b. Inconsistency of rating by different supervisors
   c. Appraisal forms that don't cover the job
   d. Dislike for the formality involved
6. The closer a supervisor can come to basing his appraisal on specific results and objective standards, the more effective his use of this management control will be.
7. The appraisal interview can make or break the entire program. It can rescue a poorly conceived program or threaten the effectiveness of the most accurate appraisals. The supervisor should:
   a. Prepare for the interview
   b. Encourage preparation by employees
   c. Arrange for uninterrupted privacy
   d. Level with the employee
   e. Encourage the employee to talk
   f. Try to set goals
   g. Appraise the interview
   h. Follow up

DISCUSSION QUESTIONS

1. Cite some specific goals or standards in your department that provide the basis for control.
2. What are some of the reports supervisors give to staff departments and higher management to help them control the larger operation?
3. What are the main reasons for the establishment of management controls?
4. What are the main limitations of performance appraisal and reviews?

5. Evaluate "the trait approach" versus "the results approach" to appraising employees' performances.
6. How do you explain the statement that a good performance review can overcome a faulty appraisal form or program?
7. Assume that you have evaluated an employee's performance on a company form. What preparations would you make for the appraisal interview?
8. Why is an employee's participation in and contribution to the appraisal interview so important?

SUGGESTIONS FOR FURTHER STUDY

Batten, J. D.
Tough-minded Management
Chapter 8, American Management Association, New York, 1963

Black, James, and Guy Ford
Front-line Management
Chapter 7, McGraw-Hill Book Company, New York, 1963

Ecker, Paul, John MacRae, Vernon Ouellette, and Charles Telford
Handbook for Supervisors
Chapter 9, Prentice-Hall, Inc., Englewood Cliffs, N.J., 1959

Famularo, Joseph J.
Supervisors in Action
Chapter 9, McGraw-Hill Book Company, New York, 1961

Heyel, Carl
Management for Modern Supervisors
Chapter 8, American Management Association, New York, 1962

CHAPTER
THIRTEEN

MAKING
SOUND
DECISIONS

THE CASE OF THE NEW ASSISTANT

Ray Ford and Burt Hall had been discussing the changes that had taken place in Assembly Department B since Burt became supervisor just fourteen short months before. The work force had grown by 20 percent. Productivity was up over 30 percent. New equipment and new methods were in evidence. And looming on the distant horizon was the possibility of starting a second shift.

"One of these days," Ray said to Burt, "I suppose we'll have to give some thought to getting you an assistant."

He said it casually, without any particular emphasis, but he started Burt thinking about the way his work load had been increasing. He was staying on top of everything. He knew he was growing in the job. No longer did he entertain any thoughts of how much easier it had been back in the ranks. But the realization that he needed help to keep on top was slowly beginning to develop.

Burt knew that delegation was a partial answer. Good delegation could relieve him of some of his growing load. It was also a way of developing some of his key men. Maybe it was this last factor that made him shy away from delegating more—the appearance of playing favorites or picking an heir apparent after being a supervisor only a little over a year.

If Ray was beginning to think about an assistant for Burt, hadn't he better do some serious thinking himself? Was Ray suggesting that Burt should have a man picked and in the grooming process? If Burt just let it ride until he had authorization from above, would the selection be made for him—possibly of someone from another department? Burt felt that there were some good men in his department who deserved the opportunity. No doubt about it, the time for a decision had come.

In the days that followed, Burt gave a good deal of thought to which of his key men he wanted for an assistant. He knew his choice would demonstrate to Ray and Oscar Palmer his own skill in picking men with management potential. More than an assistant foremanship was involved. The man he picked might very well be the supervisor of the second shift when it started. He might become Burt's successor if a promotion were ever offered to Burt. Having a capable man ready was just good insurance.

An analysis of potential assistants brought three men to the top of his list. Each had definite assets. Each had some minor drawbacks.

Sam Pitman had been a real problem for Burt when he was first used as a trainer. Both Burt and Sam learned a few things about training from that initial trial. Sam had matured in his understanding of the learning problems of new employees. No longer was he sarcastic. His tendency to show off and become impatient with slow learners seemed to be under control. Results from the people Sam trained were good now. Sam was sharp. He was young—just turned twenty-eight—but still he had over ten years of experience in the department. Few people in the department, even those with much more experience, knew more than Sam about the total operation. No one could top Sam's ability to produce. He took pleasure in taking a tough job and licking it. Although he wasn't an introvert, his superior ability as a producer tended to separate him from the others, and he was regarded as something of a loner. In many ways, Burt thought, Sam was a carbon copy of himself a few years back. Maybe that was why he liked Sam so much.

Clarence "Squeaks" West had distinguished himself as a trainer in Burt's first attempt at delegation. Squeaks was a favorite among new employees because of his helpful attitude, and he was very popular with his fellow workers. Everybody respected Squeaks for his job knowledge, for his ability to produce, and especially for his ability to get along with people.

Squeaks was the most experienced of Burt's three candidates. He had sixteen years in the department and over eighteen years with the company. Squeaks' reputation for being cost- and quality-conscious was well known by both Ray Ford and Oscar Palmer. His knowledge of total departmental operations was equal to if not better than Sam Pitman's. Burt frequently called on Squeaks for trouble-shooting assistance and always found him extremely helpful and cooperative.

Squeaks was forty-three years old. His intelligence was high, but he had never finished high school. At the beginning of World War II, he had dropped out in his senior year to enlist in the infantry. As a sergeant, Squeaks distinguished himself in combat. His wife and three teenage children also reflected the expert direction Squeaks gave his family as husband and father.

Jim Raymond was a relative newcomer to be given such serious consideration for supervisory responsibility. He had completed two years at the university in mechanical engineering before having to drop out for financial reasons. Determined to get his degree, Jim was taking courses at night. Six to eight years would pass before he could complete his degree work. In the ten months he had worked for Burt, Jim had drawn attention to himself in a number of ways. Constructively inquisitive, he demonstrated a sincere interest in making improvements on every job he worked on. Many of his minor suggestions and two of his major ideas had been implemented already.

Jim confided to Burt that he wanted to get ahead and that he was willing to work at anything that would help him learn the ropes. He demonstrated his sincerity by tackling every assignment Burt gave him with enthusiasm. Being quick to learn, Jim already had a keen understanding of what it took to make a smoothly functioning department. He frequently discussed his university assignments with Burt to get the practical side. Burt enjoyed these discussions with Jim. He noticed, too, that Jim was extremely well liked by everyone he worked with. At twenty-four, Jim had tremendous potential. He was intelligent, popular, anxious to please, a quick learner, and dedicated to his work. To top it off, he wanted to move up into supervision. Burt could only guess about this last factor as far as Sam and Squeaks were concerned.

In maturity, experience, and popularity, Squeaks commanded the greatest respect and probably would be his first choice, Burt thought, but— But he knew that a high school diploma was a minimum requirement of the company for supervisors. Also, forty-five years of age was the cutoff point for supervisory appointments. Two years could easily pass before an assistant might make supervisor. On the other hand, Squeaks still had over twenty years ahead of him before retirement.

Sam was the number one producer of the three. He was both young and experienced. The only question Burt had about Sam was about his leadership ability. Sam really hadn't had a chance to show what he could do on this score, but there was enough evidence of his being a loner to cause some serious concern.

On the basis of dedication, interest, education, and enthusiasm, Jim Raymond stood out. With a year or two of assistant supervisory experience under his belt, Burt did not doubt that Jim would make an excellent foreman. But there was his youth and lack of experience to consider. Burt also wondered what would happen to morale if he moved such a new man up ahead of those with more experience.

One afternoon when his shift had left for the day, Burt sat in the quiet of his office and wrote down some of the alternatives he had.

1. Do nothing, and wait until the position is authorized.
2. Push Ray Ford to get formal authorization before going any further.
3. Select a man and tell him that the position isn't authorized, but start him learning some of the jobs he'll do when the appointment is announced.
4. Discuss the merits of each man with Ray Ford and use the discussions to get Ray's evaluation of them. This would also serve to stimulate Ray to think more about formalizing the position.
5. Select the man, but say nothing to anyone. Quietly go about giving him assignments to test his ability and let him learn.
6. Start on a program of grooming all three with growth experiences. This way Burt could delegate more, get a better evaluation of each one, and be in a more solid position to recommend the right man when the position is authorized.
7. Wait until the job is formalized, and then recommend all three to higher management, giving the strengths and limitations of each. Then management could make the decision in the light of company policies and their greater experience in making such selections. Since all three were acceptable, Burt could live with any decision management made.

Having written down the alternatives, Burt put them in his desk, turned out the lights, and left. He knew that he might get another idea or two overnight and that he could evaluate the alternatives more clearly in the morning when he was fresh. Whatever he decided, he knew that carrying out his decision would have to be very carefully planned.

1. How can Burt's feeling that the time for a decision had come be explained?
2. A common step in the analysis of a problem is the defining of the problem. How could Burt's problem be defined?
3. Evaluate each of Burt's alternatives. What are the advantages and disadvantages of each one?
4. Are there any other possible solutions?
5. What might Burt have had in mind when he felt that carrying out his decision would require careful planning?

THE MANAGEMENT–MINDED SUPERVISOR AS A DECISION MAKER

When all is said and done, a supervisor is paid to be a decision maker. He probably makes as many as forty decisions a day. His value to his company is in the quality of his decisions. The supervisor's worth to the team is found in his batting average. How often does he make successful decisions?

The supervisor's position exists because there is a need to make decisions on the front-line. These decisions will require varying degrees of skill and knowledge. Some will be routine. Some will be big decisions that set precedent.

Decisions will concern people, equipment, methods, maintenance, production schedules, use of personal time, etc. Every time a choice is made in the course of a day's operations, a decision is made; and even a seemingly insignificant decision can have far-reaching effects.

Some supervisors find the job of making many decisions a day a challenge to be met with enthusiasm. They find their greatest job satisfaction in improving their decision-making batting average. They see that their effectiveness and future as managers lie in the quality of their decisions. This is the management-minded approach to decision making. On the other hand, we have all seen the supervisor who throws up his hands, crying that his job would be all right if it weren't for all the decisions required of him. Or consider those supervisors who can't make a decision and whose mental or emotional health is adversely affected by the pressure of problems waiting for solutions. They would be better off in nonsupervisory work.

There are many types of supervisors, some of which are discussed below. Supervisors should be able to recognize their weaknesses and try to overcome them by developing a management-minded approach to supervision. Can we recognize decision makers we know among the types discussed here? More important, can we recognize ourselves among them?

The impulsive type

He's not nearly as interested in his batting average as he is in setting speed records. He gives little consideration to facts, feelings, or funds—he makes a decision and moves on to the next one. There are always more decisions to be made. He frequently doesn't realize that his impulsiveness gives him more problems to solve. His pride is in the volume of decisions he makes and the speed with which he handles them.

The pipe smoker

His philosophy is that most problems will solve themselves if left to incubate long enough. Strictly a low-pressure operator, he doesn't let anything upset or excite him. Time to him is the great healer of most management ills. He sits back, puffs on his pipe, and says, "Let's think about it for a while."

The bull in the china shop

His job is to make decisions, he says. No one is to question his authority, his wisdom, or his method of implementing his decisions. If feelings get hurt, that's life. The important thing is to get things moving regardless of what people think.

The fence-sitter

This felow is usually unable to make a decision because of his unwillingness to inconvenience anyone. When opinions or feelings are in conflict, he is stymied because he wants everybody to be happy and have his way. He recognizes the need for developing alternative solutions but can never choose between alternatives. He takes forever to make a decision. He doesn't like to take risks, and he glosses over the fact that not making a decision at all also involves risk. His delay usually results in more crisis-type decisions, thereby making his position on the fence more and more uncomfortable.

The professor

He is the analytical type. He never makes a decision without all the facts. The catch is that all the facts are seldom available, but that doesn't stop him from trying. Like the pipe smoker, he can't be hurried. If the problem solves itself before he acts, it only proves that there was nothing to get excited about.

There are others—like the worrier, the timid type, and the operator. But our concern is for a constructive management-minded approach to our decision-making responsibility. First, the types of decisions supervisors are called upon to make should be identified. Some problems repeat themselves, and the decisions become routine. Perhaps there are a few variables, but the decisions are geared to past practices, and little judgment is required. Ordering supplies for stock and routing shipments are examples of situations calling for routine decisions. Whenever possible these decisions should be delegated to allow the supervisor to concentrate his efforts on situations that can truly be labeled problems and that require a great deal of judgment.

THE ANATOMY OF A DECISION

The purpose of this chapter is to examine how the decision-making process breaks down, what happens in each of the major phases of the process, and how all other chapters in this book relate to this critical responsibility. Knowledge of human relations, communication, discipline, initiating change, and the management process all contribute to the wisdom of a supervisor's decisions and the skill with which he implements them.

When the decision-making process is broken down, three major phases are identifiable—*alert, analysis, action.* In the *alert* phase an awareness develops that a decision must be made. Something goes wrong. A need becomes apparent. A request is made. Having been alerted to the need for decision, the next phase is an *analysis* of the problems that bear on the situation and the possible solutions that form the basis of a decision. Selecting the best decision leads then to the *action* phase, in which the decision is implemented. In major decisions, each of these phases requires the best that the supervisor can give. It's in such situations that the managers are separated from the clerks.

Phase 1: Alert

Most supervisors and executives, if pressed for an answer to the question, "How do you make your decisions?" would answer that they don't know. Yet most would also agree that making effective decisions is synonymous with good management. Developing a sensitivity to problems in their embryonic stages—before they become critical—is essential to the supervisor who would avoid being a crisis manager. He can see that problems nipped in the bud require less momentous decisions. He knows the truth of the adage that an ounce of prevention is worth a pound of cure. He knows, too, that tension and anxiety are less likely to confuse his own and others' thinking if he acts quickly.

Management-mindedness for a supervisor is being alert to potential problems, having skill in his analysis, and being willing to act decisively. Waiting to be pushed into a decision is a failure to accept management responsibility. The result of such failure is a pressure-ridden supervisor jumping from one crisis to another until he or someone of higher authority decides that the job is too big for him.

An analysis of the major problems that demand decisions usually reveals that symptoms had begun to appear long before the situation developed into a problem. Burt Hall demonstrated admirable sensitivity when he determined that the time for a decision had arrived. Even so, there were symptoms long before he became alert to the need to select and groom an assistant. Ray Ford's offhand remark about an assistant simply triggered Burt's decision to get moving. His increasing work load, the departmental changes, an increasing work force, and the growing realization that a second shift would some day materialize all pointed to the fact that a problem was emerging. We could even criticize Burt for not acting sooner, but it seems more appropriate to give him credit for his determination to face the challenge positively. After all, he could have let the situation ride until he was asked to pick an assistant. He chose instead to anticipate the day when the position would be authorized. The day might even be advanced to his advantage.

Every day conditions around a supervisor may be pointing to the development of a problem and the need for action. An operation starts producing a little more scrap than usual. Absenteeism increases slightly. Down time on a machine starts to exceed reasonable limits. Deliveries of critical materials are late. Accident frequency rates begin to rise. Housekeeping performance slips. Employees complain more than is customary about working conditions. Production bottlenecks develop. A good employee misses deadlines or production quotas. None of these symptoms perhaps is serious in its early stages, but if left unattended, each is a potential crisis. Somewhere between the earliest symptoms and the crisis, a supervisor is alerted to the fact that something is wrong. The more sensitive he is to a smoothly functioning department, the quicker he will be alerted.

The decision-making process begins with the alert, whether subtle symptoms or a crisis bring it about. At the time a supervisor becomes aware of the need for decision, he demonstrates his management-mindedness. He can ignore the symptoms, wait for something more definitive, or start immediately to define and analyze his problem. Most major decisions a supervisor will make involve some risk, and it's the risk involved that causes him to procrastinate. It should be recognized that not making a decision can also be highly risky. A supervisor might develop a reputation for indecisiveness and jeopardize his management future. It is also possible that the decision will be made elsewhere—not always to the satisfaction of the supervisor, who should have made it in the first place.

For example, Burt Hall could have turned his attention to more pressing work until the position of assistant foreman was formally approved. There are those who would claim that he was sticking his neck out unnecessarily until that time. To follow such a course, however, would be to risk the possibility that the position might never be created or that someone from another department might be assigned to him. In either case Burt would not have the chance to develop and advance one of his own men. By being alert and ready, he stands a much better chance of getting what he wants. He'll also be fulfilling his responsibility to have someone in his department ready to step into his shoes if the need develops.

Decision-making ability is developed by making decisions. Confidence is an important attribute to the successful decision maker. Confidence comes only with making sound decisions repeatedly. On the other hand, shying away from the making of decisions leads to uncertainty for everyone—the supervisor, his subordinates, and his superiors.

An early definition of the problem is a part of the alert phase of the decision-making process and is the transition into the analysis phase. We seldom question the saying that a problem well defined is half solved. It contains a great deal of truth, but it's likely to be an over-simplification. The first definition of a problem will likely be a statement of the symptoms—something is wrong; a situation needs improvement; a difficulty has been encountered; the boss wants action. Careful analysis of the facts and factors affecting the situation in all probability will call for a redefinition of the problem and give direction to the sound development of alternatives. Once the initial definition of the problem has been verbalized, either mentally or on paper, the decision-making process moves into its second phase, the phase of analysis.

It should be noted that what we are talking about throughout this chapter is a systematic approach to making effective decisions. The impulsive approach is commendable only to the extent that it demonstrates a willingness to take the bull by the horns and make a decision. In all other respects it fails the test of intelligent decision making. For difficult situations, the analysis phase is critical. Sensitivity and thorough understanding of departmental standards alert the supervisor to the need for decisions, but a systematic analysis leads him to reach successful decisions.

Phase 2: Analysis

The alert phase of decision making is inescapable. Sooner or later the existence of a problem or the need for a decision penetrates the awareness of even the dullest foreman. The analysis phase, however, can be overlooked and frequently is. Problems go unanalyzed, and snap decisions are made every day. The consequences of such actions are familiar. Supervisors who persist in circumventing the analysis phase eventually become the victims of chaotic conditions in their departments. Sound decisions follow intelligent analysis just as guided practice improves a skill.

"Get the facts" is a seemingly overworked phrase. Yet getting the facts that bear on a problem or a decision is so fundamental that the analysis phase cannot be discussed without stressing its importance. For example, Burt Hall possessed many vital facts to help him reach his decision. How could he make an intelligent choice of an assistant without identifying the strengths and limitations of each candidate, as he had done so well? It is also easy to see that he needed more information before making his decision: What is the company's policy with regard to educational requirements? Can job knowledge and experience ever be substituted for formal education? To what extent is seniority a factor? How do Squeaks and Sam feel about accepting supervisory responsibility?

Let's consider some of the factual information a supervisor might want to secure before arriving at his decisions. What company policies, procedures, rules, or practices bear on the situation? What is the past production record of the equipment or employee? How do those concerned with the problem feel about it—the boss, the employee, the union? Do contracts with the union or the customer limit the possible alternatives? What costs are involved—either in creating the problem or in recommending a solution? Have solutions to similar problems established precedents that should be evaluated? What company or departmental goals will be affected? These are but a few considerations. Individual situations calling for decisions will undoubtedly point to other sources of desirable information. A questioning attitude is essential in the analytical phase. The planning questions discussed in Chapter 10 provide a solid foundation in our search for the facts—*what, where, when, who,* and *how.*

Hand in hand with getting the facts is the need to identify accurately the real causes of the problem. Exit interviews, for example, may reveal any number of reasons why employees wish to terminate—more money, a job closer to home, more desirable shift, etc. Dealing with these symptoms individually could easily go on for some time until it finally is determined that poor supervision or lack of opportunity is the real cause for the high turnover. Similarly, substandard work may be assumed to be the result of faulty equipment or poor materials, when poorly trained operators are the real cause. Jumping to conclusions by attacking surface symptoms is an easy trap to fall into. Thorough fact gathering and a genuinely questioning attitude contribute significantly to the ability to determine the real cause of problems.

Having identified the exact cause of the problem, the supervisor should reexamine the first definition of the problem. Is it a true statement of the real problem? In some situations a clear statement of the problem may be no more than a restatement of the cause. The supervisor should, however, guard against setting forth the solution in the problem statement lest he limit his consideration of possible alternatives. In the turnover problem mentioned above, for example, there is a difference between these two versions of the problem: (1) How can we reduce turnover in the department? (2) How can we get rid of the supervisor? To be sure, the supervisor might have been the cause of the turnover, and eliminating him might be one alternative—but certainly not the only one. The first statement opens the analysis of the problem to a wide range of possibilities, from training the supervisor to transferring him. The first version allows for the consideration of other causes such as poor working conditions, low pay, and lack of opportunity. The second begins with the decision to get rid of the supervisor as the primary cause and leaves only the question of how this is to be done.

Before being satisfied with a redefinition of a problem, the supervisor should check the possibility of its relationship to other problems. Will putting out this fire leave several others still burning? Is this only a part of a much larger problem? The ability to see the big picture is a distinct assist to the supervisor–decision maker–manager.

At various times supervisors have been given advice like, "Get all the facts" and "Never make assumptions." It sounds good in theory, but realistically it can't always be done. Seldom are all the facts available. To get all the facts would frequently mean that a supervisor would never get around to making a decision. He does have to make assumptions or, more accurately, educated guesses. Intelligent decision making does not rule out making assumptions but does require that the decision maker realize the difference between facts and assumptions. Confusing assumptions and facts leads to difficulties. When assumptions are made, special consideration must be given to their validity. In view of the available facts, is it a safe assumption?

Short of asking Sam Pitman if he was interested in becoming an assistant supervisor under Burt, the only way Burt could consider him as a prime candidate would be to assume his interest. From previous conversations and from Sam's attitude and performance, Burt could make this assumption with reasonably good prospects of being right. With Squeaks it might be another matter. Why, after all these years of topnotch performance, had West been passed over? Was it because he didn't want the job, or was the lack of a high school diploma the main reason? It's easy to see that an assumption here would be risky without some concrete evidence of interest. When assumptions are necessary, they should be checked against the best information available.

With the facts gathered, the causes of the problem determined, and the problem clearly defined, the supervisor is ready to start what he's been straining to get at—the development of a solution. All too often the temptation to jump from the alert phase to the first solution that occurs to him is irresistible. Yielding to this temptation, however, results in a higher percentage of poor decisions than a supervisor would want on his record.

Creative, high-quality decisions are usually not the first ones to pop into a supervisor's mind. For this reason giving special care to developing as many possible solutions to the problem as possible pays dividends. The creative-thinking specialists have good advice to offer concerning the development of alternatives—avoid judicial thinking, and use only creative thinking until as many solutions as possible have been identified. Judicial thinking inhibits the creative approach. It tends to evaluate the solution and discard that which is unusual or hasn't been tried before. By developing many alternatives, a supervisor goes beyond the obvious. The obvious solution frequently is not the best—at least he'll never know until he explores several alternatives. Very often in striving to develop a list of alternative solutions, a supervisor will find that a combination of two or three of them gives him a more comprehensive answer to the problem.

Burt Hall developed a list of several alternatives to his problem. Any one of them might prove to be workable. It will take additional effort on his part to evaluate each of them, but how much better it is to be able to choose from several possibilities. Combinations of his listed alternatives also reveal still more possibilities.

Confidence and pride in his decisions are more likely to result from a supervisor's having thoroughly explored and evaluated the alternatives. He can say with conviction that this is the best decision he could have reached. When he must defend a chosen course of action, he is in a better position when he can say, "I considered that, and my best judgment points to this decision for these reasons."

Evaluative or judicial thinking follows the listing of possible alternatives. Avoiding evaluation in the listing of alternatives tends to generate more ideas. Now sound decision making requires that the best of the alternatives be selected. Careful appraisal of each alternative is the most practical method of arriving at the decision which represents the supervisor's best judgment.

A few key questions will guide the supervisor in making his evaluation. He should consider whether or not the decision will correct the situation or reach the goal he has set for himself. If all the alternatives are likely to fall short of accomplishing his purpose, he will want to explore other approaches. Other criteria against which he should check his decisions are apparent in the following questions: Is the cost justified? How will it affect other people or other departments? Is it in conflict with established policies or contracts? Will it set a desirable precedent? and How will it affect production?

The result of this thorough and systematic analysis, of course, is the best possible decision, and the transition into the action phase of the decision-making process begins.

Phase 3: Action

One of the most satisfying experiences a manager can have is to lick a tough problem. The satisfaction increases if he has thoroughly studied his problem and if he sees his decision supported and smoothly implemented by everyone involved. Such satisfaction isn't likely to happen by chance. It follows more often a well-conceived plan for implementing a decision. Failure to plan how an otherwise sound decision will be put into action can easily result in confusion and frustration.

Decisions frequently involve change. Resistance can be expected unless a plan for overcoming it is formulated. Chapter 4 discusses the problems involved when decisions create significant changes. Taking action on major decisions should include these five important considerations: (1) a well-planned procedure for taking action; (2) the participation of those affected; (3) the communication of the decision to all concerned; (4) follow-up during the implementation; (5) the evaluation of results. Each of these considerations is critical in realizing the goal of a successfully implemented decision.

Planning the procedure for taking action

Once the decision has been reached, the decision-making process has not been completed. The supervisor is still faced with the problem of making it work. Many good decisions fail because action was taken at the wrong time or because important details had not been anticipated. In considering several of Burt Hall's alternatives, it's easy to see that the critical factor would not be in what he decided to do but in how he planned to take action. For example, let us consider the possibility that he decided to begin grooming all three candidates without committing himself to any of them. When should he start?

What assignments could he give to them? Should Ray Ford and Mr. Palmer be informed? Should assignments be rotated among them, or should each be given his own area of responsibility? Similar questions would have to be answered for any of the alternatives Burt listed if it were to have a chance of succeeding.

In preparing the implementation of a decision, the planning questions again provide a simple systematic approach. What steps need to be taken and in what sequence? Who should do the work, and who will be affected? When is the best time to start, and how long should it take before the decision is fully operational? What difficulties are likely to crop up, or what could go wrong anywhere along the line? This last question is particularly important to consider in order to avoid unnecessary complications. By anticipating possible trouble spots, the supervisor will conceive his plan to avoid them and ensure his success.

Participation of those affected

We have discussed in previous chapters the importance of participation from those whose cooperation the supervisor needs. No matter how carefully he analyzes his problems and reaches his decisions, his subordinates will ultimately determine whether or not the plan will work. The degree to which he can involve others in his decisions will have to be an individual determination. In some cases he might decide that his subordinates can profitably help analyze the problem, participate in developing alternatives, and help decide what should be done. This would be a very high degree of participation and would be more likely to gain full support of his subordinates.

Often the decision is one which the supervisor alone must make. It is still possible to outline the decision to those affected and to get their ideas about its workability. If the supervisor is flexible and open-minded, both his boss and his subordinates can offer suggestions to improve the plan of action. Finally, if the decision is a firm one from which no deviations can be considered, he can still build in participation by allowing a discussion of the best ways to implement it. Support for his decisions is much more likely to come from those who have participated and feel that they are a part of them. This applies not only to subordinates, but to the boss and other department heads as well.

Communication to all concerned

Any supervisor who has ever complained of learning about a management decision from the union steward can appreciate the importance of the proper timing and proper channels for communicating a decision. We defined communication as the creation of understanding. Understanding of what decisions have been made and why they have been made is of vital importance to a supervisor's superiors. Their need to know what is going on in his department is essential if they are to coordinate or manage several departments. The boss should never be surprised by learning of his decisions from other sources. Informing him promptly of the decisions he has made or discussing them with him beforehand is just one of the may ways the supervisor can support him. Supporting the boss contributes in no small measure to his desire to support the supervisor.

Employees who will have to abide by a supervisor's decisions or who will have to carry them out can make them look silly or sound. Their cooperation is essential and is dependent on the degree to which they understand how the decision will affect them. They will want to know what their responsibilities are, how they are to proceed, what the decision is intended to accomplish, how they will benefit, and how they might be expected to change their behavior. Anticipating these questions and communicating the answers beforehand will help avoid needless difficulties and anxieties.

Other departments should also be considered if their operations are affected. Will the output from a supervisor's department in quantity, quality, or time put additional demands on others? Common courtesy dictates that they be informed of the decision to help them cooperate. For example, in discipline and grievance decisions, the supervisor will want the support of the labor relations department and must keep its members posted. A decision to change a production schedule may affect the shipping department, other production departments, or the sales department, which has promised delivery.

The timing and method of communication will be determined by the individual situation. In relatively minor or routine decisions a verbal instruction or phone call is probably adequate. When other departments are affected, a memo is advisable. Decisions resulting in new procedures should be carefully written, and copies sent to everyone concerned. Decisions which affect company policy or which are likely to set a precedent might combine a spoken explanation to the boss with a written report on how and why the decision was made. Decisions affecting administration of the labor contract should generally be put in writing after discussions with the parties concerned. In those cases where the feelings of a group might be involved, a meeting should be considered so that everyone gets the information at the same time and has a chance to react.

Follow-up during the implementation

The best-laid plans, the saying goes, often go awry. To ensure the successful implementation of a decision, the effective decision maker will follow closely the action he initiated. In planning his course of action, he did his best to anticipate everything that could go wrong, but he knows he can't afford to issue directives and forget them. Is everyone performing according to expectations? Has any resistance developed? Is everything on schedule? Are materials up to standard? Is equipment functioning smoothly? Are desired results being realized? Follow-up, if the decision-making process was conscientiously carried out, should be no more than a few routine checks on progress. No one is so perfect, however, that every decision he makes will be carried out exactly. Catching deviations early may save both time and embarrassment. Slight modifications, accomplished early, can be the difference between succeeding and failing.

Evaluation of results

Naturally all supervisors are interested in their decision-making batting average. Their primary concern is whether or not their decisions achieved the results expected. Their interest in self-development as managers requires that they periodically look at their decisions and evaluate their effectiveness. "If the desired results were achieved, could I do an even better job next time?" "If I failed, why did I?" They can learn from failure just as surely as they do from successes. Every decision they are called upon to make is a challenge. "How do I meet challenge—with enthusiasm and determination or by turning my back and waiting?" In the final analysis, supervisors are paid and promoted for their decision-making ability—an ability that can be improved with practice. This chapter provides the kind of guidance that

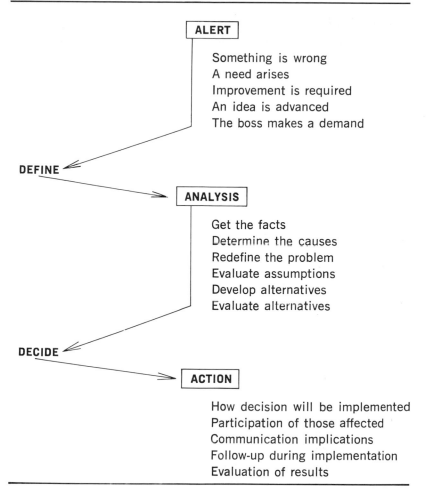

ALERT

Something is wrong
A need arises
Improvement is required
An idea is advanced
The boss makes a demand

DEFINE

ANALYSIS

Get the facts
Determine the causes
Redefine the problem
Evaluate assumptions
Develop alternatives
Evaluate alternatives

DECIDE

ACTION

How decision will be implemented
Participation of those affected
Communication implications
Follow-up during implementation
Evaluation of results

Figure **12.**   The anatomy of a decision

leads to better decisions. It's up to each individual to decide how he will use it.

Each chapter so far has concluded with a summary of highlights— not so this chapter. Figure 12 diagrams the anatomy of a decision. It not only incorporates the highlights of this chapter, but represents, we hope, the fact that every subject discussed in this book will be reflected in the quality of a supervisor's decisions.

A LOOK AHEAD

A member of management—that's the supervisor in business and industry. Being a member of management involves meeting challenges to his abilities; shouldering tremendous responsibilities; experiencing satisfactions and frustrations; and bearing the burden of his decisons. Looking at the job ahead of him, the supervisor should be able to see opportunity in every direction. Those opportunities may be labeled problems, challenges, uncertainties, demands, puzzles, and confusions, but they are all a chance to show that the supervisor is worthy of being identified as a member of management.

There are no simple formulas for success in management. No prescription, no formula, certainly no book can ever provide specific answers to specific supervisory problems. An attempt has been made in this book to stimulate thinking about what it means to be a management-minded supervisor. Guidelines have been suggested to give directions to the awesome responsibility of managing human resources in the hope that the supervisor can enjoy the satisfactions of a job well done. The problems of Burt Hall have been presented in the hope that they are typical and will stimulate the study of common-sense approaches to resolving them. Managers can never stop studying and learning.

DISCUSSION QUESTIONS

1. Think of a decision you have made that didn't work out well. Can you trace its failure to overlooking one of the steps discussed in this chapter? What should have been done?
2. Why is so much stress placed on developing many alternatives or possible solutions? Can you cite an example where having several alternatives has paid dividends?
3. How do you account for the fact that many successful executives say they can't explain how they made their decisions?
4. Should a supervisor take a problem to his boss before he reaches a decision? If so, under what circumstances? If not, why not?
5. When would the systematic approach to decision making be most helpful? Are there situations calling for decisions when this approach can't or shouldn't be used? Explain your opinion.
6. What are the primary benefits to the supervisor in using the systematic approach to make his decisions?

SUGGESTIONS FOR FURTHER STUDY

Drucker, Peter F.
The Practice of Management
Chapter 28, Harper & Row, Publishers, Incorporated, New York, 1954

Gardiner, Glenn, and Associates
Managerial Skills for Supervisors
Chapter 3, Elliott Service Company, Mount Vernon, N.Y., 1960

Lateiner, Alfred R.
The Techniques of Supervision
Chapter 8, National Foremen's Institute, New London, Conn., 1954

Schleh, Edward C.
Management by Results
Chapter 10, McGraw-Hill Book Company, New York, 1961

INDEX